TEACHING TOWARD A DECOLONIZING PEDAGOGY

Teaching Toward a Decolonizing Pedagogy outlines educational practitioner development toward decolonizing practices and pedagogies for anti-racist, justice-based urban classrooms. Through rich personal narratives of one teacher's critical reflections on her teaching, urban education scholarship and critical praxis are merged to provide an example of anti-racist urban schooling.

Steeped in theoretical practice, this book offers a narrative of one teacher's efforts to decolonize her urban classroom, and to position it as a vehicle for racial and economic justice for marginalized and minoritized students. At once a model for deconstructing the white institutional space of US schooling and a personal account of obstacles to these efforts, *Teaching Toward a Decolonizing Pedagogy* presents a research-based 'pueblo pedagogy' that reconsiders teacher identity and teachers' capacities for resilience, resistance, and community-based instruction. From this personal exploration, emergent and practicing teachers can extract curricula, practices, and dispositions toward advocacy for students most underserved and marginalized by public education. As an exemplar of decolonizing work both in classroom practices and in methodologies for educational research, this book presents tensions and complexities in school-based theorizing and praxis, and in teacher implementations of anti-racist pedagogies in and against the current US model of colonial schooling.

Victoria F. Trinder is a Clinical Assistant Professor in Curriculum and Instruction whose scholarship examines critical examples of teaching and teacher education in the context of the colonial project. Dr. Trinder currently directs the undergraduate Urban Elementary Education Program at the University of Illinois at Chicago.

TEACHING TOWARD A DECOLONIZING PEDAGOGY

Critical Reflections Inside and Outside the Classroom

Victoria F. Trinder

Routledge
Taylor & Francis Group

NEW YORK AND LONDON

First published 2020
by Routledge
52 Vanderbilt Avenue, New York, NY 10017

and by Routledge
2 Park Square, Milton Park, Abingdon, Oxon OX14 4RN

Routledge is an imprint of the Taylor & Francis Group, an informa business

© 2020 Taylor & Francis

Library of Congress Cataloging-in-Publication Data
A catalog record for this title has been requested

ISBN: 978-0-367-86207-7 (hbk)
ISBN: 978-0-367-37643-7 (pbk)
ISBN: 978-1-003-01767-7 (ebk)

Typeset in Bembo
by Taylor & Francis Books

For Colette and Simon, all day everyday;
for childhood and wisdom, their magic and coexistence,
and the souls here whose patience in teaching me astonish
me still;
for my current teacher-learners, teaching me pueblo and
pedagogy;
for the memory of Patricia Trinder.

CONTENTS

FOREWORD

What image best illustrates your teaching experiences and practices? Or, in another register, what icon expresses your teaching aspirations and your teaching intentions? What metaphor might adequately capture the excruciating contradictions—the ecstatic highs, the crushing lows, and the never-ending doubts—that punctuate classroom life minute-to-minute, and day-by-day? And perhaps most important, inhabiting those images and metaphors, how can you live a teaching life that doesn't make a mockery of your teaching values?

These questions animate every page of *Hiding Idols*, Victoria Trinder's robust account of her odyssey as a teacher. As she comes to terms with the colonial nature of the school system she's enmeshed in, and vows to decolonize her classroom and liberate her teaching, she faces epic challenges—tumultuous storms, dangerous whirlpools and coastal shelves, seductive siren songs, and her own monstrous doubts and fears. And while there are no quick or easy answers at hand, Trinder's tale of courage, perseverance, and tentative triumph sweeps us along and challenges us, then, to wage our own campaigns for schools that embrace students and stretch toward a humane future.

The contradiction at the heart of Trinder's work—a decent teacher struggling to teach in an indecent system, a moral actor operating in an immoral world—is illuminated by two recent films about schools and teaching: *Class Dismissed,* a French film about the boredom, isolation, irrelevance, and violence of education in the colonial mode, and *Rabbit-Proof Fence*, an Australian film dramatizing schooling as a weapon of control, and the inevitable resistance from below. In the US we're reminded of the Indian Boarding Schools whose mission was to "beat the Indian"—language, culture, systems of belief—out of indigenous children, and whose echoes can be heard today in schools for the descendants of formerly enslaved people, children of the poor and recent immigrants from poorer nations. This is the fundamental contradiction of teaching in the era of neoliberalism and resurgent empire.

"The starting point of critical elaboration is the consciousness of what one really is," Antonio Gramsci wrote in his *Prison Notebooks*, "and is 'knowing thyself' as a product of the historical process to date, which has deposited in you an infinity of traces, without leaving an inventory." Gramsci articulates a sense of the infinite and the ineffable tied up inexorably with the concrete and the real. Students and teachers and each of us is made of the traces from each and all—and from the facts of nature and the sweep of culture and history—but we can never be adequately summed up, once and forever. We are always more, always arcing forward, always a site of potential and possibility.

Vicki Trinder and teachers like her are engaged in a front-end effort for a more human world, a world based on the as-yet-unrealized ideal that every person's life is of infinite and incalculable value. This is the revolutionary idea of *the unity of humanity* meaning that, in the context of school, the full development of all is the baseline for the fullest development of each, and that the full development of each is the condition for the fullest development of all—a commitment to education as the practice of freedom, education as humanization. We resist, then, white supremacy, colonialism, racial capitalism, and all the other constructed hierarchies of human worth and worthlessness as base and ugly—wrong in the sense of inaccurate, as well as wrong in the sense of immoral. Her stance (and our stance) must become identification *with* students, their families and communities, not identification *of*—the latter in effect an act of surveillance in both theory and practice.

Seeing her students more and more clearly as three-dimensional beings just like herself, she discovers that each one brings into the classroom not only a body and a mind and a set of experiences, but also a spirit and a culture, a history and a community. Each of these unruly sparks of meaning making energy is on a voyage through life, and each brings parents and grandparents as well, family members and ancestors, languages and unique ways of seeing and being. Suddenly the classroom is crowded, overflowing with the essential joys and the pains of being human, and while this can be overwhelming to some teachers, it can also become an essential engine of inspired and honest teaching.

A belief in the preciousness and the infinite value of every human being can shape our work as teachers and as community residents. It insists that we gear our efforts to helping every human being reach a fuller measure of his or her humanity. It invites people on an immense and ongoing journey to become more thoughtful and more capable, more powerful and courageous, more exquisitely alive in their projects and their pursuits. An unyielding belief that the unity of humanity—always revolutionary, and never more so than today—is never quite finished, never easily or adequately summed up, and yet it is central to achieving both a decent classroom and a just society. Neither a commodity with readily recognized features nor a product for consumption, that ideal is an aspiration to be continually nourished, engaged, and exercised, a dynamic, expansive experiment that must be approached and achieved over and over again by every teacher and each successive generation if it is to live at all.

This fundamental commitment—the solidarity of humanity—is a principle easier to articulate than to live out on the ground, easier to uphold as a slogan than to enact in the real classrooms, schools, and communities we actually inhabit. To take one complicating example: we embrace stories like Helen Keller's, books like *The Miracle Worker, My Left Foot,* and *Under the Eye of the Clock,* each a story of overcoming adversity, each the tale of a teacher who recognized inside a broken or disabled body a human spark to nourish and encourage and blow into a blazing flame of triumph and redemption. Beautiful. Moving. Inspirational. Wildly popular in our culture.

And yet we can't help noticing that the families of these youngsters had advantages and privileges, access and means and social power to intervene in tough circumstances and to fight against seemingly unyielding systems. Nor can we deny the casual disregard of the humanity of millions of young people, including the students Vicki Trinder and many of us work with and worry about every day, students who were born poor and who hold no currency, students who have limited access and little recognition. The inspirational stories, then, remain bright baubles, Hallmark cards, and romantic turns rather than calls-to-arms.

But Trinder provides a rallying cry for teachers who work with young people whose humanity is routinely tossed aside, teachers who see dehumanization as both policy and practice, and yet desperately want for our young people those miracles and transformations, those hard efforts, enduring hopes, and generous investments. This is the territory of our determined efforts. We work every day so that our students might become seekers after their own questions, authors of their own scripts and not bit players in stories already written for them by others, actors in their own dramas, artists and composers of their own lives. We are mindful of the young man's outburst in Gwendolyn Brooks's "Boy Breaking Glass": "I shall create!" he cries. "If not a note / a hole. If not an overture / a desecration." But I shall create.

Children and youth desperately seek a sense of their place in the universe. Everyone needs to be recognized, everyone wants to be special and distinct, and everyone wants to leave a footprint in the sand: I am here; I am somebody. Like all human beings, students want to know that they are valuable and valued, that they can be of use. If they are always treated as "objects" and taught "subjects," they will be pushed away from their deepest hopes and their greatest promise.

Teachers who understand the unique capacity of human beings to shape and create reality through conscious purposes and deliberate plans are poised to transform their classrooms into sites that provide children with ongoing opportunities to exercise that latent resourcefulness: to solve real problems in their real communities, to act, to change, to make a difference.

We work with our students to embody the change we want to see in the world. We show them (and ourselves) what it means in practice to live purposefully, honestly, ethically, fully. We can't wait passively for someone else—the school board, the state legislature, the union, the principal, the federal government—to get it right about teaching and schooling, about citizenship and learning to live together, about engagement and social responsibility, before we ourselves get it right in this corner of this specific classroom. We will all become more powerfully engaged if and when our hearts and hands are working to improve our daily lives and surroundings. We must change ourselves in order to be worthy of the larger changes that we long for—a world of peace, kindness, love, and justice. That world just might become an apt description of your classroom.

While not a blueprint, *Teaching Toward a Decolonizing Pedagogy* is a light in dark times.

~William Ayers

ACKNOWLEDGEMENTS

If learning is living, I have lots of people to thank for all of mine.

This book belongs nearly entirely to Kristy Ulrich Papczun who served as its fearless and tireless champion, doula, and lieutenant sergeant. To her and Boyd Bellinger, who never let it go, and helped me balance the demands of program leadership and scholarship: it didn't happen until you, and I am grateful.

I can't say enough about the mentors pulling for me for decades. I owe eternal debt to Peggy Mueller, Demetria Iazzetto, Deborah Appleman, Bardwell Smith, Nader Saiedi, John Ramsay, and Paul Wellstone. Their teaching lay the foundation for my trying to get it right. I am lucky for colleague-mentors who live with me in the lucky world of thoughts, Danny Martin and Maria Varelas, whose versions of me I prefer, and whose lives and leadership as education scholars I aspire to; Cathy Main and Michelle Parker, who model the brilliance and grace of academic leadership in the programs we conspire to run transformatively; Bill Ayers, Anita Skeen, Greg Michie, and Karen Bean who believe in teaching, writing, and me.

There is a school at the heart of this book tirelessly committed to justice through the leadership of Tamara Witzl, its principal, and the brilliant teachers, artists, and families whose inspiration and collegiality I pull from still. To my team teacher, Alfredo Nambo, thank you. To all the Telpochcallis, I am grateful.

I am grateful beyond words for the teacher candidates who pursue goals of racial justice and reparative schooling, and allow me to engage a lifetime of work to theorizing a decolonizing and reparative undergraduate program for them. I am buoyed by your brilliance, and inspired daily in all ways, always.

I will never know how I got so lucky, but my lifetime of camarilla teaches me every day. I am grateful for friends who have stayed longer than perhaps they've wanted: Joung Sohn, Michelle Takemoto, Patrick Alexander, James Bechtold;

Madeline Khan-Roberts, Liz Chase-Vivas, Anne Jacobson, Tanya Merriman. I am grateful for the program faculty colleagues who share and indulge collectively critically-reflexive practice, and have filled my professional life with love and ideas: Torica Webb, Michael Thomas, Greg Larnell, Lali Morales, Marlynne Nishimura, Kristine Schutz, Lori Redding, Edward Podsiadlik, Josh Radinsky, Arthi Rao, Becca Woodard, Nate Phillips, Aisha Griffith.

Thank you to my families given and found, the global side and the THQs; the local side, and the hogar tan abierto. I have such a deep gratitude for all of you, and carry the honor to make good on your life investments every day. To my parents whose love for me is oxygen still, and the geographies that are my mind's eye's landscape: Adderbury, Jumping Bean, Man O'War, *zócalos*, SUMC. I am grateful for the faces and spaces behind my eyelids, and the ways my heart sings at both organ music and norteñas.

Thank you to Rodolfo Morales, whose image "Abrazando al pueblo" captures so beautifully what I couldn't visualize for years, and to his estate for the generous permission to have it grace this cover.

Thank you to my teachers, Judie Roman and Steve Taylor, who sparked a lifetime of joy through learning, and whom I haven't thanked enough. I am deeply grateful for the parenting I borrowed from Patty and Larry DeMooy, Judy Luzak, Harry Russell, Anne Hansen, and Janie and Charlie Tanner.

The children-now-not-children whose names are changed within these pages, but not in the carvings on my soul. I'll never not be heartbreakingly grateful for our time together in 251 and beyond. My heart isn't big enough to contain my joyful memories of you, nor are these pages homage enough either.

Grateful for the honor of being mami to Colette and Simon Delgado, whom I cherish all day, everyday. I am immeasurably proud of you, and indescribably in love with the people you're becoming.

Gracias a la memoria de Perla Lepez, and the lesson to open all doors when asked. Thank you to the memory of my mom, Patricia Trinder, and the lesson to go through them whenever I can.

PROLOGUE

That I process slowly might be the real abstract of this book, but the decades between the praxis narrated here and my ability to construct meaning and literary analysis of that story arc—as well as the one between its articulation and birthing—are glacial eras in today's contemporary academic and political worlds. While my metaphor and foundation for developing a decolonial praxis reflect the more long-view timelines of history and its centuries of violent impact, I recognize an inherent complication in the narrative worth exposing.

Power and voice in teaching are inextricable from each other, and in the personal debating of whether or not to embrace my narrative, I was yet again entering educational norms and values where my own white normativity and whiteness-centering sensibilities were at play once more.

There were other reasons beyond self-critiquing research methodologies that kept me from sharing beyond my teacher education programs and courses. I felt a great responsibility to the people represented here, as my learning could not have happened without them, and their lack of voice here does not reflect the collective way we built a community and school.

It is also true that there have been changes since its writing that made it difficult to return to.

Most importantly of all, however, is the protection of the once-children agentic here in the text, but not directly. The characters here in this book are fictionalized in an attempt to protect the students, who didn't ask for me to be their teacher or to have me convey a story that I still hope appears centered on them. In the publishing process, I have sought approval from many souls reflected here in these pages, though it is essential to acknowledge that my characterization of them— fictionalized, amalgamized, poeticized, and analyzed—is mine alone. I received their words. They were the gift to me that I have tried to reciprocate. They are the gift from them I long to share with my current emergent urban educators.

But there is no doubt that these words are mine, and I am responsible for any issues within their placement here. The words are ultimately a reflection of the complexities of practice as an attempt to model Fine and Weis's "critical bifocality" methodology as best I can here—merging academic access to large ideas and the space to entertain them with socio-political lenses on history that the epistemologies of entertaining ideas can be the colonial tools themselves.

The arc itself is fictionalized, too, as any narration of so complete a political and epistemological shift in my understanding did not happen so cleanly over twelve significant months. I work hard to fill each month with the ghosts of all my teaching months past as well as with aspirational mirages of what I had hoped might follow.

This tidiness of shifting one's consciousness toward the realities still less visible in their largesse is a persistent hope in students I've worked with in their pursuit of a justice-oriented teaching life. It is the gift I wish I could give them. It is the elusive hope that can never be—and it is my hope here to dispel any longing for tidiness by turning this tidy twelve month arc on itself, and have it convey instead the unraveling in beautiful messiness that founds anti-imperialist teaching. If there is any concrete formula or template to be found here in these chapters it is only that when hoping for a template one must turn toward the source of the discomfort—knowing that there specifically is the learning. Knowing in those moments, as students subjected to enforced whiteness in schooling understand, that those templates, authored by few and imposed on many, are fast prisons—both of our own making as well as by the architecture of history, confining of the learning and unlearning, but within which all resistance takes place.

I don't know what absolutes make excellent teaching. I don't know that there are any that do. What I do know is that the most damage enacted in classrooms upon children is through the antiquated notion that when student struggles manifest in legacies of inequity, they and the adults who serve them are to blame. The great con is that we continue to not blame a system that needs legacies of inequity to fund itself. We perpetuate the colonial architecture by not naming the system that exhausts generations of young people with a pedantic sense of self-worth attached to productivity.

Until I could unlearn these values I had no hope of interrupting those inequities. Currently my students extend their days, weeks, years—and their hearts, minds, and souls—toward an interruption of the colonial project that is based in shared voices and shared work. They commit twice the number of learning hours than their undergraduate peers to an unrelenting process of unlearning. They jump through the hoops and hopes of licensure requirements to land in a realm of perpetual fight against compliance and its restraints. They subvert their own needs toward the collective work of eliminating great injustice in the communities we serve.

This book is for you, and that effort.

1

JULY

Hiding Idols

There were many reasons not to go.

Two weeks into an immersion tour in the worlds of education, arts, culture, and history in Mexico had left me overwhelmed, drained, sick, and on unstable footing. Whether it was the infamous altitude of Mexico City or a sudden bout of homesickness, I was feeling shaky and a bit daunted by the realization that the day's activities involved a 90-minute bus ride over mountain roads.

I could have chosen not to go. I could have spent the day in quiet isolation, sparing my nomadic collective any physical contagion, resting from the hyper-sociality of our research and study fellowship. I could have tended to the relentless nausea that made sustaining any kind of nutrients nearly impossible, as well as the emotionally intellectual crises I'd felt over the course of the two-week immersion in the center of an intense and complicated city, itself at the center of an intense and complicated national history.

I could have decided not to go. I could have spent the day in quiet contemplation of the transformative things I'd already learned—at the Plaza de las Tres Culturas, where historic artifacts from Mexico's different heritages were located and memorialized as much as the student martyrs of the 1960s. I could have written down the details of our tour underneath the Catedral on the main zócalo—the central plaza of Mexico the city and country—where the ruins of the indigenous temples lay sequestered from public consumption meters under the marble floor over which parishioners made their pilgrimages to the massive crucifixes. It might have been wise to sleep, dreaming of our recent coasting through the canals of Xochimilco past the seeds of indigenous harvest, in homage to the early commerce of the original inhabitants of the city. I could have painted my mind with the walking tour of Coyoacán and its cobalt blue that spoke not just to Frida's aesthetic but more profoundly her take on the world. If my condition improved, I could have repeated our studying of the timeline of Mexico's early pillar civilizations and the different archaeological treasures of each at the Museo Nacional de Antropología. I could have sat in the hotel café watching the patrons, and internalizing the lessons learned of the purposes of cold leadership on show at the castle at Chapultepec.

There were still three weeks ahead of us, so I could also have been proactive and protective of the diverse experiences yet to come. In a mere week I would be on a gallery crawl through Oaxacan streets in the strange light of dusk, watching colors in the sky reflected in the Rodolfo Morales painting that sang to my heart. Somewhere in between, beyond the recollection of nearly all of us, I would be sampling the benign and vindictive tequilas of the Puebloan deserts. After a sing-along bus ride across the waist of the country, I would spend hours taking notes on the language-acquisition policies of Xalapan schools, seated at wooden first-grade desks. On a Sunday near the end of the trip, we would be carted to a retreat from the teeming streets, and wander freely across the coffee trade history lived through an epic family drama of one hacienda in the Veracruz hills. We would leave soon after observing world heritage artisans dye their own spun wool in the purees of local plants of Michoacán, thinking of the chocolate-sipping at dawn with sweet bread in the footsteps of rural Mixtec radicals. We would take maps locating the radio tower of a Lake Pátzcuaro Purépecha-language station and break pace from the group, walking the back stalls of Morelia's largest outdoor mercado in search of a hand-made guitar.

I was possibly forsaking all that. I was potentially ruining future years of good health. I was sacrificing it all because this was the chance of a lifetime and I had much to learn.

Something whispered this to me, and so I went.

The bus pulled onto the dirt road outside the cathedral and abbey. We disembarked and allowed ourselves to be herded in the manner we'd grown accustomed to through the wrought iron gate and the heavy oak door. Despite the heat of a mid-July much nearer the equator than any place I'd ever been, the hacienda-style cloister was cool. The building stretched both to our left and right and was lain out as a square perimeter around a central garden, replete with a humble fountain and brick seating area beside the far wall.

There were murals in random locations around the small garden, and the faded colors gave them an eerie but historic air. They conveyed different moments of spiritual doubt from ancient texts, and visually communicated the messages of the different parables connected to each. At one point in time, I might have been able to call up the stories connected to the images, but at this moment the murals were simply an allusion to events yet to unfold.

The large cathedral was to our left upon entering the hacienda, attached at the back of the northern wall by a covered walkway. We'd seen this layout at several different churches around the capital city, but the architecture hadn't really yet struck me until I saw personally its height and mass here, without any people, and up past the distant mountain ranges into the clear blue sky that felt closer than the steeple.

I was familiar with the architecture, personally and intellectually, from my travels in Europe. The church where my ancestors were buried, as I eventually will be alongside them, looked strangely similar to this one, especially in the simplicity of its faded pale ecru exterior color. The earth tones made me think of the different geologies that must have perplexed the original colonists, expecting to replicate their beliefs, and themselves, here in the new world.

The guide was talking to us about the different uses for the cloister but I was focused on what looked like mountainous desert surrounding this oversized monument to Christianity. The terrain we'd passed through had been daunting even by vehicle, and I couldn't imagine a hubris large enough to attempt it. I felt certain they did not have the materials necessary to re-create a world left behind for the disappointments of a slow and unfulfilling conquest.

Monuments to one's own people across England were at least generational gifts that could be eventually appreciated. What arrogance had made them think after the decades to build this, there would be anyone to remember why it was built?

I couldn't place the hue of the soil and wondered if my eyes were finally caving in to the illness that had wrought havoc on all my systems. The mountains seemed orange—imbued with a light whose source I couldn't place. As I looked down at the slate under my feet I noted the same color, and its marbling in the brick walls painted over with several different coats.

I had nothing to help me believe I was there.

It was as I had perhaps always imagined Mexico to be—from my own tinted lens of heritage and experience.

I'd been alive twenty-odd years before I realized the brutal sense of loss my mother had felt at her isolation from the geology of her youth. Though I'd been back with her to England on previous trips, I'd yet been too young myself to see it as anything but different than the world I'd grown up in. Then in my early twenties, it somehow felt deeply familiar—as though I'd affected the connections to the world I'd adopted through my parents' migration and was now dropping the façade—as though geology had reached out and grabbed me from beyond the constructions of culture I thought I'd made.

On my first return with her as adults, I watched my mother's shoulders drop and her neck straighten and her skin glow in the Atlantic air that had fostered her growth. In looking at the faces filing in and out of the market stalls, I'd seen them differently—their broad faces and solid gaits—and realized there is a community for everyone.

I wonder what emotions flowed in the intersections of lives here in this mountain valley. One long route of history for the people who had always lived here, were of here and for here. These were the people whose joy in their surroundings emanated from them in welcome to those who would take from it what they wanted. Those people on a long perpendicular route, tense with a deep homesickness, desperate to enforce upon others their values and punishments, so homesick for a spire to break the horizon they'd just met, and blind to the spot for all its layered meaning it had before them.

I thought suddenly of the marches we'd just participated in to speak out against anti-immigration school policies spreading across the US. We knew that facing the foreign on our own soil seemed to bring out the ugliest natures of the US. We watched how, despite the ways in which the indigenous of this special place had indulged the Spanish need for spires, their descendants humbly settled without complaint in our gritty and overcrowded section of the city where they'd come simply to save their families.

I considered these two book-ended moments in history, and the ways in which I'd been greeted and treated as royalty here in my students' homeland while my own government failed to acknowledge its accountability in the phenomenon that forced them northward—only to then treat them as criminals.

My thoughts were hanging heavy on me and I needed to get some air, so I asked if I could head outside and over to the cathedral while the rest of our group studied the artifacts protected in the abbey. One of the guides was happy to oblige and escorted me through the garden and over to the back door.

It was stunning inside—simple in its white walls and wooden pews. I recognized again the elegance in its humble placement of ex-votos and storied mummies. I saw the peaceful blend of the peoples of those two eras only in the graves found inside the floor of the chancel.

I'd been in churches like this all my life and never would have imagined the power of this one on my life, at this moment, in this place. There was a learning here I'd been prepared for but didn't know—the blend of what I was without knowing and what I knew without being. An aesthetic and knowledge I'd inherited enveloped me and filled me at once with peace and shame.

I wondered where my students in their mestizo lineages stood in relation to these things. We'd seen for ourselves on this trip how important and integral a part of the national pride of Mexico the colonial era was, and I'd been surprised. While the iconographies of popular murals and paintings I'd seen north of the border harkened back to the indigenous eras primarily, I was astounded to learn how reconciled people were about the conflicts in their histories. The only word I could find to describe it was "mature"—that in the developmental trajectory of a country, they'd reached an achieved identity beyond even my own individual abilities, let alone my adopted country's.

The group was filing back in and our guide was telling me he had the best treats yet for our visit. I couldn't quite imagine what more might be there, as the whole purpose for writing our federally-funded grant for teacher development and studying so hard through the last weeks seemed suddenly to have manifested already—and I was internally more ready to really see my students in front of me, those of the last few years and those I was going to teach for the first time, and our work together, in a new light.

We ascended the back stairs up to the choir loft. There, tucked into a corner, was a centuries-old pipe organ. It looked uniquely small in the otherwise empty loft space, its wood chipping away from being unfurnished and subjected to climates it was not intended to experience. I realized that I'd seen the pipes from the pew down below and not even registered them, but now I could see them connected to the source. I wondered when was the last time anyone had ever played it and thought briefly of my two grandfathers whom I'd never known yet who had sat at similar instruments inside similarly small and peaceful churches thousands of miles away, on the other side of this history.

There beside the crippled organ, I suddenly knew that despite all the nuances of difference, there were powerful elements of our human experience that bound me to my students and to the crazy world we all shared far away from here. In the attempts to read the world for any reflections of ourselves within it, we were also deeply tuned to the absence of such reflections —and the ways in which substantive inquiry might erase the distinctions between us.

I had images in my mind of the enormous labors of the Herzog masterpiece "Fitzcarraldo"—the teams of hundreds of South Americans who had hauled a 300-ton steamer up a muddy hillside to fulfill some random imperialist dream— and thought for a moment of the legions of people who'd also possibly labored to bring this instrument here to this place, most likely with less of a connection to it than the one I felt. The metaphor also elicited the thought of my students earnestly expending all their energies in order to master a curriculum designed to erase them and which fulfilled the dream of some neo-imperialist far removed from themselves. In the muddy climb to some elusive apex, where would I find myself in the chain of events, I often wondered, and how was this different than the story behind this pipe organ?

We had other places to travel to that day and so were being ushered back down to the chancel of the church. I could feel my color starting to return and the hint of a spring in my step. This sense had been missing since the day beneath the Catedral of the capital, where we'd descended to the ghostly Aztec ruins, overwhelmed and subsumed within their conquerors' Christian versions. We scattered ourselves throughout the pews. Our guide stood to the north side of the chancel and drew our attention to a medium-sized cross. It stood toward the back of the open space about three-feet tall and built of what appeared to be burnt house beams. Some of the beams looked to be in poor repair and we were intrigued as to the role of something so banal and homely.

The guide held up an old journal protected by a plastic sleeve. It suddenly dawned on me that we'd seen more artifacts here than present-day inhabitants. The town appeared to be no longer much alive in its perch atop a hill surrounded by other mountains. The guide began his story—our heads turned over our left shoulders and our left arms resting on the backs of the pews.

"As we started to uncover the history of the village," he began, "those of us interested in keeping up the convent and cathedral came across this old diary. It was written by one of the missionaries over a hundred and fifty years ago. One of many priests recounted here his stories of struggles and difficulties as they worked to bring Christianity to the people.

"For the most part it read like most documents of the era. Except for a notable detail. The priest reported here the course of different religious celebrations that had been thrown for the whole town. These fiestas included different ceremonial elements, including a procession for which they used this cross to lead themselves to the square and back.

"On a couple of different occasions, the cross was struck by lightning. Not while it was being carried but there in its station in the middle of the plaza. The first time, the priests were stunned —and took it as a sign of God's approval of their work. They congratulated themselves and dove more deeply into their intended efforts to serve the people.

"The second time, a year or so later, when the cross was again struck in the same place, they were slightly frightened, and deliberated together to try to determine what indeed their god might be trying to communicate to them. For years they considered that there was a meaning in the two strikes but that because they were not able to read into the message, they should store it away in a secret place so that it would be protected until they could come to a consensus about what that message was. The priest who authored this journal briefly hints here that some people thought the message might be a directive from God to discontinue their work, but that was quickly dismissed and the cross lost to the inner closets of the convent. This diary, in fact, never mentions the cross again after that.

"Decades later, new missionaries came across it and brought it out for religious services. Within a couple of years, reports were made that it was again struck by lightning and then placed at the front of the church. Reports were made to the head parish in the capital, and someone there had remembered incidents from years past. The consensus was that there was a message to be interpreted, but that there was no certainty what that message might be.

"Until decades later, when the cross was brought into the city for study. With the advent of x-ray technology, scientists were able to locate a small metal idol placed at the heart of the intersecting beams. It appeared to be an idol of one of the gods of the original people here."

The priests had been reading the miraculous events from a lens that reinforced their own worldview.

They'd not been able to see what they'd never known about the kind and patient way in which the human beings they'd sought to "save" had instead maintained their core beliefs—while humoring those who so desperately clung to the need to make others into versions of themselves.

I felt an added layer of sadness to the historical narrative of colonization in this region. There was the overwhelming tragedy of a people targeted at the heart of their self-definitions in order to conquer and control them that made me think carefully about my role as teacher, but there was also the deep remorse at the lost opportunity for the clergy to know more deeply what they'd been involved in; whether in order to change their ways or simply to have a better understanding of the complexity of the people they'd underestimated.

I felt the urge to lament their fear of learning the deeper meaning behind the lived realities of their desired converts as well as to glean a more complete understanding of the commonalities that existed within both religious practices, and perhaps at the core of the collective humanity shared between them.

The clergy had been unable to face those realities, locked in the reinforcement of their imperialist culture's theft of power and their self-righteous beliefs in a religion that would 'save' those they had encountered. If the privilege and boldness of that kind of synthesized class, race, gender, and religious privilege couldn't steel them for a difficult truth, how could we expect to find honest and sincere treatment of these issues in today's world?

We could only if we learned from their mistakes, I realized.

★

In my studies of religion, I'd come to learn the importance of parables—of the humanity of stories and the grace of a well-told series of events. There was a purity to the importance of a narrative universal enough that people could see themselves in it but specific enough that it rang true.

How ironic that those missionaries and the befuddled clergy would be the source of the parable of my life—of the questions around acculturation and resistance, of interpretive lenses and optimistic narratives, of being inside culture but not of it, of internally believing one creed while marching in-step to another, and imposing one march upon others, while unaware of a dance they were hiding from me.

There was no mural to this parable on the walls of the convent, and yet its history had made it visible and clear. It was an unintended lesson, forever etched in my mind as the ultimate metaphor in a life of crossing cultures and teaching against oppression and for empowerment.

I saw the invisible writing on the wall, and longed to paint it to fruition.

★

So was I the journaling clergyman, in my earnest desire to realize some vision I had for my students—one that I believed involved their own betterment, but was perhaps locked inside a skewed worldview?

Or was I, like the people of that community before him, working within an education system that I didn't believe in—while secretly carrying a different idol that the system couldn't see for its hubris?

Or was I the possibility of either, or both, at simultaneous and distinct moments?

And who would tell me?

How could I know?

And how would history tell my story?

I knew it was time to start writing it down—to support the indictments that might lie centuries into the future, or to tease out the nuances that might be missed in the broad strokes of investigating post-colonial teaching in a racist society.

Either way, I had work to do.

I had to find a way to be my own x-ray, and let my community reap the benefits of truthful learning, and not just the descendants who would narrate my foolishness to future travelers.

★

The months to come would provide me ample opportunity to watch the lightning blow open the façade of my teaching, and I planned to use the insight garnered here in this place to work at hearing and seeing the message my students were trying to tell me—and the nuances of my role in their education lives.

I certainly felt that I'd already been struck by lightning enough times. Maybe if these particularly befuddled clergy and their ilk had had a bit more fortitude they wouldn't have hid away the cross and shied away from whatever messages they thought they were getting.

I was ashamed to say I certainly understood how they felt.

Here in this place, however, I felt I'd been given a challenge to go back into my teaching year ready to unfold its layers and think and rethink this theory being generated by a metaphor from a couple of centuries past.

I stood there and admitted to myself that teaching oftentimes felt like parading myself, and all the things I believed, up and down a mountainside I knew nothing about, hoping that others would buy into what I was promoting and follow along—secretly afraid that when they were in fact falling into step that they were doing it just to humor me.

I thought frequently on the ride back through the mountains I now knew about putting myself away in a back room and shutting the door on those episodes—without following through on them.

If I hadn't yet done this, I hoped there was time for repair. I was still standing in the center of a plaza and letting the things unfold that I'd been long fearing—and then learning from them no matter how painful the lessons might be.

★

While moments of crisis were encapsulated within all my teaching days in some way or another, there were particular moments across my career that would serve as lightning strikes and break open the institution I thought I was promoting and expose it for the hidden treasure my students had wanted it to be all along. These moments highlighted for me the nature of working under the colonizing umbrella of education in the US while hoping to promote a de-colonizing and equity-directed and social-justice-focused life of learning for my students and their community.

What I saw that day in the mountain villa in near ruins was how tenuous such a paradigm would be. I had to face how nuanced the realities of our cross-cultural classroom in a colonized and oppressive society were, and the historic challenges of changing that for us all.

We were returning knowing that the best way to stay true to our cause was to drag it out of a back room and put it on display, so that one day the history could be told and unfolded in parable and stark reality.

I'd been writing most of my life in order to sort my mind out, and try to construct a meaning beyond the way I'd initially experienced events. While teaching had exhausted me to the point of not continuing that practice, I now saw also that I'd run from the deeper understanding as the journal-writing clergyman, and tried to tuck those experiences away in a back room soon after they were lived so as not to have to sit with them and the thoughts they sparked for the discomfort I felt.

I'd thought—or maybe subconsciously hoped—that I'd learn simply from having lived them.

I stood outside the church and the relics within it and realized the artifacts did not make the history, but instead the excavating of the stories and the interpretations shared with all who came close. Just being inside my classroom and its community did not make for the platform from which to engage in social-justice teaching. Just walking from school to home and back again did not open up the notions of community engagement. I had to stop and take it all in and then offer up the honest processing both for those who shared it with me and those who might have a future moment like mine with this small idol inside an old and ugly cross.

The items, I realized, had no inherent beauty or attraction but were there to serve as a catalyst to the deeper beauty of learning—of seeing as clearly as one can from all directions and then continuing to stand in a moment that hurt for its painful revelation.

A year of crisis moments of my teaching—of my learning—of the lightning strikes that exposed it all—was yet to come and would, as told, expose me for the centuries.

2

AUGUST

Pueblo Pedagogy

Archetypical ghosts in tow, and literary foils having set up camp in my head, I had some excavating of my own to begin upon my return to Chicago.

I hadn't been ready for that "torpedo fish" moment until then, and knew I had some texts to organize around myself. To make sure the connections I was making were authentic and others-directed, I welcomed the company these old friends afforded me in setting out to undermine the colonial project.

I found the texts I'd held close for years, and who came to mind in that complicated cloister.

I knew first to find Horton and Freire, Anzaldua and hooks, needing their histories of empowered communities whose invisible knowledges serve as tools toward their emancipation. I found Valenzuela and Cummins on the same shelf, the impact of their socio-cultural frameworks for language and education a testimony to interweaving theory and practice. An imaginary dinner table conversation for us all might include advocacy for worldwide communities outside the culture of power and the ways in which education can foster spiritual, academic, and social change.

As I buried myself in the theoretical framework of small activism in communities and the layers of investment in education they make, I realized that not only had they facilitated my understanding of the hidden idols but they had also given me strength to stand inside this tension and live inside the discomfort. Their company made it possible for me to look deep into my own unfolding narrative and see the versions of it I hadn't heard or seen. Dog-eared pages and well-worn covers, these texts sat lowest on the shelves over my desk and were never farther than an arm's reach from my thinking. They were the moonlight for this journey of culture-hopping and nuance-claiming teaching for empowerment inside the darkness of school institutions designed to prevent it.

I knew I had more research to engage in yet, like Frost's snowy woods, and spent the next couple of weeks in my library sorting through philosophies that would carry me into and through the year ahead.

I located the voices of Delpit and Ayers, and began to question the ways in which one can embrace a pedagogical practice of listening to the people in one's classes to grow with them toward a new sense of equality—and how power could be diffused in the articulation of it. Such power was the blood of the society that implemented education as its transmitter of the status quo and I turned to Ladson-Billings and Spring to help me remain open to the not-so-benign history that created the inequalities my students currently faced in our schools. I realized that the history I'd drawn so close to and elicited my life's question from was in fact the out-of-school curriculum so eloquently theorized by Schubert, Pinar, and Eisner in their inquiries into interpretive notions of what we choose to teach and what's worth knowing.

These essential questions included also the languages that communicate our choices as well as the ones we construct daily with students. I thought of Krashen and Faltis and the ways in which culture and developmental approaches to language acquisition had fed my soul as both language teacher and student, and how evolving theories of trans-languaging spoke to the liminal imaginings of the decolonial feminists of my initial academic pursuits.

I unpacked the texts that had frightened me in their power and clarity—the revolutionary and anti-imperialist brilliance of Lugones, Fanon, Moraga, and Hulme. I hoped in my own spiral curriculum for an entrance to the challenges they offered me that I had not seen in previous attempts.

As I pondered the ways in which I'd made meaning of all these different active theories in my teaching life, I considered, too, the collective efforts of Cochran-Smith and Lytle toward the recognition of creative teacher reflections as a critical field in the world of educational research, and how narrative inquiry unfolded via Clandinin and Connelly who theorized it through its subversive role in academia and nurtured its intellectualism in an increasingly narrow definition of thought.

As I rounded out my physical and mental libraries, I paused for a minute at the texts of the late Senator Wellstone, who'd written his actions into theory, and then back into action in increasing spheres of influence, along with many of the Liberation Theologians like Gustavo Gutierrez, who asserted a preferential positioning of the poor in the institutions of the catholic church, and pushed the inverting and centering of oppressed colonized communities in text and subtext through Vatican II.

My perusal of the ideas that had rested within me brought me next to the ways in which notions of equality and justice in education had reached beyond the context of the field in the critical narratives of Paley, Kozol, Michie, and Kohl. I thought about the power of voice, and exerting it even when it is intentionally unheard. I knew that silencing of our pueblo-focused labors was part of a society that chose to know very little about them, and settled in to this chorus I hoped to claim as my own.

As I looked back at the roots and trunk of this tree from my one small branch, I was humbled by the hope that we might still be in our early decades, and that the centuries between the hidden idols and me—in which these personal and literary conversations had taken place—would be but a blip in the long run of empire and its deconstruction, and that the continued excavation of my students' work with me to weave new co-generative theories into our practice would convert into an oxygen to promote the tree's long life past our moment.

*

I knew at that moment what context of history my own endeavors were part of, and why I needed to open up the experiences of my year as I felt them, and why I'd wanted to be fortified by those who had come before and spoken about these issues at length and the implications for a world of teachers and students.

I thought quietly for a moment of the women who had populated the teaching force before it qualified even as a profession—of the women who took the role of caretaker into their hearts and gave of their lives to children. I thought of the ways in which our society used to force the choice between teaching and experiencing life, and laughed self-consciously at my hermit-like first years, when other leisure and creative activities fell to the wayside and I tried to stay on top of the huge responsibilities I'd been given.

For reasons like those I wondered how many teacher narratives had not been—and would not be—written, and how herculean it must have been for Ashton-Warner and Paley to get their stories into print. How many women had co-constructed meaning, language, and safe spaces to explore the inner truths of their work without ever being noticed? I would take the opportunities (and technological advances of the age) to acknowledge the grains of wood and small successes and failures involved in such a life—not just for my own x-ray examination, but also for those women and the ways in which they couldn't, as contextualized in the theorizing of Greene, Grumet, Miller, and Noddings.

Valenzuela would appear on the shelf closest to my mental desk, along with Kumashiro, as their deconstructions of caring and social justice in teaching would guide me toward a deeper examination of what those notions meant for my students, and for me, and in which ways our orchestration of them managed to be additive as well as anti-oppressive. I'd hinged my analysis on his critical notion of crisis, and placed the text on the end for better access in crisis moments.

I dug out, finally, after the reminders of the contexts, two of my most treasured books—the first by anthropologist Victor Turner, whose humanitarian vision led him to see magic in individual uniqueness and communally-created self-definitions. Turner's appreciation of the powerful bonding between people sharing a journey helped illuminate for me why I was so drawn to my ultimate favorite text—Herman Hesse's canonical bildungsroman

Siddhartha, in which education for the protagonist was the very act of living, constantly redefined in light of the concentrically-circular communities in which he traveled, and through which his river ran.

★

As the world evolved around me in its continued spiral outward from the simplicity of the indigenous people of that mountain village, I considered how notions of identity and community were unfolding in new and scary ways. I thought about the ways in which Gee worked to categorize these new definitions of self in collective. I thought about the potential overlap that rural transplants from different homelands might feel in a shared context, and to what extent the affinity identities we claimed might supersede our natural or institutional identities—not to mention those we acquired in an oppressive discourse.

This led me to the paradigm-shifting and life-changing scholarship in critical race theory and critical whiteness studies in the texts by Ladson-Billings, Bell, Sleeter, and Leonardo. I wondered how I had thought before hearing Crenshaw and the framing of intersectional oppressions that re-illuminated dangers of essentializing urban students. I contemplated the brutality of the imaginary worlds of Erdrich and Cameron and the ways in which Spring chronicled cyclical oppressions across cultural groups, and all through the institution of schooling. I searched deep within me for the harrowing framings of Fanon and the perils of incrementalism—and hoped for future learners to frame our school-based pueblo pedagogy as urgently revolutionary as well as complicit.

I loaded up my humanities heart with philosophies and histories that also exposed the empire in the etymology of empirical research, and took faith in what I knew and how I knew it.

I knew it all because it had revealed itself in physical artifacts of a resistance so complete as to have been rendered inexistent.

★

In order to do the lightning work ahead of me, I not only had to be clear about whose tree I belonged to, but also who I'd been in my different contexts—as well as the reasons I believed that I'd ended up in my community beyond the books that had pushed me there and the invisibility of community idols that made me stay.

Re-entry after our teacher-development study program into my surroundings and culture proved harder than I'd imagined that summer. I was trying to come to grips with the extremes of my summer experiences on a hot day in August that made the neighborhood feel like it was downwind of a concrete factory. There was dust everywhere—it never ceased to amaze me how thick and black it got as it gathered on the old windowsills of my apartment. No matter how hard I scrubbed, it seemed to settle in between the grains of the woodwork, altering the pigment of the white paint to the point of disconnect from its original state. My partner Gilbert and I sat in our second or third outfit of the sweltering day on the broad front steps leading up to the front doors of the two-flat whose upstairs we occupied.

It was one of the stifling days in August that make you not hungry, but we were counting change so that we might buy an "elote" from the woman on the corner in front of the Laundromat. As we pondered who between us most needed to eat, I thought long and hard about the dreams and efforts of global migrants to create a situation better than their previous one for future generations. I thought of the first people of those generations—those born into a new country but not entirely of it, like Gilbert and like me. Our ambition was supposed to propel us to heights beyond the dreams of our parents, though most of the time our current situation would have appeared to our ancestors as "derailed." I was more sensitive about my betrayal of my parents than Gilbert seemed, but the immediacy of hunger was making any deep thought difficult in that moment. I knew that lives committed to teaching and art-making would do less than validate our parents' immigrant hopes for a better life. Sitting there in the ugly, smothering, and sooted gray heat of Chicago's southwest side I knew I was not meeting expectations of the generations before—and not banking the capital spent on my behalf. I was also not creating the capital hoped for to establish security for the generations yet to come. I was failing the immigrant line of succession.

I'd seen this play out in nuances all around me and this was the reason I locked in: immigrants, children of immigrants, and third and fourth generations all dancing around the issues of responsibility and security. I noted the quiet seriousness of the families of recent arrivals in my classes, and the hope in the eyes of their parents at drop-off. As an ESL teacher I worked closely with the families who were most immediately post-trauma. Like my grandfather after his POW days of WWI, they were reluctant to speak about what they'd been through in their migrations, but the impact of it was communicated non-verbally in nearly every exchange. I read in the averted eye contact and constant movement stories of survival and loss, and profound nobility in having journeyed for entirely selfless reasons—to find a way to attend forever to those left behind and be the good ancestor for all those ahead.

I knew also in each interchange shared expressions of knowing, that for the relief of those who had succeeded and arrived, there were stories I would never know and descendants whose lives would never be, of those whose sacrifices were final.

Though teachers' labors don't produce wealth, I knew I was personally driven by motivations similar to the legacies I perceived in school parents for much of my life. I knew my parents' sacrifices and lonelinesses, and focused relentlessly on making good on them through the only avenue I saw open to me: school. I was lucky in that it was a good fit for my individual quirks: the privileging of personality styles in American schools fit my personality and tendencies, if not those of loved ones around me. I carried a pride through my efforts that because of me there might be vindication for my parents' choices, and a restoration of happiness that at times felt missing. This motivation continued to bring good things, on paper, until I graduated from my elite college wanting deep within me not to read the tea-leaves of the current economy, but instead to find others whose lives paralleled ours—and provide linguistic, cultural, and psychological support through the liminal exercise of learning to learn in American schools.

In the tournament of my own childhood, I'd had a "bye" for many years, and I currently considered my own transition to the US educational system as gradual. Apprehensive about the lack of character and clarity in the American society writ large, my parents scanned our new city for alternatives. My siblings and I ended up in a small haven of a Montessori school on Philadelphia's outskirts called, appropriately, "Walden." As I realized the emotional ties I felt to that institution, I also realized simultaneously that the people who comprised it had been a crossing-cultures safety net, and I worked hard in the hope that my students might one day feel similarly. With the lack of any non-mainstream options, it was a big responsibility to provide that service, and not one I took lightly. From the high floors of our school, however, one could see a skyline laced with as many steeples as industrial smokestacks, signifying a safety net outside our school. Whether formally or informally, church was a place to connect across cultures. I wondered if parents felt comfort or heartbreak at the schooling options within some of them. I knew that tuition precluded many from this option. While I understood the many dimensions that were attractive about the parochial school system on the south side of Chicago, parent articulations of hope centered on cultural connections over religious indoctrination—a phenomenon I would come to appreciate profoundly in the adult relationships I would develop.

These were locations that reflected the values and meaning of the word "education" back to families in easily recognizable ways.

For my own "drawing out," Walden's magic had also been in its small size. While I couldn't remember any specific learning activity in detail, what I had ample memories of were moments when I knew I mattered—as part of the community, as a younger version of the person the teachers had hoped I'd become, and as a life full of moments large and small that all built toward that goal.

★

If I was 100 pounds that August I was lucky, and certainly less consequential than that. While I did not feel entirely back to myself, I needed to take advantage of the days the school was open and get myself settled as much as possible. Most of those days were split between the hands-on busy work of creating a nice environment in my classroom—putting colored construction paper up on the bulletin boards with inspiring catch phrases and "dichos," setting out bright folders for different workshops in our cozy corners housing the carpet remnants gifted us, and somewhat-steady chalkboard easels that would capture students' thinking. I spent time each day organizing book bins by theme and sticking on them the colored dots that referred vaguely to levels of difficulty, and tried to contribute in some way to the building of our community of adults by catching up with colleagues and asking about their summers.

Those of us who had been shepherded together around Mexico needed less of this—and perhaps space from each other more than bonding—but I was happy for the growing camaraderie and sharing of our anticipation for the year ahead. I'd come to feel also a communally self-righteous bond with those of us there for long days, all of our own free will, eager to get back to work. Trying not to feel too aggressive about my own nobility, I had a short conversation about my fears for the year—and a more specific conversation about strategies for setting up exciting centers for writing workshops—with a good friend and then headed happily back to my classroom, humming and feeling like a student set free in the hallway.

Things had been so stressful the year before as we worked to start up our small school, recently granted autonomy from the large elementary one that had been housing us for years, that I hadn't been very good at tending the social soil supporting our work. I avowed this year to make this a priority right from the start. On my long walk down the hall, I saw the door open to our 5th grade classroom and decided to see if the teacher was back. Having had her own grants for summer travel, she had not joined our summer expedition, and I was eager to compare notes—and maybe test the waters to see how much my previous-year failures had resonated outside my own head. I had also hoped to touch base about the students she was passing on to me—those I had known from my ESL classes and the others who had later filled out that grade level and her class—before the year got underway.

It was already unsurprisingly a glorious room, and I found Sylvia seated on the floor in front of her file cabinet. She'd been here at work for weeks, I guessed, and already I could feel a trickle of competition and inferiority make its way to my throat as I caught glimpse of all the things she'd already done: her new students' names and helpful charts invitingly affixed to their desks; the windows brightly decorated with silk fabrics in a variety of strong, warm colors; gorgeous mobiles of different animals and student names hanging over the neatly-arranged desk groups around the small room.

My own new room was perhaps twice this size—not from earning it in any way, but more because the school had agreed to give the middle schoolers their own nook in the building—but I realized that I had a long way to go to make it even remotely this inviting. This admission surfaced in me like a confession as I respond to her bright "Come in!" and climbed through the portal.

I had hoped to connect personally, but my nervous chatter was no cover for the difficulties I felt in crossing the several divides between us. I was surprised when Sylvia gave no response as I expressed the fear that she'd set the bar pretty high and that the students she'd sent to me might be pretty disappointed to realize they'd left such a cozy space for my absent domestic talents and decorating skills. I recognized her lack of interest in assuaging that concern or heading down the road of how I fared in comparison to her—and the truth was that I had come in today feeling really confident but was starting to feel that slipping away and wanted her help.

These were entirely selfish reasons to disturb a teacher in the midst of working hard on her own time, I realized, so I tried to get the conversation back on track and get us both back to work. I decided to ask about her travels overseas. Sylvia's fascinating bi-cultural background and adventurous spirit made her radiant beauty and excellent teaching even more intimidating. When I tried to process these feelings, I realized how much I attributed her successes and self-assurance to the fact that she both shared a background with the students and also knew intrinsically about other worlds I struggled to access. As much as I tried not to essentialize her cultural place, I'd always feared that mine was somewhat deficient in comparison, and projected into our dynamic this unhealthy and complicated, inappropriate assessment.

To ease my feelings of inadequacy, I tried hard to remember back to my "flow" teaching year and the day Sylvia was completing her observation hours at our old school and chose to spend her last couple of weeks in my classroom. She had spent several days with us in the middle of a "Five Senses" unit in which we'd integrated music and science. The students had been presenting their final projects—songs and homages to the different senses as found within the communities of their present and past worlds. Sylvia had been emotional that day in our debriefing as she talked about hoping to craft units like that one for her students some day; she had even given me a children's book in Spanish for my classroom library called *Calor* ("warmth") and thanked me sincerely for letting her observe. I'd been so happy for the feedback and more proud of my large group of students than of my own efforts, but also really honored to be so recognized by someone whom I deeply respected.

I'd promised her I knew she had amazing years of teaching ahead, and really meant it.

It was hard to hold that memory in my head and reconcile it with the dynamic I now felt between us, and I struggled both to locate the source of any current problems and also to let it go. The truth was that I both wanted her to see me and my practice in that way again, and that I wanted to see it that way myself, too. It was hard not to feel that I'd let that emergent teacher down by my own devolution, as well as suffer the recognition of how fragile my claim to success had been.

I didn't want to accept that I was both wonderful and horrible at teaching—or that this was entirely visible to others.

I wanted to push through the challenges I'd felt and try to get back to the person I'd been during her field work so I tried to orchestrate a flipping of our mentor–mentee roles so that I could soak up the successes she'd had while I'd been flailing. In that moment, too, I was hoping to find out in which ways she was planning to implement her own Fulbright learning from her trip to India—would it be a unit or a series of lessons that carried on throughout the year? Had she brought back artifacts or school contacts to help the students get a more personal sense of life growing up on the other side of the world? What similarities did she encounter in children from complex cultures very different from our students'? What kind of impact did her time there have on her personally? I felt behind, in a way. I'd spent the long summer in Mexico trying to catch up to what my students already knew—to where they already had been without me—and now was realizing that Sylvia had taken the opportunity to go to places new to her and the students, and to bring back a whole new set of ideas, perspectives, and literacies to infuse into their learning. I suddenly felt the need again to catch up—to try to glean parasitically from her knowledge and make some connections to it for my new students, even though it hadn't been my experience to share.

In fact, while my summer enrichment experiences had always contributed to my teaching in small, concrete ways, their impact had often been more personal and diffused throughout my being than my teaching—and this past communal trip to Mexico had been no exception. I wanted so much to put this feeling out to Sylvia, and hoped to connect on this level and share some insights about the humanness of the profession and craft, but was yet again too fearful of my own shortcomings.

It was a moment I would forever regret—as it would never come again.

Syncopated and difficult, the conversation meandered into directions that didn't mean as much to me as the one I was too fearful to move toward, but I still felt I had some work to do to get us back to a space of sharing and collegiality that had been erased by events of the previous year. I hoped merely to open myself up to a shared ridicule by recounting the aspect of my own travels that had been the most humbling and humiliating: my run in with what I'd heard labeled as "Montezuma's Revenge"—a socio-political characterization of the gastrointestinal battle fought against those who represent the colonizing forces that had once wrought their own hell of disease and devastation. For me the illness had been the unavoidable reminder that I remained a complete outsider to that which I had been seeking to join.

As I shared what I felt had been perhaps the cause of the illness—a squash blossom at a posh rooftop restaurant off the zócalo in Mexico City—I was hoping for some validation of my self-awareness and to offer an invitation to share in the ridiculing of my outsider-ness. I wanted to say that perhaps despite my best efforts, I'd learned there was no gray area when it came to biology—we are who we are, without affect or intention.

My inelegancies at communication had prevented all that, however. I was derailed from that pursuit and stopped abruptly both by her words and the change in her demeanor. "Your system's been too pampered," she asserted without smile or collegiality.

"I don't know – it was pretty sudden and –," I was cut off.

"If you've grown up eating that way, there's no shock process and little damage. That's the payoff, you know."

I could sense my own futile back-pedaling and struggling both to come up with the right way to redirect the conversation to where it had been, and to identify what I had said that was so offensive and upsetting.

"But in my earlier trips, I ate more riskily...."

I was trying to present myself as more than just another white tourist-voyeur, but also as too naïve to dismiss the nuances in our cultural differences.

"Everyone always makes it about the food, or the water, or the way things are done in Mexico; I thought you'd see it differently given everything."

I had the strange sensation that perhaps I hadn't totally recovered even, because I wanted to sit down and take a minute to catch my breath. Surprised by the fact that she had thought I'd be more resilient—why, I'd wondered—I couldn't even begin to grasp the fact that she was angry.

"It was more a feeling like I was weak, over everything else. Why did I get so, so sick? And why was everyone else doing fine? I kind of felt like there was something wrong with me, but I didn't think it was because of my growing-up, really, ever." I tried hard to read her face but it had fixed in its changes and was inscrutable.

"Maybe there's a lot more about your growing-up that you should look at."

★

It was an intentionally small school, so by design there was hardly a person who didn't know this exchange had taken place. I retreated from the room with a quick and ungraceful back step through the portal and headed down to my own. I'd left a couple of students waiting there for me—happy to transition slowly to school life and eager to contribute to the ways in which their new classroom might unfold—but I was so shocked by the exchange that I worried it would over-whelm my happiness to see them. If I hadn't seen the animosity beneath the surface toward my difference, where else was I blind to ripples and waves of my racialized presence? In what ways was I being blind or naïve to think that my attempts to bridge the differences had been effective, even genuine? Should I have not been so comfortable talking about some of these more nuanced topics? Was I being inap-propriate putting myself and my whiteness on the table?

I hugged each of the students around the shoulders as we entered the new room. Boxes and books strewn all about, I had fallen in love with the space already—one long wall of bookshelves, another one all windows. If I craned my neck through an open one, I could see my apartment's back stairwell, and the church parking lot perpendicular to it.

Pedro and Ricardo helped me dive into the books as I was still wrestling with the aftertaste of my confrontation with Sylvia. I wondered anew about the divides between us—between me and nearly everyone in this community—and longed to surface these ideas with my companions. Besides my mangled and emergent Spanish, my new status as the students' teacher and neighbor compli-cated the issues. I'd known these students as long as they'd been in school, taught them English in first grade when I'd lacked all preparation for the real things I'd need to know: how to help people find employment without documentation, how to build space into a day so that children can finish homework at school, how to provide parameters and consequences for children not dependent on repercussions in their volatile home lives, and —most importantly—how to see students constructing their learning and identities in classrooms, and center the work of teaching around those comprehensive and complete efforts.

Part of the learning I knew I'd underappreciated was the importance of language in a culture. Hoping I'd have access to my students' lives and their issues turned out to be naïve and impossible without some understanding of all the languages at play—that of their parents and homes, that of their shared world-straddling, and that of urban teaching.

It was important to me, so I took it on—teaching English by day and then studying Spanish in the evening. I learned both from real-life contexts and through books. I used my emergent language skills in parent-teacher conferences, in meetings with parents and students outside of school, and in after-school activities like soccer with the students. I learned the different Spanish words for "goal" and "effort," for "value" and "meaning," and for "humility" and "bravery." Most importantly of all I learned the meaning of those words beyond their surface definitions—by seeing them all in action and learning to see the knowledges and values from which they manifested.

I thought now in retrospect perhaps I was conflating my emergent language skills with deeper sharings of culture and community with the students. In my archetypal white female teacher identity, I'd been hoping both for pedagogy and politics to supersede any ethnic, racial, or cultural divides. I could see now that learning was supposed to erode that archetypal lens—that for every good intention, there'd also been a level of hubris—and it was up to me this year to spell out the nuances between.

Apparently this was all very evident to Sylvia. Immersed in my own anthropological lens, I'd failed to see that I was also being studied.

★

Stepping back into my role as teacher was tainted somehow as I wondered anew what my agency in these circumstances could be. As I saw it, I had three options: teach thoroughly from my location of privilege and bias within a system that reinforced that—without questioning and without critical reflection; play no role in the transmission of cultural dominance through my own actions in the classroom and leave teaching—adopting the critical theory that to teach from my position was a fundamentally and inescapably racist act; or build a resilience to live inside the tensions placed before me—"be" the privilege I couldn't escape and its correlative agent of whiteness while working to interrupt its impact and violence. Could I be this third possibility in the paradigm? Could I enter the public school system every day while working to tear it apart at the same time, and while facing the dangers of representing things I didn't believe to my students, my communities, and to the world of education in general? I had to consider the work ahead as my main lesson: how to deconstruct the racist beliefs in the benevolence of a white woman sacrificing everything to help children who desperately need her.

I wrestled with the knowledge that, perhaps, my students didn't really need me. I felt, in fact that they often learned despite me. What I was certain of was that I needed them—terribly—to fill out the gaps in my own education and to sustain a hope that education could be the great equalizer still. I knew that that exchange needed to found the learning to build a force for resistance and for shredding whiteness in the values as forced up on them.

There's no nobility, however, in being paid to teach where the person learning the most is oneself. While I knew how much I could continue to gain from the experiences, I also knew I had to figure out a way to do that which I most hoped to do—teach students who greatly impressed me with their knowledge and talents that which would help them gain access to the knowledge our culture valued and economic success in this their adopted country.

I had to recognize that perhaps there were legions of people better prepared than I to provide these experiences for my students, but because I thought I might have a fighting chance, I decided to walk right into the stereotype and its history of damage, and try to weaponize it on their behalf, from within their schooling itself.

I thought repeatedly about Vivian Paley—about her work and about the discussions around her role as a white female teacher and also as a critical educator. I forced myself to recall how she never shied away from these controversies but instead lived inside of them. I went back to my library to re-read how once she had started to feel secure and complacent in her teaching role, she knew then that she was in danger of veering off track. While I had veered off track, quite clearly, with my colleagues in different positionalities, I rested on the colleagues in my library and their complex reads of difference and humanization in schools.

I thought almost every day about the moment in which Paley realized how much work she had to do on herself—when she had experienced the shame of racist policies that she and her colleagues fought for in debate with the racially-pathologized parents of her students.

I couldn't justify to myself knowing the truth about those experiences in my own teaching and then simply walking away.

For the time being, I knew the work was to stay.

After the initial shock and hurt of seeing myself and my role in the school through Sylvia's eyes, I realized how fortunate I was to be afforded that lens. While it hurt my pride to be challenged on a level I couldn't do anything about—despite my hard work and heralded good intentions—I knew that this was really the level on which I wanted to think about teaching. I'd struggled throughout my preparation courses and early years in the classroom with labels I'd heard in reference to some of these visions, and here they were in front of me highlighted in red.

I needed a card catalog in my library to help sort through my nagging questions. Could I think of myself as an urban educator? Yes—it was certainly demographically appropriate, but why did it matter? Despite the dominant discourse about urban education in which the issues were framed as blame against students for their own struggles, I was hesitant to pick up the mantle. My feeling about the issues behind urban education was that they lay in the large oppressive bureaucracies that failed to provide equally for low-income students and their communities. While we truly were dealing with what were typically recognized as inner-city issues, I had learned to see in segregated Chicago a wide variety of different "cities." Our city was urban in definition, but so were the schools in the community on the north side where I had originally lived—and they looked nothing like the schooling opportunities my students had. So where was that nuance inside the label of "urban education"?

Others tried to point to our work as "teaching for social justice" —incorporating the critical examination of society into our daily work with children. I felt that on the level of intentions, I could embrace this title, but I knew in impact the title was empty. I felt wary of making any claim framed in my role in the lives of others, and knew I'd never want a causal reference attached to my positionality. Mr. Neville named himself the Chief Protector of the Aborigines while he ushered a holocaust against indigenous families in Australia. Should I see the activist titles as parallels? Who was I to say that my work was in any way a contribution to equalizing the playing field for my students? How was I to know if there was any justice at all for my students down the pike? I clearly remembered a day in my own growing up when a mentor had struggled to break it to me that I should only expect injustice in the world—that life was hard for girls and that I shouldn't get crushed by the constant re-realizations of this along my path. Though unclear to me at best, not only was I worried about claiming my work as contributing to some broader justice in the world, I was also nervous about preparing my students for a reality that would not be realized for them. There was no name for activism that taught resignation, but I hoped they would find a way to work toward equity somehow on their own.

I was always too uptight to be a hippie, so no one even mentioned a whole bunch of other labels that might have been appropriate or not to the work I was doing.

I thought back frequently to my student teaching days—and the framework that incorporated all of my pre-certification work in Chicago classrooms. The Urban Education Program (UEP) had existed since the early 1960s, espousing the kind of critical practice that I had hoped to model and live out. I felt honored by that tradition and the decades of teachers who had come before me—namelessly and without desire for any recognition—through that program and others. The UEP held at its core five pillars of pedagogy and practice—the first of which was that teaching was a political act.

This became the tenet to which I held most dearly—the recognition that in both positive and negative ways there were political ramifications for all of my work with children. I believed recognizing both sides of that equation was part of moving everyone forward. I felt a kind of peace when I saw hints of this in others with whom I shared my successes and failures.

While I struggled to find a way to articulate my work, I felt steeled by being able to recognize the same dedication in others—label or no.

Eventually I knew that despite our surface tensions, and differences in both belief and social place, I shared this in-between space with Sylvia. The space had pillars of a sort all its own: between claiming an agenda and blindly adopting one imposed on me; between social positions of race, economics, and history, we saw in our potential contributions the same hopes; and between "liking" what we saw in each other and not, in the dialogue and discourse we laid the seeds of a deeper practice as teachers.

We shared an in-between space much like the one I shared with my students—a space that was more profound than someone being "good" or "bad," a space where the moment a label was adopted it was obsolete. We constructed multiple spaces where language and history were fluid and expansive—Spanish and English intermingling with the hybrids being created daily and differently by the diverse students in my class. I felt our realizations of these elements caused our space to facilitate transformations—my deepest analogy to pure education, because learning is about becoming a new version of yourself and seeing a new version of the world—that lay inside every moment small and large.

The internal dance I had to do each day was also the academic dance I needed to engage in as a teacher: act, reflect, repeat.

Learn hard so that I could teach. Build outside of myself for new opportunities for my students and me alike. Be a new version of me so that I could offer a new version of the world to my students.

Simply and ever not-so-simply, I stayed.

3

SEPTEMBER

Pretty Books

This was the time last year that I'd almost thrown it in; found something else to do with my life; volunteered in someone else's classroom; re-discovered my love of waitressing; headed back to school to figure out what I'd missed.

Like winning the first set soundly in tennis through an exciting and eye-opening first couple of years, I now felt as though I was losing serve despite myself and getting bageled here in the second. How could things have turned around so quickly in my teaching? What kind of nerves had I lost? Had they ever existed, and if so where had they gone?

One short year ago was supposed to be the grand beginning: we'd worked throughout the whole summer weeks without students trying to get our little school up and running—hashing out visions and issues both large and small, like deciding who got what room—as well as what kind of shared government we should establish. The days of summer had placed us in hot and stuffy former schools with old-system computers on which to place our orders. We'd filled the months with the questions of what kinds of resources to purchase, to how we might replace the formal grading system. We examined notions of culture and curriculum, the context of our community, and laid the foundation for integrated units we hoped would incorporate all the different experiences of diverse bicultural families.

Time was short for all of that, and the summer ran out on us. Mid-stream in our theorizing, we had lessons to plan and rooms to organize. While my head had still been mired in our internal and external pedagogical and political debates, September arrived without any furniture or materials. All the elements of teaching that I'd dismissed so universally had centered themselves now in our whole project—resources enough for everyone, or even just enough to share, standard methodological approaches giving students time to practice their learning, and

—that which I had maligned most of all from my cozy and safe position as resource teacher—an organized norm-and-values plan for our classroom society.

Like the early colonists, from my safe perch of my fifth grade classroom, I'd loved the design and architecture of a new territory, but my utopian aspirational ideas (wielded unkindly and arrogantly) needed revisiting as we staggered into our new selves.

As the first days had unfolded before me, my enthusiasm for a split classroom at new sixth and seventh grade levels waned. My thinking degenerated from "what hands-on activities might I come up with that could help the students transition from the top-down systems of our home school to the more democratic approaches we hoped to shape our legacy around?" to "how am I going to keep the older students from bullying the younger ones for five minutes so I can get my head above water and figure out what we should be doing next?"

In what way could we market a utopian architecture, with aspirations of enacting social justice? Wanting to come on strong in the first few days as a brand new school, we'd instead had to deal with non-intellectual nagging questions of what about our offerings would be so different from the school that housed us previously? Even the unpalatable notion of marketing was easier to face than the complete overwhelm we experienced via the things we did not have ready. I had innumerable metaphors for the chaos unfolding, but collectively we clung to the perennial metaphor of boat architecture that needs to float simultaneously to its construction.

It was hard to hold on to the essential truth that this was the school we'd always wanted. This was the moment for our vision to come to life, and somehow I was entirely off my game. The new version of us we'd been planning for for so long was motivating; the new reality of us was terrifying. A split sixth and seventh grade class, these were brand new grade levels for me. I'd been hoping in my early years to build toward the middle schoolers, but I realized we were all embarking on a new developmental phase without some of the key Urie circles. The students who'd been assigned to me were nearly brand new students whose families had taken a leap of faith to join us in the commitment to a vision steeped in arts, culture, and language—but also unique was the school that was so new that it lacked the infrastructure to even provide the paperwork.

So much trust had been given, so what gave us the right to envision that we would come close to giving them a return on their investments? They were parents of preteens, and I realized they knew more about reading facial expressions and body language than most—and that mine must have read completely for panic. The most common subject in the first few days had been the parents' unfailing enthusiasm as they assured us they would jump into the pool with us at the deep end—not knowing they'd have a teacher who might have forgotten how to swim.

It wasn't even that I'd forgotten. It was that I had no concept that swimming was what I should be doing—the water was different, the dimensions beyond my vision, and the surrounding context clues completely foreign and the rhythm of days entirely staccato. Nothing carried from one day to the next, and we were gearing up too routinely not to burn out.

We collectively had little infrastructure to help us settle—the artists came to help us construct routines around the openness, but there were no prep periods to help ground the days, no one to watch the students during the non-educational, non-classroom time, no one to provide meals or after-school supports. We were food, shelter, water, and care, 7:30 to 4, until parents returned, in a long repetition of days. I'd looked forward to the students whose stories I had anticipated, but after two weeks we had seen enough of each other to last us through to Thanksgiving. In the echo chambers of our empty classrooms, we'd forgotten our primary work in facilitating the critical development of young people's minds, and had turned into utopian child-care providers.

I arrived every morning at seven to try to prepare for the long day, but mostly sat in my stark classroom, frozen, unable to produce much of anything to help me, paralyzed at the immensity of the work and its fractural nature. After monitoring school entrances and drop-offs, and shifts of taking students to breakfast in the adjoined building, I'd been full of fear when I faced my students. Children are the world's best ethnographers, collecting data, coding it, and analyzing it for meaning—and the clarity of their read of me was matched by the lack of clarity I had for us all.

I'd tried to establish routines that might create some kind of comfort for us all—morning transitional journal time, read-alouds, centers—but we were missing the important element of trust that comes from sharing a clear road map. Each new idea became a new battleground, and why wouldn't it? I'd been unable even to connect with these excited and adventurous new students and convinced of my failure long before I'd invited them in to our shared space.

The tests of who I might really be as a teacher came in close sequence those first few months. I was out of ideas to reinforce the limits I'd wanted to establish while they were also being pushed, and my colleagues were stretched beyond the usual workloads of teachers also, so any common supports schools manifest for their teachers who are overextended by circumstances were missing, and there was little help to be found beyond my door. In our immaculately placarded mission statements around the school testifying to our beliefs in the wonders and importance of collaboration, we'd failed to understand the basic ecology schools rely on for their existence, failed to imagine the heavy need for time, space, and energy in the initial stages of putting theory into practice—and underestimated the importance of materials and books.

★

It wasn't like the flailing of individuals had really been a secret to the community. I'd learned long ago that teachers excelling in the classroom often went unnoticed, but one struggling with elements of the comprehensive tasks was obvious as neon.

There were teaching clichés we resisted universally, but I was holding fast to one of them: that as difficult as a situation can get, there is also always room to turn it around.

★

While I was not the person in charge of my classroom, that didn't mean that no one was. Diana, one of the seventh graders, ultimately called Ms. D. by the other students, was a student with whom I'd had little contact in our previous incarnation of the school. She was abrupt and loud with her friends, and intimidating and fierce with new people. Like one might hope for in a new classroom teacher, she enacted a clear vision for us and a tone that facilitated its surfacing. I'd been unprepared for the sheer force of her will, lacked the important initial response in defense to such a good offense. Diana's student identity metamorphosed in front of us in the gap left in leadership. She wore a clear affect of authority and the students gravitated to her in kind. Unprepared to start the year, I'd naively hoped for an eventual stabilizing, forgetting the essential framing of the first days of school.

Of course I had left the whole year open by not having that initial week ready. The work for me in reflecting was to determine to what extent I'd had agency or authority in the smooth first days behind me. I was suddenly uncertain if any of those environments in my classroom were connected to my philosophy and pedagogy as laid out for students. Was I not just taking credit from a communication from the traditional schooling that had long-established how students were to view and respond to me? I laughed at how self-assuredly I had thought I excelled in this arena. I'd prided myself for years, and in our summer plannings, on not having to raise my voice, of facilitating students' intrinsic motivation for healthy community participation, even as we numbered more than the room would allow. Down to the technical school mandates, any resistance I modeled was facilitated by the mutual "enemy" of autocracy as school management. One of my favorite events with my 40 fifth graders, after all, had been to follow the norms of straight-line travel between classes, in the binary way we constantly reinforced gender, and resisted it from within. My students stood taller than me, hiding my quiet communications with them during those passages that were invisible to the larger school community, whose mandates we were superficially performing.

Within a year, of course, we'd seceded and had no constructs to resist together, no boss to discuss and mock, no identities among us that weren't permitted, and a path forward perilously clouded over.

The hallway pilgrimages were suddenly the least of my worries—I wasn't the only one struggling to establish mutual motivation for baseline decorum, colonial in all the connotations of that word. In after-school meetings and informal debriefings, we all expressed similar frustrations—we had anticipated more enthusiasm for intrinsic development of school culture and the tandem support of self-determination. We watched instead the corrosive power of loosening reins, and the loss of the values we held primary: respect for self and others, high self-expectations, generous listening.

In the death spiral of anti-racist teaching, our own lack of structure slowly slipped into "these students" narratives, particularly focused on questions about capacity for freedom. We'd devolved in shorter time than it had taken us to evolve into our current school model. With the absence of what we'd believed ourselves not to be, we'd lost what we were.

In my compounded struggles day after day, I was walking the new teacher tightrope three years late in my teaching: feeling the treachery of objectifying, judging, and essentializing my students. If I'd had a capacity for quality lesson planning, I'd have built a unit around literary irony. Exhaustion and the negative loop of self-talk had metastasized into anger and resentment before the end of our third week. I knew the dangers of racialized devolution and held tightly to a positioning of ourselves as still on the same side—and as co-excavators of a different version of ourselves, and steadied my discourse before it articulated what I didn't mean.

Desperate to claim the lack of control as external to my own actions, I sought out the easy scapegoats of Ms. D., and even previous teachers. I'd heard comments echoing my internal thoughts for years at our old school and now embarrassingly considered my self-righteousness a lack of experience and expertise.

★

As I organized reading workshop folders, my new class in my new room of new sixth graders took out their books. I shuddered to remember the anger with which I'd written in my last-year's journal about seeing myself not like "these" students. As I looked out on my new group with the distance of experience and preparation, I was humiliated to know that all my internal processings the year before had never been as hidden as I'd hoped. My fear of the lack of structure—and then of the students themselves—had emanated from me like heat off the summer pavement and ignited mistrust in my students. My fears seemed to have been the reason behind the spiraling lack of control I'd had, and I'd been too consumed by my own angst to realize it. I'd been so surprised by assumptions about my students' capacity to internalize discipline amidst our living example of the power of rebellion that I hadn't been able to perceive the ways my inability to see and hear clearly had aggravated the situation.

They were telling me that they'd been aware of the inner-workings of the system all along.

I hadn't seen that I'd been totally transparent—it was obvious that I had a lot invested in the expectations of the institution that when given the opportunity to build a new one, students felt free to exploit the gaps in my own self-awareness. The regression felt nearly complete, and my handle on the ladder back to the surface was loosening daily.

The students had known it. Not only had I not, but I also had bulldozed past insights they might have shared.

★

With our new year I had a chance to make things better—to try to improve my reputation as the "corajuda" in the building, and to construct my aspirational environment out of the ashes. With many teaching Septembers behind me, I actively performed Type-A characteristics not organic to my identity by anyone's definition. If our peaceful coexistence depended on it, I would effect as much organization change as I had capacity to do.

I had a vision for our lives together that was not a performance, however. I saw a new hope for the year and eagerly put core expectations on the wall, planned for trust exercises and democratic decision-making routines, and chunked my day into balanced and rewarding sets of time. I knew to offer instructional times that were predictable and varied in length. I knew to construct opportunities for students to believe that classroom routines were from their own ideas, and I offered weekly meetings for talking through challenges arising in our micro-society. To anticipate hiccups that might befall our community, we role-played potential issues, as culled from my disasters with last year's group. To internalize expectations for ourselves and our peers, we wrote letters we would use to respond to our best and worst selves when they surfaced along the way. I made clear our human expectations for both, and a plan to get through them, and placed myself as an example of some of the worst we might see.

For the most part it worked. Students began interacting within the norms we set and began taking ownership of the process of determining parameters for our life as a group, and what we would do if they broke down. We put our academic expectations into writing and then chronicled evidence of progress we might make toward those goals. We looked to each other to redirect us with understanding and consistency when we diverged from ourselves. To connect our contained community with the extension of it outside my classroom, I asked students to bring in one sanctioned item from home that would help connect the spaces, and I made arrangements for home visits, wanting parents to feel directly that these connections were in place. I asked parents and students to author our experiences, and to credit their own development by being transparent about their happinesses and challenges.

I promised I would do the same, and led with the confession that I had reconnected with my own joy for teaching.

★

Not once during those first weeks did I feel any kind of externalized negativity toward my students of the broader expressions of their identity, and I recognized what I had stolen from last year's students. In guilt and newfound joy, I decided to invite Ms. D., now an eighth grader, to visit my new classroom.

It took two other teachers to get her there.

Daniel and Ian, the two men of our teaching team, smiled at me wanly, quietly doubtful of why I would insist on causing more harm than previously, and why my evolution couldn't afford Ms. D. the space to do the same.

I smiled at her and inquired that if I promised she was free to leave whenever she pleased, could we excuse the sentinels? She nodded but looked at them hopefully—as if to plead the silent request that they not be far.

Ms. D. had always fared a bit better in the classrooms of men—whether due to gender, generally calm dispositions, or some intersectional space I couldn't see. I'd had to rule out my race and gender as the core issues for Ms. D. after seeing her and our lead teacher enjoying a laugh together on the first day of school. I realized that day how much I had longed for that level of interactivity with her—and how sad I'd been to devolve into that other person.

I'd had an easy time admitting that my issues with Ms. D. had simply been all about me. While my race and gender had not been Ms. D.'s issue, I'd projected them to protect me from my profound failings. I had needed not to see the extent of my damage so profoundly that my clouded lens remained through the first weeks of this new year. In the breaking of the clouds, I saw a chance to make things right.

I gestured for her to sit down in the armchair next to my coffee table, covered with thick and heavy art books. "Nice," she said, not to me.

Stereotype threat along with burned bridges made any new construction between us nearly impossible. I could see that I was already on the brink of ruining things. What was I thinking I could do here anyway? Once again, and to her detriment, I didn't have a plan. Her very tone had made me entirely self-conscious and defensive, and in that brief loss of focus my intentions were flipped on their heads. I'd hoped to talk with her outside the context of teacher–student, but this shared history was inescapable and present in her embodiment of self. She let me know that she was aware how different I was being with my new group—comfy chairs and all—and the implicit injustice of it all.

I tried anyway. "How was your summer?"

Her even gaze met mine as if to say, what was this? A writing prompt? If I'd really wanted this information, wasn't there an easier way to go about getting it?

Projecting false authority hadn't worked with Ms. D. and the whole class last year, and so I decided to go with straight-up honesty. Abetted by the distance of not having to work together for a while, I toughened up to continue.

"I know I'm probably the last person you wanted to see, and I agree that you've earned the right not to have to talk to me again. But it made me sad to know we'd be in the same building and not able to smile or acknowledge each other."

As an act of yet more resistance, she offered a flat stare.

"So I wondered if you would be interested in helping me out this year."

She offered only silence in response. This was going to be a monologue, I thought ironically. I'd have given my right foot last year to get this small of a reaction from her.

"Right. See—here's the thing. I miss you." But did I? "I mean, I miss someone keeping me on track." I doubted the sincerity of anything I was saying, and considered bailing then and there.

"I guess." I didn't realize I'd said this last part out loud, so she laughed.

Finally she had responded, and it was a laugh.

"Ok. As you know, I need some help. I don't know how to give 'peiscas'. I don't know how to pull a student's ear."

I had her attention now, and a glorious hint of a smile.

"But I don't mean physically. I think I could do it, if I had to. But I don't know how to do it without hurting anyone."

"I don't get it."

"Oh, but I already know that you do. My students might need me to be the kind of mentor–teacher you've been for me."

★

We talked for close to an hour —once I'd broken down the barrier with a little bit of the self-deprecating humor I'd sorely been lacking in our time together, the hour seemed to fly. Eventually we shared notes on the kinds of moms we knew in and around the neighborhood, and which kinds she thought were doing the best job. We talked about the people who'd been filling in for her mom during recent financial issues that I'd not heard about. In her own estimations, these troubles had played a role among the reasons Ms. D. had got tough, perhaps shadowed only by her longing for her mom in those absences.

She'd got trapped inside that strategy even when it was working against her.

I told her I completely understood, and that I'd share of those things whenever she thought it would help.

I wanted to talk with her about the issues I understood personally about moms and hard times, but more so I wanted to share with her what I understood about the injustices of adultifying too soon our young girls of color, both through structural issues beyond the control of their families, but also through the implicit biases our society enacted daily in culture, media, communities, and schools.

I asked her to help me by being my eyes and ears with the new students. I told her I didn't think that they had the will to stand up to me in my weaker moments, and so I'd need her to challenge me on their behalf.

I told her that while I didn't know if it would make me a better teacher—after all, last year had been my worst year—I was certain it had made me a better person.

"I think so," she kindly confirmed, and put her feet up on the table. This version of adulthood was the one I wanted for her—comfort and companionship—and I put my feet up next to hers.

★

The motif of transformations and important life moments was a concept we tried to come back to repeatedly in our work with the students. In a couple of months I'd be able to talk with my new students about the powerful transformations I felt I'd experienced with them as we embarked upon an integrated mini-unit on metamorphoses. Pivotal moments of catalytic change are critical in all subject areas, so this theme was something we embraced across the grade levels and curricular areas. I was eager and looking toward our place in that spiral curriculum, and excited to get started.

As students compared notes on crucial moments in world history where peoples and countries had been catalyzed into new versions of themselves, we researched and analyzed the scientific processes of converting energy from one source into another. As we chronicled growth and devolution over time, we graphed and categorized literary elements of plot and resolution, and demonstrated growth of characters in mathematical processes, redefining numbers and amounts. As students contributed to cluster-wide pools of academic analogies, we organized the different subject matter we'd studied and looked for interdependent changes. We took every academic action to pivot our whole curriculum on the hope that had brought us here and would take us into the years to come: complex and cultural notions of change.

These units would be assessed in several different ways—personal reflections on the parallel processes of transformation across the subjects. We used curricular materials to orchestrate presentations to their cluster peers of an example of transformation outside the ones we had been studying, either this year or prior. We captured the theme in cultural and historic wonder, also, through an artistic and creative-writing project we referred to as "Retablos." Taken from the traditional folk religious acts of paying homage to different saints through acts of pilgrimage and accompanying "ex-votos," we celebrated this practice of gifting metal paintings documenting critical moments in the pilgrims' lives. Students gave witness to this dimension of their cultural heritage by considering conceptualizations of gratitude and miracles, and of the will to suffer as an expression of all these things. To concretize the learnings and the integration of other curricula, we focused our activity on moments in which our students' humanity had risen to the surface and served to catalyze domains of their identities.

Students wrote essays about their experiences in Language Arts classes, and toyed artistically with the academic exercise of writing "abstracts" as we asked them to distill their stories to their cores. For writing development as well as artistic messaging, we pulled from their writing what could be added on top of their painted images. Students also selected appropriate media to convey their transformations in visual form. We allowed them to choose to demonstrate their change moments descriptively, symbolically, or in a combination of the two. Whichever visual decisions they made, students understood that their written narratives were to accompany and complement the works in our public gallery opening at the local museum.

For early adolescents in the middle of dramatic and occasionally tumultuous trajectories of development, this unit afforded us successes not just in the academic and artistic areas of instruction, but also in the growing empathy and community they were experiencing among themselves. Students were deeply invested in the transformative experiences of their peers, and eager to name patterns that paved academic as well as social connections. The students' capacity for drawing personal and intellectual parallels from our multiple activities was facilitating open conversations in which our otherwise-struggling students had found a space safe enough for them to participate.

This experience was also a chance to share with the students some of our personal and professional transformations as teachers, in a presentation on the broader history of the development of the school.

Students pored over the draft of the Origin and History document, and many referred to it in their own future academic presentations. They connected our beginnings to events as diverse as the Mexican revolution and the emergence of butterflies from cocoons. They connected the process of slightly departmentalizing to the math tasks of changing fractions to decimals. They made connections between their own narratives and the character vignettes in Paul Fleischman's *Seedfolks*.

★

It was just as I was experiencing my own roots growing that the books were almost taken away.

My classroom library was greatly enhanced by a generous organization dedicated to filling teachers' book bins and shelves with student-friendly texts. As teachers across the city began to fight the standardized-testing version of reading instruction, we in language-learning classrooms understood this new model as nothing less than the torture of students for being different, and punishment for a meta-lingualism we tried hard not to see.

The organization expected a lot from us in return, however: enrollment in workshops they designed to be helpful to us, in the strengthening of our abilities to put the books to best use.

I believed in the program in many of its aspects, but after years of giving up summers and weekends to professional development, and being boxed out of the workshops due to the deep professional learning we had experienced in Mexico, I felt confident in my own development as a professional as well as frustrated at the continued framing of teachers' issues being that we just didn't know enough. I had lots of experience listening to other people's versions of how to teach better, and was a little self-righteous about the growth opportunities we had designed for ourselves. On top of this all, I was developing a resistance to white-normative reform approaches and a persistent inapplicability for us teachers in language-rich classrooms.

Their workshops were provided by master teachers who presented innovative and exciting ideas, but in the return from our Fulbright fellowship, I knew that the work ahead to improve my teaching had to come from within me. I was certain that absorbing any more external envisioning of literacy justice would extinguish the spark I had found, and was tired enough to commit the ultimate crime in education circles of just letting it go.

If I had learned anything from the year before, it should have been that deciding what is best for oneself is only met with scorn, retaliation, and negative summations of one's being.

I felt entirely like Ms. D. as I watched the director of that philanthropic organization head toward me down our long hallway, flanked by her assistant and our lead teacher. There was nowhere to hide—and while in essence they weren't really after me as a person, they were coming for my personhood via the instruments of my transformed instruction. Their belief that I had not earned the books properly and had benefitted from gifts I was not entitled to emanated from them in all its white-woman judgment. In my efforts to complexify that in myself, I stood my ground and tried to smile.

"Hi!" I know white-woman worlds well, and the necessity of a good offense, as the saying goes. "You want the books but I don't want to give them to you. What do we do?"

"There's not a lot that we have to talk about. We were pretty disappointed that you failed to meet our standards of professional development required for the award you were given."

"I know. I'm sorry. I just didn't know how little time I would have, and I didn't organize it as well as I could have."

"I'm sorry that happened, but we're hoping you have the books organized for us so that we can give them to someone more deserving and willing to commit to our program's goals."

This was a smart approach. Indeed, I wanted other teachers to have the opportunities and books I had, but I knew the catastrophe this loss of resources could be. I knew, honestly, that I needed to learn and still wanted to learn, and that I'd been happy upon the award announcement for the workshop opportunities as well as the classroom library, and knew that I would enjoy them despite what I saw as culturally-narrow approaches. Beyond my own understandings of culturally-relevant teaching and learning, notions of equity and equality raced through my head—was there someone whose need was greater than mine, and more deserving due to their compliance?

I thought of Ms. D. and the other students who might have felt just like me in that moment—when so much of their life was about hard lessons that we with power over them would never have to experience but had all the opportunity to make it harder still. How was a system that claimed to be in their interest designed to hold the power away from them? Why was there no opportunity to negotiate the hard rules of our schools, especially when the rules prevented important things?

I knew in that moment I'd make it without the books.

It was about the validation.

I'd cleared my head of everything but my core resistance, and felt a final grace in the parallel I'd drawn to my own mistakes when I thought my epiphany was causing me to hallucinate—a miracle moment worth telling on my unmade Retablo. Ms. D. was coming out of the room down the hall.

"What's happening over there?" It never ceased to amaze me how fast news traveled in our micro-society.

"It's ok, kiddo. Just trying to explain a couple of things."

"Like what?" Piquing Ms. D.'s curiosity only intensified her rebellious streak.

"Let's talk later," I pleaded. "I'll need you."

"I'm sorry to tell you this but I think you need me now."

Our lead teacher looked back and forth quickly from Ms. D. to me—and smiled.

I was learning again the strength required to stand up against the myth of white benevolence—a brilliant theory into action that I had spent a year patho-logizing as defiance.

"Your teacher has some things that belong to someone else," the philanthropist informed her.

"Really? Like what? You mean those books she hauled up here the first day of school?" I thought two things simultaneously: Where had she been that she'd witnessed that? Why hadn't she helped me? "Why would she carry them all this way if they didn't belong to her? Do you mean that they belong to us students?"

"Well, no. That's kind of what was supposed to happen, but things didn't work out right and these are now supposed to go to some other students."

"Then why'd you give them to her?" I hadn't been able to see last year for my personal feelings about our interpersonal tensions, but it was clear Ms. D.'s talents of argumentation and strategy were unrivaled, and would serve her well in a future of litigation.

The philanthropists were silent. They could have said, "We were wrong to think she deserved them."

"Isn't there some way for her not to give them up?" Ms. D. was trying a concessionary tactic. "Isn't there some way you could agree to leave them here?"

The women were tough for not having been in the classroom in many years, and they weren't easily deterred from their mission. Quite aware of my own deficiencies, I'd long resigned myself to this outcome, but was shocked suddenly to see my deficiencies framed positively by Ms. D.

"But she hasn't done her homework. When you didn't do your work for her, what kind of response did she have with you?"

"What makes you think I didn't do my work?" She put her hands on her hips. "You see, you got it all wrong. She's been doing her work since before she even thought about asking you all for some pretty books. You all just don't know it."

"Let's see if you can tell us then."

"Oh, I can tell you, but you should know it already. Teaching is hard. Sometimes you just can't do everything you're supposed to. This girl hasn't even had time to write her pretty poetry. She's tired. Do you know how much energy it takes to feel bad because you got students you want to help but can't? How crappy it feels when you want them to learn to love to read but they can only do their homework in a bathtub after everyone's gone to bed?" I stood there stun-ned, shocked by her astute assessment of my struggles, a profound empathy for her peers, and a keen awareness of my weaknesses beyond how they affected her. Our lead teacher was nodding emphatically and beaming.

"So how is it that you're gonna help her? She doesn't need classes about reading. She could stand to be taught to get her head out of those books, instead. She needs help doing some other things we've got set up for her—you all got classes to help her with that? She needs some classes like the ones we give her here. Like what it means to be white when nobody else cares about it, but we all have to know about it all the time."

My own transformative experience had been more public than I thought, and to the one person I thought had not been paying attention.

She looked the visitors up and down. "Let her have her pretty books."

She turned to walk back down the hall but bellowed over her shoulder in that way I'd come to know all too well. "You know, I think maybe our classes have got some openings if you're interested."

I realized I'd won no matter what they decided—quite possibly, I never needed to win anything again.

I went back inside, pulled up a chair at a table and graded some character collages, happy to find that what I loved about my pretty books was often realized in my pretty life: we are always in the process of changing, and if one is reading, listening, or watching, it's the best show in town.

I thought too about the master class I'd just been given about the pitfalls of white normativity. Thinking you already know the outcome and evaluating others based on those expectations, you will never see the magic of metamorphosis for what it is: agency in action.

I never heard from the philanthropists about the matter again.

4

OCTOBER

Huapango

I decided to be proactive after noting how terrible it felt in the previous year to be so out of control and slow to react when called upon. I tried to craft quick and tight integrated units that would help propel us through the curriculum but also provide us with some possible memories beyond that.

Quick was the harsh reality of the unit upon us that October. In an effort to meet the external and unmovable deadlines for a couple of dance performances, we jumped into the unit feet-first and decided to work the assessment piece in isolation, ahead of the other curricular components. It wasn't the optimal decision—and positioned directly against much of what I believed about integrated curriculum—but we had little choice given our constraints. The elegances of instruction are for adults more than students, and the responsibilities of compromises belong with us as well. I still hoped the unique motivation in the students would support the deeper learning intended, as they were intense about their work for a cause they'd requested. It was my wedding we were preparing for.

The first month of school raced by leaving uncompleted tasks in my personal life that paralleled uncompleted tasks of each school day. Among all the small school-startup details to organize and sort out, there was one that made me the happiest—the work we were doing to choreograph this dance for my big occasion.

In collaboration with our dance artist, we did a quick frontloading of folk dance history, and applied the relationship between history and tradition through our focus on Huapango. While we only had a few days to pull the efforts together, it was important to all of us that we be as grounded in the history of the dance as possible. Its roots came from the Gulf of Mexico region, what had been my fast favorite Fulbright destination, through a week of exploration in Veracruz. My study group assignment that week was to collect artifacts and analyses of history while the other two groups rotated through arts and culture. I had immersed myself in my favorite content area and the specific colonial history of its haciendas, and formulated some ideas for my own academic interests as well as vast and detailed information we would implement in our school curricula.

The Huapango tradition fell into both categories. Because the Huapango meter is based on factors of six, we were able to craft correlating math activities for students to explore and understand the connections between two, three, and six—and how these entities played out in different portions of the song and dance. We were able to break down our chosen song into verses and refrains and examine each for its metrical value—and also begin to explore what unique mathematical meaning we could attach to each portion of the dance. For the moments when the rhythm was weighted on two beats, the students choreographed themselves in pairs, also reflecting a tradition of the dance. They layered these meanings in their proposal—the mathematical justifications, the particular history of this dance, and the hope to honor symbolically the pairing of our wedding.

For the measures and verses that were based in three-beat measures and groupings, the students decided to broaden their pairs into different variations of triads and trinities. They wove their traditional moves through the joining of pairs and the dispersements into triads—embodying a hope in their proposal that a joining of two in marriage was an expansive act in one's life that included the care-taking of oneself, her partner, and the entity itself of the pairing.

The dance artist and I laughed that the students had been interviewing their parents, or possibly watching too many novellas. We both processed together with the students the different mathematical constructions as well as the philosophical renderings of love and marriage, and the students and I set out with him to put the pieces together with the music.

I hoped that I could live up to their belief in me.

I'd never really intended or perceived that I would marry. Marriage had resulted in pain for my parents, and I'd seen early the nuances of love, cohabitation, and commitment. I'd witnessed also the self-definition that can break apart when a marriage does. I had grown up wanting to alleviate my parents' pain, and felt certain I knew how to avoid it my own life. With the arrogance of youth, I'd assured my parents that I would take a route different from theirs. I believed naively at times that I was assuaging any fears, but knew by now that the quiet of their responses was the kindness of letting me find out for myself.

The prospect of marriage was unanticipated curriculum for me, then.

That curriculum was infused with cultural learning as well. In the years I'd lived and worked in Pilsen, I was coming to realize the added dimensions of self we find by encircling ourselves with loved ones. I had found ways to detach from the individualism of my previous thinking, and pushed toward a deeper appreciation for why so many for so long risk the pain I'd seen. To live without it was worse.

Philosophically, culturally, and interpersonally, it had turned out to be nearly impossible to see the world through my previous assumptions and be the kind of teacher I wanted to be. During my first teaching years, I'd thought I might perhaps present as a good role model of independence for future young women who would also be able to strike out and survive on their own.

I didn't know enough about the values I would absorb to realize just how alienating this perspective was for my students. In my first years in the classroom students had interrogated me somewhat frequently about my life status: Husband? Parents? Children? Land of heritage? I'd laughed off the questions in a demonstration of the unkindness and insensitivity whiteness sometimes concretizes into. Whiteness in its bravado had also prevented me from seeing that cultural elitism for what it was—a hurdle to my own understanding, the value that broke through and helped me chip away at the blinders.

With my students I often smiled in non-responses. While I felt no personal connection to the categories of life that my students so valued and that peppered their inquiries, I felt connected to the sincerity of the people who cared in ways profound enough to open up to whatever this might be that they had to teach me.

★

Love comes when you're least looking for it, I'd always heard. I was at a particularly arrogant peak on my independence mountain when Gilbert started working at our school. I was stubborn and resilient beyond being independent, so I ignored any kind of emotions that had been generated in me as well as the kind and off-hand comments shot at me by students and colleagues. I worked hard at my teaching and at the preservation of my blinders in the first year we collaborated. Gilbert challenged both directly and indirectly the core identity markers I'd claimed and bragged about, and I was afraid that conceding any of them would initiate a domino effect in all the others.

Strong-willed and petulant, I tried to hold fast to certain "rules" I believed people should anchor their lives on all the way through, and the first of those was not to enter into a romantic relationship with a colleague. The source of that articulation was less clear than that of the second: not to consider a relationship with someone already committed.

This archetype had been present already throughout my childhood, and I feared the emotional capacity to process it in myself. To that end, I had needed some persuading.

When I finally started to cave in beneath the weight of my self-imposed romantic exile and began to allow the whispers of "why?", I began to see more clearly the image of me my students had maintained. I recognized that rather than being exposed to someone made strong through self-sustenance, I'd been the image of someone not whole enough to invite others in. I'd misunderstood their curiosity as wonder, when in fact it had come more from sympathy and worry, and from the profound compassion I would come to recognize as the most prominent of cultural traits in that community.

I had the opportunity to relive this awareness daily in the planning and rehearsing of our new Huapango and to realize how much of good teaching was to listen rather than speak. Though I had been fearful of centering myself in my students' learning and adding to their labor in order to indulge my wishes, I had actually managed to get out of the way and let the students speak to me clearly and in layered melodies about the version of themselves they wanted to be visible, and about the complexities of their developing worldviews, including a deeper joy from giving than receiving. In the repetitive trinity of the chorus, I let these new understandings swirl around me like the brilliantly-colored skirts in my classroom.

★

It was a good thing that I had lots of opportunities to revel in the goodness of the changes that were unfolding for me because I was off-rhythm in other areas of my life. I feared my betrayal of my sister would be irreparable as I hadn't checked with her for availability before scheduling our wedding date. I was afraid also that the corrosion would extend to my parents and other sibling, and that this unexpected and joyous development in my life would actually divide me from the rest of it. My mother's high expectations for me had always motivated my successes as well as a long-term desire to please her, but in this quick series of dangerous events, she feared that I was either not quite the person of her estimation or possibly not making these decisions fully of my own accord. Either way, in her eyes, I was conceding cultural practices to those of someone else, and she worried for the implications far beyond this one day.

These misunderstandings and disappointments afforded an opportunity to surface some issues that had long lain beneath the surface of my emerging adulthood, but I was nearly devastated to see the impact my unprecedented happiness was having on that of my loved ones. In a moment when I'd felt whole in new ways, I was also ironically being questioned about the integrity of all my different selves, and didn't know how to find a way out.

The rhythm of my days, in pairs, triads, and sextets had fallen nicely around an event that would exclude the choir I'd sung with, the small family I'd known, and a past I was working to integrate into a present.

★

Being an individualist claiming to work for community empowerment was like showing up fully-clothed to a nudist beach: both pathetic and rude all at the same time. I wasn't blind to it, and suffered a perpetual awareness that everyone around me was navigating the work in ways both trusting and open, while I suffered some pervasive fear of exposure steeped in superiority.

My intensive covering exposed me as even more transparent. Inside that metaphor, for all the layers it brought, I was walking the beach in my tweed suit while the pitying and happy bathers spared me ridicule despite my unsightliness, choosing to leave me to my own perpetually-twisted interpretation.

Nuances of skin tone and colorism's history had surprisingly arisen in my teaching more than a few times, in ways that not once centered on me. Cisco had been the middle child of a kind family that lived a few doors to my north. It had been clear in my ESL classes that he was among the most popular boys in the school. My routine often intersected with his sisters as they returned home nightly from track practice to take over the care of their younger brothers as their mother went to work. In the summer months, as I sat outside on the parkway, the girls often joined me under the old trees as the younger boys played. Cisco had a sense of humor even in third grade that was particularly charming—kind and jovial in a tranquil kind of way.

When he'd been in second grade we'd written ballads for Valentine's Day, and he wrote his about his love for the butter cookies in the cafeteria. I often saw students wrap the cookies in napkins to share with their siblings, parents, or friends at some future time. It was one of my earliest lessons to note the ways in which my students had learned a cultural value invisible to normative whiteness—pure generosity and the deeper joy felt when good fortune is shared—that made such an impression on me as to adjust my lenses on cross-cultural experiences as well as assumptions about the nobility of children.

These sappy reflections were not, however, the content of Cisco's song ballad he wrote for class. He took the tradition of Spanish-language ballads to a new level with a moody rendering of distracted days spent longing for his cookie, how the joy negated the smell of the cafeteria, and how his poor under-resourced school couldn't cloud this joy. The class had organized a competition in which they rated each other's ballads, and Cisco took every recognition and honor, as well as a couple of bows. He concluded with a mock acceptance speech in which he thanked his mother for making cookies not quite as good as the cafeteria's, so that indeed he could produce this song.

Teaching language was truly the most co-generative fun I'd ever had.

On one of the summer afternoons I sat with his sisters, I noticed aloud to his sisters that Cisco was sporting long sleeves despite the stifling heat, and his sister Beatriz let out a long sigh.

"It's so frustrating, Maestra. He doesn't want to lose his color."

It took me a long moment of watching him to absorb what she was talking about. The discourse about skin hues had been one of my big surprises in my early years in the community. When new babies came into the school, among the cooing and doting from all the adults, one could consistently hear commentaries about preferred levels of melanin—often framed as gratitude or regret at the light or dark skin shading amidst a quick reflection of one's ancestral antecedents and their location along mestizo lines.

I hadn't quite known what to make of these situations and in my conspicuousness often kept quiet, acknowledging the irony that in my white world it was common practice for people to spend time and money bronzing themselves in the sun—or in substitute machines—and that there were status attachments to these skin shades that coordinated with the amount of time one was able to spend tanning.

As I sat here on the parkway, I realized the extent to which our racialized Americanization of the world had been absorbed by locations of the post-conflict world much like toxic ultraviolet rays. Cisco had seen and understood clearly the class differential of race here in the US and in his home country. My students were subject to the nightly reminders offered in popular novellas whose formula included a white wealthy protagonist family tended to by a darker or indigenous person portrayed as lesser. This formula was broken only by worse models where indigeneity was centered but only as the focus of ridicule, as in the eponymous title character of "La India Maria."

Cisco was strategic in his efforts to keep his lighter skin.

The inheritance of different skin tones often varied within families in our school, in a nod to the mysteries of DNA in the historically-significant mestizo blending of heritages. A decade later I'd be reminded of Cisco and his sisters when my own mestizo children would be born entirely different in their phenotype, and celebrated socially in fascinatingly intersectional commentaries that would mark those differences.

Beatriz had a healthy sense of self—she was the best runner for a ten-mile radius and performed consistently well in school. She wanted Cisco to build up pride in other aspects of himself connected to his wit and humor, and not define himself purely on his pale skin capital. She confessed to me that she dreamed of forcing the issue by throwing away all his long-sleeved shirts and leaving him exposed to a sun that had not yet blessed him.

★

Cisco was one of the students to take the lead early on in creating our Huapango, and one of the only students who knew beforehand the song we'd selected. My students had academic levels of pop culture awareness and could report to me at length about movies, music, television, and radio in both the mainstream and indie margins of both their cultures. In my own immersion into my future family, I had developed a sense for myself about ways in which artists I liked had blended multiple cultural backgrounds over the years. We chose for the performance a song from a Chicano L.A.-based band, an exceptional group of musicians in their own right who crossed musical canons as well as folk traditions. Musically and lyrically, the group reflected contemporary interpretations of transcultural life, and were the solid favorite of my new in-laws and friends.

Cisco had been the only student familiar with the song; the friends of his father whom he visited on occasional weekends were fans of the band, and he'd grown an affinity for them that the other students hadn't yet internalized.

This meant center stage for him as I let him present to the class about both the lyrics and musical style of the song.

A benediction of sorts to youth and innocence, the song we'd chosen paid homage to the ways in which people integrate their different selves across the ages. We'd had to dive into the interpretations quickly upon the beginning of the school year, and Cisco had been a big help.

Perhaps the least reluctant or worried to dive in was our dance artist. I'd not had much luck in previous years getting Roberto invested in the academic components of our integrated units, but for whatever reason something had struck him about the personal nature of this current effort. He was a tremendously gifted dancer, famous in Mexico for his work with its premiere dance company—a fact I hadn't fully appreciated until getting to see a performance myself in the capital city that previous summer. He'd been the sole interpreter for the famous "Danza del Venado," an athletic and syncopated solo act incorporating fluid physicality and Olympic-level leaps, all in connection to the drum-led music.

We knew we were lucky to have him on board with us but had not yet been able to fully connect him to the world of our students. And in the tumultuous years behind us, we'd not really had the chance to take on the subtextual issues of class, race, and tradition within Mexico proper—Roberto hailing from a privileged class that had not belonged to the majority of my students. While I'd only reluctantly learned the hierarchy of skin tones in greater Mexican culture, I'd not yet grasped the intense bifurcation of the classes in part created by the increasingly invasive role of the US in an increasingly globalizing economy.

We'd weathered these transnational dimensions of diversity, and hoped for opportunities that provided emotional connections between him and our students. It was here in this song that paid tribute to the fluidity of culture and the magic of youth that those distinctions had begun finally to slip away. The students' mathematical constructions for meters of 2, 3, and 6 would eventually lead to a mathematical performance of all of us as a whole. More than the complicated path that had been laid to our wedding day, the learning involved in musically reaching these new understandings was worth our celebration. Through the immersion of new knowledges, I'd found a way to de-center myself from the activity—and to ultimately bring us all into the same octave.

★

One of the elements of the original design of the unit had been to tie the students' artistic statements about the dance to some other phenomenon in nature, society, school, or other domain. Students had been given free rein to choose the connections they wanted to make, and so when it came time to present their findings, we had an intricate tapestry of concepts that fell under the umbrella of the dance. One of the groups chose to talk about the metric basis of the song and presented different formulas that might be used to create different kinds of stanzas and verses. Other students explored the water cycle in its connection to the "river's flow" mentioned in the song and presented a large poster to the rest of the class. Other students gave a mini-lesson on the role of trees in nature, while yet others explored the ways in which cities grow from rural networks into urban metropolises. To complete the activity was to earn the ticket to present the dance to the rest of the school, and the collaborative nature of the project had helped those students who might otherwise have faltered to remain on track with us, and I noted that once again there had been a deeper lesson to learn from my students.

★

I'd tried on multiple levels to have our unit and performance help me underplay the events of the wedding. We had planned for a simple, local, and not-drawn-out lead up to the ceremony, particularly to help me avoid extended focus on us. I'd really just wanted my family to come out and stand around us while we shared some things we loved, said other things to each other, and then simply signed some papers. My expectations focused on the work following that day, and I'd reluctantly allowed even this small focus so that we could celebrate our community rather than the other way around.

I'd been a consistent disappointment to my mom in this regard and her exasperation was heightened by the shortened preparation time leading to our day. "If I cried at every birthday party you ever threw me, why would I want the big spotlight now?" I'd tried first to make it about me. It had infuriated her that I couldn't get through the birthday song until I was ten. Her British impulse for many years was to push me through it and that eventually I would get over my fears or shyness. My memories of that were an important guide for me in my teaching as I encountered all kinds of intelligences that had no correlation to social anxieties or comfort levels with forced extroversion. We hadn't explored some of these issues during my childhood years, and in my seeming reluctance to abide her, I approached my birthdays with trepidation. Something about this extended to other holidays as well. If I could have performed as my mom wanted me to, I would have. I wanted nothing more on those special days, or others, to make her happy.

These issues had surfaced during my college years, also, as she reeled at my chosen career path. Traditional images of teaching centered teachers as performers, even as our understandings of the enterprise shifted significantly. Beyond even mainstream culture's misinterpretations, her own schooling in mid-century England had fixed an image of teachers' necessary desire for control and strong sense of self—schools were a particularly rigorous engine of English society, and I wouldn't have fit them as a student and was certainly far from the image of a teacher.

I brought her out to see the kind of classroom I was building—where the spotlight stayed on the students through careful organization of activities and learning experiences. She got to see ESL centers—for vocabulary and reading, speaking and articulation, writing and self-expression, and listening and fluency—that repositioned me in the room as the guide, and as a yardstick for themselves to check their developing understanding. Students came up to me with their decoder maps to show they'd been listening to the recorded clues and directions, and my mom worked with groups of students and occasionally stepped back to take it all in. I'd planned different activities to make her feel at home, and to let her know how much of her spirit I held central in my own life. Her love of maps and exploration was something I shared, and also a key instructional tool with English Learners. I watched as she gleefully took the reins with that center and explored with the students their own imaginary places.

In my own schooling years, my mom had attended every parent-teacher conference, curriculum night, and open house. I loved her strong connections with my teachers—and her investment in my love of school. When I was devastated over a "B" in a science class in seventh grade, she'd refused to talk to me about the grade and talked with me about building a less-reactive sense of self. She was brilliant in all the unrecognized ways of the day, and had been unfortunate enough to intersect with a version of school that didn't see her vast intellect and worldly curiosity. I couldn't imagine a system that didn't value her. I knew in myself that her tireless work ethic was the source of our survival. Her affinity for patterns and intuitive reading of people were the foundation of my happiness. The societies that privileged our whiteness were the base of our successes.

What she'd expected my days to look like from the other side I had consistently imagined—and I knew that her worldly wisdom had not included the cultures and histories of my students. Happier than I in the spotlight, we asked my mom to tell us about her own migration and her struggles with it, and then had her lead a writing activity with the heirloom she treasured most. She talked about the sheer volume of American vocal patterns shocking her at first and still today, and how once she realized beneath her acculturation the ways in which she was allowed to retain her own heritage, she had made peace with such adjustments.

There was a general rapport established quickly with the students, and at one point one of the boys even asked her for her autograph—and told her he thought her accent made her sound famous. She told him she thought the same about him. She later told me how much she realized all the ways in which our school was trying to allow my students to retain their own heritage, and how she had related to the students in ways she hadn't expected. She warmed entirely to them throughout the day, and began even to ask them a few questions. This led organically to a conversation about my grandfather's picture that I'd had taped to the chalkboard.

My mom's dad was a soldier in the First World War. He had been only seventeen when he left home, and the youth in his letters astounded me when I finally had the chance to read them. While attempting to avoid the censors of the German wardens at the POW camp, he'd painted a rosy picture of his detainment in order to keep his own parents from worrying too much. Retained and restrained, he managed to narrate his daily existence as positively as he could. Word had it that my great-grandparents only began to worry once the letters had stopped.

My students sat riveted as they listened to this piece of history they'd only abstractly ventured into in classes. As my mom conveyed the epic ending to the tale—of her father's odd release and journey home with one wooden clog, alternating it foot to foot, she passed the photo around for the students to see for themselves. The students wanted to know how he'd got across the English Channel as depicted on the map, and a couple of the students alluded to the body of water they themselves had crossed in their own family migrations. Other students noted the generosity of spirit of those who'd housed my grandfather in whatever bombed-out domiciles they'd still had, while yet others connected with the hardship of trying to communicate urgent messages in places where there was no access to such communication—and the worry about the active imaginations of the loved ones left behind.

Later in their writing students would remember different pieces of the story—and would comment on all kinds of different aspects of my mom's talk with them. Different levels of English proficiency, as well as the complicated issue of memory and its tricks, caused the students to write up this oral history with all kinds of different details. My mom thoroughly enjoyed the renditions and the ways in which students were placing themselves in the story subconsciously. She'd also been amazed to hear details of some of their own family sagas infiltrating the narrative, and began to make sense of the ways in which I'd been connecting to a community I found hard not to explore.

I was thinking about all this and the possible culture clashes ahead of us as my well-shod family rolled through Ohio and Indiana on their way to me. They'd decided not to come see me the night before the wedding, and so I'd been granted another evening to ponder the potential tumult of the next day.

In an attempt to push aside our concerns, we took our friends up on their offer to grab a bite after setting up the hall for the next afternoon. After having arranged the tables and chairs, and set out the arrangement for the luxurious buffet of food provided by my suegra and her vast network of comadres, I felt certainly ready to relax with people who were both excited for us and not overly attentive to the nature of tomorrow's event.

As per the usual at that time of our lives, our conversations turned to the ins and outs of our teaching lives and the political context that enveloped them. As we discussed some of the community events ahead, we found ourselves in an animated conversation about nationalism. It was the one element of my new community that I had struggled most deeply with, but our friends were interested in the nuances of that reaction and how both Gilbert and I had arrived at such a position.

I wasn't sure on both of our accounts, and tried to present a parallel in my own national heritage and the ways in which I felt proud of that lineage but careful not to fall in lock-step with its actions across the centuries. I expressed that I knew that I was born of and talking about the ultimate example of colonial violence and empire, and so perhaps any nationalism I might feel would be laden with an oppressive mentality I'd hoped not to adopt.

Our friends agreed that this would shift my sensibilities, and that once a country had been colonized, nationalism might serve as an empowering technique rather than a claim of privilege. I agreed that there were nuances in the hierarchy of global power but also felt that nationalism in Mexican society had been used to squash autonomy in its poor classes and maintain a classist status quo.

I'd seen my students at their most animated around the Independence Day celebrations every September and had struggled within myself to come to grips with it. There were a couple of teachers at our school who felt awkward about pledging to any country and stood apart every year at the whole-school recitation of the Mexican national anthem. The fact that most of those teachers had been white did not go unnoticed, although people's generosity and granting of us the benefit of the doubt helped brush it under the rug as a mere symbolic act.

I knew I needed to challenge myself, and I felt the safe space with our friends to raise the issue. I'd experienced the deepening awareness of centering my focus away from my individual needs toward the community as expressed in the students' dance and wondered if there was still a crucial point I was missing as that communalism played out in versions of nationalistic pride.

My friends perceived a tighter conflation of the ideas, though they were uncertain if they'd think that way if they didn't have such deep connections to their homeland. What caused them to wave the flag and cheer their country in sporting events was a deep affinity for the people, not the government, and everyone they knew seemed to feel similarly. They wondered aloud with us, however, how much of that communalism might have been exploited by a government that was infamous in its oppression of its poor, and seemingly hell-bent on maintaining a rigid order of classes.

For our students, we agreed, the nationalism was a bit more innocent—mostly manifesting itself around the soccer leagues. I was wary, I confessed, of our role in promoting nationalistic tendencies in the young, with the possible result of numbing any critical-thinking impulses that might lead them to push to transform their beloved country. If anyone might stand a chance to help reorganize the system, it might be this generation of students with all their added insights gathered from transnational experiences.

We knew, all four of us, that to similar degrees we had also had those experiences—as would most of the people organizing themselves on our behalf tomorrow. I felt a sudden affinity for everyone with their lineages so disparate in geographic location, but so similar in tone. I thought of my appreciation for this conversation, and for the close relationships in that room—including the one I had with my spouse-to-be—and not just because I shared my daily living with all of them, but also because I believed whole heartedly in the power of the perspective that comes from having to continually cross borders.

In some ways this had been the message from the student choreographers crafting their gift—that there was a fluidity in the ways in which human beings can grow when engaged deeply with other people—that the exchanges between individual people facilitate much more than just a sum, but stretch and grow to include whole histories that would eventually intersect if we were able to travel long enough. I anticipated the celebration tomorrow with all of them, of the dances of intersecting and separating that were inevitable across a life lived deeply—a sure way to maintain the core of what was good might be to hold on to the knowledge one had had all along—and flowed throughout like a free river of youth.

5

NOVEMBER

Day of the Dead

"Do not learn anything from this." There was no thinking myself around this horror. If I could survive it, I wanted it contained here, tonight. How stupid to consider that teaching might be a series of crises teachers discretionarily respond to. Thinking myself around possible actions and the way automatic responses victimize kids already victimized by a system now felt childish. I had thought of the micro-moments of these kinds of decisions as crises. I wanted to scream. I knew nothing, and if I could go back to knowing nothing I would do that in this second. I wanted not to be anywhere inside of this.

Detached from my mind separating itself for as many seconds as it could, my feet continued slogging through the ugly late-fall Chicago rain, gray to the point of allowing no other referent—just dark and biting, this first day my sweet classroom helper was living without his sisters.

The rain felt like hand slaps, intentional in their assault, as we paraded toward the basement space now housing the family in its new version.

I'd heard the sirens the night before as I sat by the window watching the weather turn from hostile and threatening into formidable and isolating. I remembered the sirens for the strange eternity of their wailing—camped south of me in a way that communicated a worst-case scenario, as they stayed in place. Eventually the sounds crescendoed again toward me and then past quickly to the north toward the hospital stationed historically within the famous Chicago park that served as a sometimes DMZ between communities.

Later I would think of the peak of that noise, the loud peal proximity that puts a staccato note on a shared space with an emergency vehicle. My moment suffering from that sound and smugly content in my own safety was the closest I would ever be—ever—to the girls. The vehicles diminuendoed north down the thoroughfare that separated my apartment from my school, and I watched in the wet fracturing of light, the spinning red and white lights dimming as if they were being extinguished as they crossed under the train tracks and turned out of sight.

The water was the thing I fixated on in both that innocent moment and in the shocked disassociating that followed in the aftermath of knowing.

I'd lived in the neighborhood long enough, and in close enough approximation to this artery that ran from the prison campus to the hospital, to escape being drawn into the trauma connected with such sounds. They were gradually being woven into the fabric of my life here, and I packed my exposures to sadnesses like layers of skin, and learned—*learned*—to shrug in the midst of someone else's devastation.

I wanted to build a life on the belief that learning is preparation, but mine had tricked me. The moment instead sliced right through the protective skin layers, and this time the wailing was mine.

If I raged at anything in the first moments of knowing, it was at the rain. It should have been of help in the face of the fire that crushed and consumed the inner guts of the Muñoz family's brick three-flat. It should have overwhelmed the single faulty appliance wired incorrectly by a long-ago nameless stranger. It should have wrested an escape for the girls, extinguished a singular path for them back to us. I fought my own brain that wanted not to accept that it hadn't. I spent hours hoping to contemplate into existence a version of the events in which the aura of the flames that I'd innocently seen had carved only a small light in the night storm before being extinguished, or that the stupid stove hadn't taken on a leading role it didn't earn, and that the girls hadn't died just for preparing each other's dinner.

Everyone above ground had managed to escape, but the girls and their cousins who were spending the night together to kick off the weekend had been trapped. I'd sat there in my apartment a few blocks away, dreaming in the quiet of the aftermath, watching the rain streaming down my front window, about the future, about the past, and about the episodes of my teaching for which I'd not yet learned to forgive myself.

The girls had been trapped.

It was possible that I'd sat there that night and thought of Raquel. She'd come by my room during a critical moment that very afternoon. She'd stood outside and waved me over; it was evident she wanted to speak to me about something. I'd gestured that she should get back to class, and that I would talk with her later—trying on a forced confidence in my new stricter approach to teaching: during class time she should be in class; we could connect afterwards. Wanting to be a better team player to my colleagues in the middle school cluster, I was trying on new "no exceptions" framings of our norms. Raquel had been one of my seventh graders in Ms. D.'s split class the year before when episodes such as these easily distracted me, and I may never know if at that moment, she had understood that I had grown in my management, a contrast to the version of me she knew before. Recalling fears I'd felt of disappointing her previously, I may also have been showing off. I may have wanted her to know I could do things differently. I may have thought I'd have a conversation with her about adolescent psychology and how hard it can be to navigate different versions of it in one classroom, with one approach. The ponderings of that night might have been all of these loose thoughts, lost in the rain, with the events that shrouded present, recent past, and near future.

I'd never know what she'd read from me in that teaching moment; it was the last time I'd ever see her.

★

As I'd tried to construct a learning environment with that sixth-seventh split that I'd had the year before, while we as a school constructed everything from scratch, Raquel had been the one student who had a connection to my teaching in the old school in my fifth grade class—when being in my class was a calm and productive affair. She and her siblings had been in my ESL pull-outs for years, she and Pedro officially during school and her two baby siblings informally in our family after-school sessions. Her mom was a nurse whose genuine intellect informed me academically as well as emotionally, with her wicked humor to highlight it more. I gravitated to her eagerly, and the warmth she radiated in all of her maternal dimensions, and the generosity with which she shared her children. I'd been impressed by the closeness of their family, knowing the adversity that hindered their lives in our community but didn't dampen their commitment to maximizing their sacrifices and building what they could. I'd visited them several times in the lost house and was grateful for the social connections beyond my official role in their lives.

Raquel had been the one I'd asked to help prepare me before the formalities of the wedding only three weeks ago, though at the last minute the demands of her family business kept her from being with me.

I'd been sad more than hurt as I understood the difficulties in planning activities when so much of a family routine depends on everyone's maximized labor. I'd felt some guilt that I had asked and put those needed hours in jeopardy, and thought about the possibility that I was centering myself in ways I ought not to. I knew deep connections with students were investments in their needs and the capacity to work with them holistically, but I was loath to consider that I had crossed into selfishness by asking her to join me.

In light of all this, I'd waved Raquel on.

I must have been wondering that night as the storm pelted my window what she'd wanted to tell me so earnestly underneath the reflections on my teaching week and hoped I would know it soon.

I might have even thought: I hope she's ok.

★

Raquel hadn't judged me once during that toughest year. She'd encouraged me onward in my Spanish development and propelled me to keep trying with the students who had learned how to successfully derail my teaching. As I got to the end of teaching units, I'd look at her work for evidence of her learning first—to know whether I could expect that learning had taken place for any of the students, and where I might work to build bridges for others. She'd been ridiculed gently by her friends that she was too studious and serious, and that she should stop sabotaging Ms. D.'s efforts with her kindness, but she never wavered from a core integrity that quieted others in the warmth it radiated, and I never once saw her bend under the pressure.

In photos of that year, Raquel is the student often looking directly at the camera in almost all my candid shots, despite my efforts to be discrete with candid shots to witness what we'd been able to do. Raquel interacted with the camera as though she were aware of the history being written and wanted ownership of the versions being told. In a project on family trees, students had drawn images of family photos they had seen or even had in their possession. Students wrote painfully-detailed explanations of the photos to practice descriptive writing and then also narrated and painted the worlds those images spoke to in their composite projects. We'd pulled all the dates from the students' charts of ancestors and chronicled eras of Mexican history inside the timeframes the images provided. Raquel's close relationship with her grandparents and Mexico-based family proved to be more than an asset for her, as she shared with us the stories her grandparents told. Her peers had varying migration stories, and many of them hadn't experienced much of their grandparents' lives. Raquel knew their lives and their thoughts, and her narration of their wisdoms became our keystone in the classroom's composite oral history.

Once the descriptive-writing and artistic components were over, and we'd created individual histories of transnational Mexico, we also charted US incentivized-citizenship programs that had intersected with generations of their families. Some students were children of "bracero" families and others related to professionals brought here through global exchanges for teachers and other civil servants. Other students had migrated collectively with waves of neighbors after ecological events or political turmoil, while others were lone ex-pat families who had experienced individualized trauma or upheaval, and were here to amass as much capital as they could so that it could all be sent to those who remained at home. In a later project on the Mexican musical tradition of "corridos," students in the school wrote musical renditions of key characters and events, and performed these catalytic personal histories in celebration of the collective migration histories now informed their current lives.

Back in my classroom in that first year, however, I was growing connected to the students' ancestors and eager to put their research and hard work to continued use—and so was stretching the activities as long and as far as I could. Our final activity was to try to create a message from the oral histories —a kind of moral of the story—that everyone could take away with them. Students needed to develop these particular oral histories with their parents' commentaries and editorials, and focus on family members' opinions about the central lessons learned. We began the sharing of these by retelling what we could with our younger mentees, in our Reading Buddies time, our weekly hour where my students read to their first-grade partner, and supported them in affective and skill-based analyses of texts.

Raquel's peers believed her story needed a bigger audience. With ten first-graders all cross-legged on the floor around her, and her peers leaning against desks and walls on the periphery, Raquel had recounted the story of her grandfather's shoe-making talents, and the entrepreneurial ways he took care of the feet of all local farm workers. He had become the cornerstone for the agricultural laborers in their rural town in central Mexico, repairing shoes, tracking physical and emotional health issues, and counseling them as they took time to rest with him while he worked to repair shoes. As the economy fluctuated and the agricultural businesses gave way to different industries, he'd maintained his focus on the men he'd known for so long, and worked his micro-economy in such ways that all his previous customers had access to what they needed.

His soul appeared in my classroom every day, and I made a note to tell Raquel's mother about the parallel between her caretaking of her classroom community and the stories we'd heard about her father. Though the world for his grandchildren had changed even more than the economic shifts he had weathered, his belief in facing one specific hardship and never conceding to forces beyond one's control paralleled his descendants' lives in Chicago. Hurdles were to be understood and discussed, but there was nothing that should shake one's core commitment to others. What Raquel remembers her grandfather saying, she shared with the young students: "There's only the doing. If you climb, climb. If you dig, dig. If you watch, watch. If you know, know. Everything else is distraction. When you know who you are, then you do what you do. Most importantly, when you don't know who you are anymore, just doing will tell you."

★

If things had unfolded differently the year after I had Raquel in my class, the year I had her brother instead, we might have coordinated similar "Advice from our ancestors" morality tales into a large public ofrenda being installed as part of our celebration of the "Day of the Dead" traditions. Every year each classroom transformed a corner of its space into colorful collections of mementos and reproductions of photos to contribute to the collective honoring the dead. Students designed strings of papel picado, and created bright paintings of marigolds. They made pottery versions of "pan" and other favorite foods, and told each other stories of the loved ones being remembered. In photos of cemeteries across rural Mexico, the candle-lit festivities contradict the sadness imbued in the grief and loss, and the music and shared cultural practices bridge any corporeal divide and eclipse increasing darkness and cold that accompanies the dreary first days of November.

The joyous rituals in these cemeteries are carried into homes as well, and the humor and faith demonstrated on the same day each year extend also into the daily life of families across the multicultural regions of Mexico. Ultimately, the inescapability of death is a part of life to treasure. That there will be a death tale for each person is a perfect manifestation of the belief in each person's uniqueness.

Every child understands from an early age the importance of remembering their pasts, and recalling the specific characteristics of lost loved ones so that the void they've left will be made a bit smaller. On the Fulbright that past summer in Mexico, I'd had a conversation with one of the museum guides in Oaxaca, a state famous both world-wide for its gorgeous traditions around this holiday, and for the spiritual elegance with which people interacted with each other. I'd wondered to him if the holiday took on a different tone for those who'd lost family members or friends in circumstances that had political overtones or had felt preventable somehow. I'd wondered if there was ever any rage that got in the way of the celebratory tone. I'd also struggled to articulate these words in the contextual ways language marginalizes ideas that aren't central to cultural tenets—it had taken me many minutes even to be able to barely articulate that question. Years later, students in a teaching program at a local university would be disappeared in large numbers[1]. In close parallel to my life, I would remember the cultural guide and his patience with my limited and linear understandings.

"Ah, I see the question behind your curiosities," he'd said. "But there is no room for anger on such a night. Anger comes from expectations—and death is the great eraser of those. We know those expectations are very Western at their roots. This holiday reflects some Western traditions but is not the same as them. What we bring out on this day is what we value most of all—and the joy you might be questioning comes from a faith deeper than any frustration or anger at things you cannot control. It is the night every year when your heart must be completely filled with love. That is the real light that brings back the dead. That is the depth of the joy even horrors brought by conquest cannot erase."

★

The absence of light was what struck me the most that afternoon as I snaked my way down the gray exterior stairwell into the cement basement where Raquel's family had taken shelter. As the cold rainwater crept in across the floor where we entered, I thought of the essence of Raquel's grandfather's advice—keep "doing," even in the face of all other distractions. I said it like a prayer: "Keep doing."

The stark reality was that I was inside an event where I didn't know at all what to do. In my classroom I had a safety net for when I felt uncertain—a tradition of teaching I'd acquired by osmosis from all my years in school. When I felt the inner questioning of the two value systems I was asked to engage, I could always resort to norms of schooling as I knew it. While I realized that those norms were borne of a culture different from that of my students', I trusted I'd later find ways to build the bridge between them.

In the cold, dark entry into a reality I didn't know if I could endure, I knew there now was no "later." With Raquel I'd fallen back on old norms and waved her away, when I could have figured out my focus on the tasks we were engaged in, and still availed myself to help her in a moment of trouble. I hadn't had to choose. I'd tried on a false, linear confidence that her need could wait, and that I could calculate my time. I'd thought I have it. I'd been wrong.

I was wrong, angry, and here on the steps, about to face the shattered remnants of Raquel's family. In the losses of my childhood, I'd had no responsibility to facilitate the process of grief. Adults around me had taken charge and constructed our comfort inside our culture as we knew it, and I'd absorbed that process and expectation subconsciously. Outside a new world I didn't want to enter, I knew that for two boys in there I was one of the adults and in a unique position to help—and uncertain about my capacity to navigate the pain of the moment and the cultural practices that would soothe it in its raw vulnerability.

In that doorway to the world Raquel's family now faced I considered the fact that once upon a time it would have been Raquel to process feedback for me about the situation. I knew even more profoundly that were she at all allowed to have survived, her first focus would have been her little brothers.

On the steps my co-teacher Daniel was ahead of me, already on the other side of these thoughts. Even as I paused on the landing, other neighbors and supports had snaked around me. There was no hesitation in the movements as I watched them enter and provide care in as fluid a motion as any I'd ever seen. At this point I couldn't see beyond the activity of these caregivers to the boys I was looking for, next to the void of the girls who wouldn't be here. I wanted a light—a flash of lightning or the fluorescent bulbs that irritated our classroom—somehow like marigolds to guide me. For an instant, I recalled the admonitions of the Oaxacan museum guide. The light this world offers its lost loved ones is a light of faith—a faith with no object. The faith is the object—it is the recognition that our being is fullest when we are in the service of other people.

I believed Raquel's grandfather would add a concrete admonishment to the spiritual analysis: when you don't know, doing will give you the answers.

With the words of them both and the ache for the girls, I went in.

★

Years later I would remember the way things unfolded, the way someone went for candles and yet no one wanted to light them, the way a lamp was brought down from the first floor, and that someone from somewhere brought a mattress for the boys to lie down on. I watched the way they fell asleep facing each other and within seconds of lying down. I would remember wanting them to rest but being afraid for them not to be awake as I watched the endless rainwater spin around the drain in the middle of the floor. The most vivid recollection would be of the boys on top of the mattress, covered in what we had, after a search for a spot as far from the runoff water as possible but also within inches of the door.

As I sat atop the mattress near the boys, I saw the way Sra. Muñoz's eyes were unsettled in their vigilance of the children in front of her and also for the children she'd lost. In her distance from us she cried quietly for her daughters and begged to see them. With the realization that she couldn't, Daniel had held her arms firm to her sides to ride the surge of anger. I wanted unconsciousness for the boys, and all the rage in the world for their mother. I wanted us to let her rage at the world, at herself, at the city, at the electricians, at the poverty that had driven them from home, at the family that allowed them to leave, at the one exit her daughters could not get to.

I'd sat on the mattress with the sleeping boys, and wondered about the tandem grief and anger that would surface in them. When they'd last slept they'd been different people, and when they awoke they'd face the brutality of events again as their consciousness would struggle to make sense of the pieces in front of them. In the immensity of what I feared for them, I buried my head in my hands. The sleep of the boys opened a space for me to mourn the loss that I felt unfolding in its gravity, but I knew the dangers in this moment of being too close to the raw emotions of Sra. Muñoz. I'd been protected by thoughts of caretaking until the boys rested, and in their absence I worried I had no caretaking capacity that could help her. I'd been drawn to her as a parent for her comprehensive and graceful commitment to her children, despite what would have been insurmountable impediments to others, and faced now the awareness that I had none of that to offer her in return.

Over the years I would remember her grief in details I didn't think I had even noticed in real time, I would realize the transitional place of her trauma and that part of what the Oaxacan guide was saying is that acceptance isn't resignation but the fullness of being. In that cold basement miles from the bodies of her daughters, there was nothing that should be done. There was grief and shock, horror and rage. Any other activity did not belong. I realized later too that we did not belong either. We were there for comfort and to act, but we were not inside her pain. We were there to guide it if we could. We could serve as a bridge as she traveled between worlds no mother should have to visit. My vigil was with the boys, Daniel's vigil was with her, and in its entirety her vigil was with the girls.

We did what we could, and when we didn't know what to do, doing helped us more. We recovered more mattresses and stopped the entering water. We assigned tasks for the morning. Someone might have located the children's father whose grief had been so big it needed its own space. Someone might have wrapped themselves around Sra. Muñoz.

All I knew was to place my own protective arm over the sleeping boys, and wait until morning.

★

In the months that would follow, I would remember more and more of the anguish of that night. In seemingly-constant conversations with colleagues and parents—and sometimes with students—we began to piece together the ways in which we'd all experienced the tragedy. There were many times we couldn't anticipate the timing or the intensity with which we revisited events in unfortunate ways.

At school, a couple of months after the tragedy, we had our first fire drill. There had been a long discussion among the faculty for the last couple of years about the typical public-school practice of warning teachers about the drills. Certainly, in the absence of real danger, it seemed silly to force young children suddenly into the cold and harsh elements without having had time or preparation to get coats and other protective layers. There was also the aspect of teachers having some kind of opportunity to alter their lessons to better accommodate an interruption—so that the drill wouldn't serve to derail high-quality instruction and put teachers in the tough position of having to re-establish rhythm in their rooms without any professional courtesy.

This time we'd experienced the terrible repercussions of a fire in the loss of our students. Discussions we'd had before felt quaint and academic. Teachers balanced pervasive low-lying guilt about the role we might have been able to play in the prevention of the girls' deaths. "What if" scenarios are common, of course, but the collective nature of them among faculty brought a keen level of anxiety to our preparation discussions. Despite the intensity, we were unable to be productive. What was a safety routine for a hypothetical future was now a play-by-play reminder of a horrific recent past.

In the months that followed the fire, we'd invested numerous hours in trying to care for the psychological health and healing of all the students in the school. We had school on the Monday after the fire, accompanied by large teams of counselors from other sites to help us facilitate both whole-class conversations as well as one-on-one meetings with specified students and teachers.

The counselor from our old school spent the day in my classroom, taking part in our class meeting. I'd decided that we should meet formally for the first hour of the day to talk about things, but then spend the rest of the morning in art activities— portraits for the ofrenda, papel picado for the hallways, construction paper sweet breads, flowers, and candles. I thought that if we had the students work in groups at different stations, then maybe they'd have conversations that weren't as threatening as if they weren't doing anything—like art therapy. The students who didn't really have a personal connection to the family wouldn't have to immerse themselves in the sadness, and the students who were struggling to make sense of it could let out some of their feelings while being productive in other ways.

At one point in the first couple of hours, one of the counselors came to arrange a time to meet with me. My friend had stayed with us for most of the morning, working with groups and talking with students in general about how to respond to Pedro when he returned to us the following Monday. The students had the most concern about that—how to be around him and what not to say. The students were uncertain about the role they'd play in trying to help him get back to learning. We tried to assure them that they should be sincere when they talked with him—that they should not feel like they needed to talk about what happened, but that they might want to open it up to Pedro to talk about his feelings whenever he wanted. I could read their apprehensions for the same kind of fears I'd had the night we'd spent in the basement. Maybe it had just been normal fear that had kept me from feeling like I could help Sra. Muñoz, not a gap in our cultural practices or life experiences fostering wisdom. I thought maybe I hadn't yet known how to help someone get through such a big moment, how to just "do" as her father would have told her. I didn't know how to have faith inside the space of anger so that your heart can stay open.

I decided at my friend's urging to take up the counselors on having a meeting. Everyone agreed I should meet with someone I didn't know previously, and so we sat in the copy room for a few minutes in the late afternoon when my students went to their gym class. I hadn't wanted to leave them with anyone else— not for their sakes but for mine. I'd soaked up the students' thoughtfulness and innocence like precipitation as I felt my emotions were dry. After the weekend of organizing food for the family and arrangements for the funeral, I'd needed their gentle laughter and to see their joy surface more easily than for me. I'd realized also what we might offer Pedro that had seemed so elusive before: the wonders of being a student.

★

In my meeting with the counselor, we spent most of the time processing the visit to the funeral home that had occurred the day before. Sra. Muñoz, Daniel, and I went at our appointment time to the converted house that sat at the corner across from our old school's campus.

At the end of my third teaching year, we'd received a grant to coordinate a small summer institute through which students would paint a mural on the wall of the Boys' and Girls' Club that sat on that same corner. In the long summer days of mixing paint and coordinating kid schedules, I'd not really noticed the business just behind us. In my short time at the school I'd heard community conversations about young people killed, and registered perhaps on some level the location of all those wakes. Detached from any emotion in response to the news, I projected the dehumanizing desensitization so pervasive in those years about gang violence and the unrelenting murders of young people.

I saw that squarely now as we approached the building. I glanced at the bright colors across the street from so many summers ago, and hung my head in growing shame. The Polish name on the funeral home sign was unreadable for me— I'd never had the skills to pull together the consonant streams in the Polish language the way I'd heard people do in documentaries and on the north side of the city. I knew that the family had run the home for generations, perhaps pre-dating the migration of Mexicans to the neighborhood. The brothers of the current generation in charge knew no Spanish and asked Daniel and me to translate as much as we could. The business element of that piqued some latent anger, manifesting more in frustration at the challenge. This particular vocabulary had not yet been taught in my emerging language. I turned to watch Daniel face his emotions, his elegant fluency unable to mask his horror at the terrible details.

Sra. Muñoz asked repeatedly to see her daughters. Inside the several responsibilities we were there to carry out, nothing was more pressing to her than this simple fact. In more need of the comforts afforded by her own cultural practices, she wanted to be with the girls as much as she could in the upcoming days and for the girls to have an open-casket wake at which family could share in a complete and collective grieving. The undertakers informed us that they could not honor this request, and tried to avoid any resistance by moving on through the rest of the details, in English so as to exclude her direct participation. Shocked at the interchange, I hoped Daniel was absorbing most of the concretes—cost, date and time, specific forensic services they provided.

We'd collected already nearly a thousand dollars from the community, church, and local non-profits, so we tried to assure the men across from us that with this as down payment they could expect the rest of the money in time. They seemed less perturbed by this than I expected, though one of the brothers commented to us with a half-smile that they were used to the needs of low-income families.

There was something about this cold sentiment and the way it was presented that set me on edge, and as we ironed out the time and day for the wake, I worked hard internally to place the nuance of what was troubling me. While I might have seen their commitment to the community as that of providing a service, there was something exploitative about the way he'd conveyed their history with neighborhood clientele. I wanted to interrupt him mid-stream as he prattled through the list of services in the package we'd purchased for Tuesday and ask him what he knew about any of the people he worked for. Did he know that this humble heart-broken woman in shock was a physician who sold ice cream from a truck because it paid more than the medical industry in her home country? Did he know that some of the gang members he'd possibly dismissed carried the hopes of grandparents and great-grandparents who had migrated here hoping for opportunity and been thwarted by an economy fueled by maintaining this marginalized class? When he looked at our old school, did he see the hopes buried there with no ceremonial services to be purchased?

Did either of them know that the girls they were going to bury for us wanted to become a journalist/writer and doctor, respectively?

I carried this anger to my session with the counselor, who tried to suggest a defense for what we'd experienced, and explained away the perils of desensitization, defending them for perhaps having become numb to the sufferings that their jobs put them in the middle of. She tried to comfort me by offering that language could certainly have been the central issue, and that maybe too they'd experienced their own history of marginalization and invisibility in this community. Ultimately, she reached across to me and expressed that maybe beyond all these contextual factors piquing my anger, death was death and cultural understanding combats the pain of this ultimate universality.

While I could see a possible truth to what she said, I was still troubled and sought out my old-school friend at the end of our long day for his take on the situation. He knew me well enough to see through some of my unwieldy assertions, and I trusted him to help me settle as much as possible. I knew myself, too, and that if anger was indeed a secondary emotion, I was instrumentalizing it at length in my responses to my conversations with these professionals. He also knew the funeral directors from being involved in the community and would know my frustrations in a very specific way.

The true difficulty had come around the issue of reuniting Sra. Muñoz with the girls. We had no hope of consoling her in the absence of that opportunity. It turned out that—for whatever reason, whether the intensity of the fire or the actions of those at the hospital and funeral home —there was no way for her to see them. Images we'd all held on to, perhaps, were disconnected from what was true for us. Selfishly, I knew I didn't know how to process what the parameters of Sra. Muñoz's capacity for horror might be, and to what extent we were replacing that imagined trauma with this very concrete disempowerment, now at the most important moment of her life. Already we weren't sure that she was able to hear how complete the devastation had been. In the beginning I couldn't be sure that it mattered, as it was hard to differentiate her immeasurable grief from the frustration at being thwarted in her only ask. Ultimately I would learn from her that it didn't.

I didn't know enough about the business, I told my counselor-friend, and wasn't certain where my distrust of the undertakers had come from other than a growing politicized lens about racialized inequities in all kinds of circumstances of access. I could provide no consolation for her, or even myself, via this perspective, and as we sat there and talked, I knew that my grief would be intertwined with anger for longer than was healthy for anyone, though I still believed that anger was a powerful tool in resistance. No version of it had manifested in justice, however, for Sra. Muñoz, and I now needed to consider other realms in which my students' families experienced this intensity of disempowerment.

I was thinking, of course, about our school. I wondered to my counselor-friend if he saw what I was projecting into the scenario. Were the undertakers doing what they believed to be right in trying to protect Sra. Muñoz? Had they made this judgment exclusively from their own position of privilege when they should have invited us in? Was there more nefarious weaponizing of the circumstances connected to the lack of social capital the Muñoz family appeared to represent? Would they invent this horrible scenario simply to avoid additional labor, believing they would not be compensated for the high costs of that work?

My mind settled on the last question, and I understood the impact of that question on the rest of Sra. Muñoz's life. In my own admission of distrust, I entertained the difficult thought that I may have acted similarly in my own professional life. Didn't I every day make decisions I thought were in the best interest of my students without taking their opinions into consideration? How many times had I projected my own values into that equation in the name of advocacy or empowerment? Which of those instances could have caused life-long trauma?

Were there any occasions in which I had stood in the way of families fulfilling one lone and last wish?

How many times had the whiteness of my role initiated trauma that might not have occurred with someone more culturally-appropriate in my place?

★

I'd appreciated the efforts of my friend to remind me of differences between me and the undertakers but my own sadness heightened my critical reflections, and the questions ached and lingered. Still we taught. After school on the third day, we all filled the funeral home for the wake. On the fourth day we crossed the boulevard to attend the funeral, made ourselves as quietly present as we knew how, and learned from the boys what kind of love they needed from us then. Through the days we counted, marking that first week, we walked quietly in a fog through our own grief. We were relieved of our own sadness by the needs of the young people in our care—knowing the emotional, educational, and cultural complexity of that important word. Our days were filled with decisions once not fraught, but that now pitted our attempted sensitivity against the required activity of late fall on a public-school calendar. Report cards were completed and shared, conferences often hushed and quick. We even kept the originally-scheduled picture day, despite its occurrence after the morning's funeral—the eventual pictures a reflection of Victorian post-mortem photography not so much commemorating us or anyone, but instead documenting and honoring the shared death among us at that moment.

For many of us, our annual commemorating traditions for the Day of the Dead ritual helped catalyze a group healing at last in earnest, beyond the performances in front of our students, and perhaps as taught and even prophesied by our Oaxacan tour guide.

We'd been scheduled as a whole school to present an ofrenda at a local community museum. We all contributed work we'd kept from the girls—either current year artifacts or items we'd held on to from their previous years with us. We assembled them all around the altar, surrounded by representative marigolds and candles, sweet breads and coffee, sugar skulls and catrina dolls of the girls in different school memories. We submitted calaveras with the customary teasing, funny poems on them, and sealed letters from anyone who'd wanted to send one. We tried to honor their unique characters with particular stuffed animals and toys we'd been able to salvage from the building.

We added lastly a journal for museumgoers and community members to contribute memories of their own, and to express their grief individually and publicly.

★

We were brought back to the present by the work we faced in helping the boys. They'd returned to us a week after the tragedy weak and exhausted, sad and nervous. As we tried not to make any presumptions about the roller coaster of emotions they must be weathering, we tried carefully to settle into the work of returning them to the routines they'd had before their world changed forever: R. L. Stine books, math computer games, globe-trotting on GeoSafaris after school.

We talked about the girls in as many ways as we could, and maybe more than they wanted us to. Everyone in the school seemed to understand the goal was to hang in there, to be present consistently in case the moment arose when big questions would come up for them.

With each other, we also asked them ourselves. We had our own existential struggles, caretaking impulses to balance, and a lot of pedagogy questions about how best to proceed in our plans—a word that stung for many of us, with ache and regret.

★

Slightly after Thanksgiving a group of us teachers traveled to the museum to take the ofrenda down, and as we sorted the items and preserved as much as we could, my colleague showed me the journal. She'd been reading through the messages, and had stopped at the weight of what she'd found inscribed on one of its last pages:

> "Wherever it is you go now, just do.
> And I'll try, too.
> Love, Pedro."

Note

1   In 2014 in Mexico, 43 students at a teacher's college were abducted. The word used to describe this type of event in Central America is "disappeared" —this term often presumes state-sanctioned massacres.

6

DECEMBER

Tianguis

I'd decided to add to my family rituals that Christmas by bringing home some traditional tin ornaments my students made and sold through our school's annual Tianguis. While we'd used materials suitable for in-school production, the "hojalata" were designed to resemble the traditional folk art we'd seen in several different towns across Mexico that summer. Cut painstakingly from tin, the brightly-painted ornaments were careful renderings of important aspects of Mexican life—characters with different instruments in traditional dress, important public sites such as cathedrals and government buildings—and we'd carefully wrapped several examples to bring back with us to the school precisely for this Christmastime activity.

December was often our most chaotic month at school. Besides Christmas, my students observed the day of the Virgen de Guadalupe on December 12th with a pre-dawn mass in honor of Mexico's most important religious character.

Guadalupe represents the best of Mexico's sophisticated efforts to integrate the duality of their history—the polytheistic roots of the indigenous cultures and the monotheistic Christian influences that came with colonial invasion and the violence of Spanish conquests. The story behind her role in the religious life of most Mexican people is that she was an apparition of the catholic Virgin Mary who appeared to a Mexican saint outside of Mexico City in the 16th century, asking in the indigenous language for there to be a church constructed in her honor. According to different historians, the apparition contained aspects rooted in both traditional Christianity and Aztec religions. While her appearance contained references to Mary in the Immaculate Conception images, the colors were also reflective of two separate Aztec goddesses and many historians reference this highest-ranking saint as emblematic of the efforts of indigenous and mestizo people of Mexico to integrate their historic roots into their colonized existence.

I'd worked in the community for a short time before realizing the omnipresence of her image. Guadalupe graced business awnings, flyers, student notebooks and backpacks, and lots of phrases in informal discourse. She was inescapable—and revered across the board by my youngest students in their sketchbook drawings, by their parents in references and vernacular expressions, and by rebellious late adolescents and innumerable tattoos sported by older men and leaders of rival gangs alike.

One of the struggles Gilbert faced as an artist in the community was getting past the ever-present iconic images when trying to convey aspects of culture and community in murals and paintings. As he brainstormed with different groups of students, he challenged them beyond their initial impulses to fill murals with the traditional images of Guadalupe or other common symbolic representations of the complex history of their history and community—the Aztec calendar, the volcanoes as warriors, the traditionally-catholic iconography, and other images I came to realize as standard bearers. As a refugee of the Catholic Church, Gilbert harbored ill feelings about the hypocrisy of the Virgen and its role in a religion that served to oppress and repress the ancestral lineage of his cultural heritage. And while I agreed with him about its role, I was also intrigued by the folk-nature of this manifestation of Roman Catholicism and so listened carefully to the stories about the services.

If December 12th fell on a school day I had to be careful to plan activities that would allow students to conserve their energy while still completing our academics before the two-week break. We did the typical elementary-school activities of trying to create gifts for the students' families in arts and crafts work and evidence of good learning. And we also struggled to provide cumulative assessments of the curriculum learned up to that point so that when students returned in January they could have a quick refresher on the topics and then move on from there.

December was complicated for us in the community, however, by the dual forces of maintaining the belief that education is of highest priority for developing youths, and an understanding of the imminent dispersal of families back to their homes in Mexico—as both an escape from the cold, and a necessary reconnection with missed families in need of money or medical supplies, or extra hands to provide extra labor. Because of the length of the journeys to return back to the towns of their family networks, many students' parents augmented the two weeks off from school with an additional two weeks to fulfill their obligations of seeing each relation left behind, and for regrouping and filling the spiritual well for another year away from the "gente" and "tierra" they so dearly loved and missed.

Given the inconsistencies of attendance and the separate holidays, as a school we orchestrated to fill Decembers with a multi-age, parent-led activity based on the holiday bazaars of small-town Mexico, the Tianguis.

The Tianguis involved the faculty brainstorming different artesanías that could be completed across grade-levels and in 90-minute-long workshops. The artesanías also needed to be reflective of different folk-art traditions of Mexico, hence the "hojalata." Other workshops included weaving ornaments, popsicle-stick houses, wrapping paper stenciled with prints, dolls made of cornhusks, and papel picado to decorate the school for the event. While traditional tianguises had been barter-based, we priced all the different items for sale at just enough to cover the expenses of the materials.

Each teacher chose an activity to prepare for and organize for each of the three afternoon workshops. Some of the affection for the process was that it was one of the moments in the school year when one could work with past students and relatives of past students we'd never had in our classes. It was nice to exploit the family nature of the school as well as build some culturally-appropriate festivities into our pre-holiday chaos. And because the tianguis workshops were not formally assessed in any way or reflected in students' grades, it also eased the burden on students who were absent for the month and made for less academic recovery upon their return.

One of the other whole-school holiday activities was to honor the "posadas" —traditional singing and food exchanging that resembled what I knew as caroling from my growing up days. Several days before the holiday from school, the primary grade cluster organized its students into singing groups that would travel to a few of the other classrooms, where our students would have a traditional "treat" of sweet breads and juice with which to receive them. For those of us in the middle school cluster this was an important tradition, because it reestablished for our students a connection to the younger students in the building. Part of our mission entailed a fight against the segregating out of middle school students from other younger elementary students. We hoped to keep our students deeply connected in the lives of their younger family and community members by participating in this activity and others like "Reading Buddies" —where once a week older students would sit with their younger partner and share in reading books and activities.

Many of my students already had domestic responsibilities that included extended time with younger students—whether their own brothers or sisters or cousins, nieces, and nephews—as well as in community activities. The seemingly vast divisions between adolescents and their younger peers didn't appear to be in existence in the community to the degree that I'd been raised with. My pre-adolescents were mostly affectionate and attentive to younger students, and extremely adept in the art of caregiving and the work involved in it.

This cultural attribute made our Tianguis workshops a treat in themselves. We were often able to assign different older students across the board to different workshops where they could serve as assistants to the teacher—both in managing the students as well as adding to the quality of the younger students' projects.

★

It was all of that good feeling and holiday warmth that I was hoping to bring with me to my own family's celebration as I packed away different items I'd purchased to hang on our tree and serve as centerpieces at our holiday dinner.

My mom's own distance from her family and homeland propelled her throughout my growing up years to open her door every holiday season to the people in her life who also lacked a home base, as well as close friends who we'd come to think of as our extended family in the US. Each year the assortment of souls changed and added to the fun and festivities in unpredictable and startling ways. We planned large feasts of roasted turkey and traditional vegetable offerings from both my relatives' English feasts and our new American traditions, with pies and desserts as clichéd as apple pie and sherry trifle.

In all of my mom's struggles to live in a new land, her resilience, warmth, and effervescence were never more in evidence than on Christmas Day. It was this openness of spirit and appreciation for cultural difference I was relying on as I brought home the treasures that symbolized my own adventures and adopted communities.

Despite the nuances of difference between the cultures my mom and I claimed, I had inherited from her an adventurous spirit. My mother immigrated to this country with the intention of knowing all its wonders, and making them her own as a political act. I had hung my hopes on her core curiosity in all the ways it manifested throughout her identity in those early days of my relationship with Gilbert. I knew well across my childhood my mom's public extroversion and her consistent excitement for meeting new people, and was now well-aware of Gilbert's wonderful gregariousness and easy empathy as well. I was not surprised that this had made for a strong and fast connection between them and never gave a second thought to the intercultural dimensions of their relationship, as I'd seen so many of our parallels between us. I had heard on occasion of issues surfacing with parents of intercultural and interracial relationships and was grateful without realizing how very different it could have been.

The first meeting between Gilbert and my siblings was equally kind and gentle. Despite my sister's law-enforcement career and new life in a somewhat socially-conservative environment, she had my mom's kindness and warmth with people that she prioritized highly in her self-definition, and for reasons possibly too complex for me to appreciate, she was private about all her political beliefs. There had been issues early on in my teaching as she'd been romantically involved with someone working as a border guard in Texas. For two Christmases the unspoken truth that the students who sat in my classrooms had escaped agents like her boyfriend resided at the table like another sibling, but we were able to protect our relationship and protect the once-a-year time we had together. Whether this act was a betrayal of my new community I was too emotionally involved to tell, and so we left our differences back in our new home states, and returned to our younger selves and my only sisterhood.

My brother's kindness is beyond both the gentle demeanor of our English ancestors and the grace and kindness handed down to him from our mom, and I've never met a person who knows him who doesn't hold him at the top of their nobility lists. I was thrilled for his excitement for this new "brother" relationship, and awed that I never saw difference surface between them ever. Their shared bond developed in the laughter produced from their talking through topics that included, from what I could translate or understand, cars and music, politics and religion, and the number of necessary commentaries about surviving us women of the family. I was grateful for and proud of my small family, and would eventually have cherished opportunities to travel with Gilbert to the small towns of the English countryside which were also "home"—and that housed a relative every third house, as we used to say.

The exciting moments of culture clash popped up for us during the holidays in the forms of our guests. That year of the "hojalata" there were lots of supporting cast members including both our long-time neighbor's aging mother, the Rush Limbaugh fan, as well as my godfather's adopted foster son, the ex-con. While we were slightly nervous about the potential fall-out in both of these cases, I was reassured by my family's support that not much would happen beyond a mere discussion, if that even.

It also wouldn't be the first time that Gilbert and I had faced racist commentary and prejudice—even from people we cared about. In fact, some of the teachers at our old school had incredibly unfortunate feelings about the students they were serving. In general for me, that was the worst offense. Because I felt that teaching was such a subjective and human endeavor, to feel negative feelings for and about the young humans in one's care was to me an egregious problem, one that was not assuaged or helped at all by continuing to practice in that environment.

Stereotypes of our students played out in different ways at our old school. I'd spent the first years of my teaching career surrounded by older white women who were Chicago-lifers. They were drawn to me in the way advanced military men might be drawn to recruits. I must have seemed terribly naïve and pliant because I received daily bits of wisdom that came to me both from a generous place of sharing hard lessons and seeking more souls with whom to share their misery. I'd been warned about this kind of teacher discourse in my preparation program and student teaching experiences, but wasn't prepared for the affection that I would feel for the people perpetrating such terrible notions of my beloved students.

I didn't really understand what kind of difference it would make if I stopped talking to them, as I saw the partisan teams squaring off and not really making any headway in either direction with each other. That dynamic in the school, to me, seemed a tragic waste and a sacrifice I didn't feel ready to make. For the most part my interactions with this group of teachers didn't center on the work we were doing. They saw themselves as my surrogate mothers and asked me kindly and consistently about how I was doing, about my personal life, and about other peripheral elements to the job. I sometimes felt that perhaps I was compromising the ideals that had guided me to this point, but I was also eager to know well the people with whom I was living out my hard-working days.

In many ways that group of older women was the reason I was able to sustain my energies for my students. They never expressed anything other than support and encouragement for my work and were always eager to hear my stories.

I felt this way about theirs, much of the time. My favorite of all the stories that didn't happen in my own classroom occurred one day toward the end of my first year. My desk was located in the basement hallway just outside the boiler room. I shared the space with the art teacher and music teacher—two very distinct and different people who were both white and had been working in the neighborhood for more years than they would say. Both traveled great distances to get to the school and were invested in their teaching, if somewhat detached from the efforts our group of bilingual/ESL teachers was engaged in to create a different kind of educational institution than we experienced there at the time.

It was near the end of my first year when I was sitting at my desk after a long day of taking my ESL show to all my different classrooms across three separate buildings. I could hear Anderson in the second-grade classroom outside of which our desks were located. She was making her way through the canonical master composers with all of the second grade classrooms around the school, and I could hear her presenting the next section on a new composer.

I imagined the thirty-three students whom I knew well—they were my first group of the day. I knew Anderson's routine with the students and could imagine them all with their hands folded neatly on top of their desks waiting for the mini marshmallows that accompanied their music lessons like a welcome alto line. She set the tone for her lessons with a friendly routine and a small treat, and brought out the content of her lessons while the students reveled in the gifts.

That the students never demonstrated temptation or jumped the gun in eating the marshmallows was a source of amazement to me. It demonstrated a willpower I didn't know to expect in seven-year-olds. I knew in the human exchange that the students' appreciation also spoke to their connecting of kindness and music, and more broadly reinforced my growing understanding of the importance and safety of classroom routines, while I bristled at times at the behaviorist model of classroom management.

As I brought my materials back to my desk, Anderson was post-marshmallow and pre-music, and with the door wide open I was able to enjoy her easy affection for the students with whom she didn't share many linguistic commonalities. I was never sure how much of the content of her instruction the students understood, and I think Anderson wondered, too. Besides the frequent requests for translation assistance and/or other suggestions, what was about to happen had made her cry.

For each of the composers, Anderson had chosen an iconic piece of music that she helped students learn the rhythms and melodies to. There were no funds for instruments beyond one keyboard but Anderson was adept at letting as many students as possible try out different musical phrases. I was aware of the change in composers and only half listening when I heard Beethoven's Fifth begin. Almost immediately, a rousing chorus of young voices exclaimed emotionally, "Beethoven! It's Beethoven!"

I could see Anderson only in my imagination and fought hard the impulse to run into the classroom—to try and get a peek at her reaction. It turned out I didn't need to, as within seconds she was outside the room and in our hallway, feet from my desk, tears spilling down her face. She'd thought to excuse herself only when she realized that she'd welled up.

"Do you mind—just watching them for a minute?"

I was happy to—in part because I could help out a friend, but mostly because I wanted to see for myself my students in this new light. I put my hand on her shoulder and hurried in.

The students looked confused and concerned. I tried to reassure them by telling them their teacher was okay, and that she was just happy that they knew the music.

One of the boys in the middle row raised his hand and I called on him.

He sweetly asked me in Spanish: "Why was she so happy? Did she like the movie, too?"

Anderson had heard the exchange from the hallway and understood the key vocabulary word of the second question. She returned smiling as the full realization met her in the doorway—they'd been excited about the dog.

★

This story made the rounds of the school pretty quickly and because she was so well liked, people were quick to offer a smile or hug in response. Our friend the first-grade "monolingual" teacher—the teacher who ran the classroom of only-English first graders—had heard and gave a chuckle the next morning as she came down to see us with her coffee. Anderson and I had been chatting about her sharing the story with her husband, also a music teacher at a city high school, who had found her sudden emotion rather amusing as he knew her to be private and reserved in general, but especially so in the workplace.

Eckman had been laughing too, but was more amused by the fact that she had believed that an entire class of poor, immigrant students knew Beethoven.

As soon as Eckman said it, I realized how tainted the episode had become for me.

Not one person in Anderson's family or network (or in mine) had expressed this opinion and yet it had been there the whole time—the possibility that the joke would be about the students' perceived lack of cultural information and the naïve belief that they should be expected to acculturate that quickly and deeply. I wondered what canonical folkloric or mariachi pieces our table of faculty would recognize, and closed my eyes at the latent worry that the students' knowledges might never surface in most of their classrooms.

For me the story had been about Anderson's emotional stake in sharing the things she valued most in her own world and culture—and how much it meant to her that she do that successfully. The thought that her young students might be deeply happy about an iconic composer and excited to be learning about him had changed her entire demeanor so completely that it had silenced the students' enthusiasm, and forced her to have to leave the room under the pressure of being so vulnerable before such young children.

For me the moment had also been about the ways in which we as people acquire knowledge in a new culture. Those emergent English Language Learners in that second-grade classroom were completely attached to an American movie and able to reference it spontaneously. They also knew that this movie they enjoyed was drawing on important information woven into this country's cultural fabric.

I knew Eckman had somehow missed these nuances and remained firmly planted in her misassessed and lowered expectations for the students. In my own personal interactions with her she'd been so intuitive and insightful. When my mom was first diagnosed with cancer, Eckman knew something had occurred with me before I had even admitted the fear to myself. I now had to reconcile the fact that I had experienced that deep level of care via the overlapping identities of being white, female, and professional. I struggled to understand her empathy if she could not see similar heartbreaks and fears in our students. I knew this was what white privilege meant—to be read as human in all its frailty and potential—and now saw the way it worked as oxygen in our educational institution.

Comments and assumptions like the ones Eckman was making that morning were the hiccup in my continued relationships with her and the larger core of white teachers in the school. I knew they had been highly suspicious of me when I arrived, and that the relationships that existed were due to forced overtures from both our sides. I imagined I was perhaps a caricature to some of them, and that several of our social-justice archetype had taken positions at the school before. I knew also that working past that image would make my adult teaching life better, but that the odds were slim that the students would benefit from any of it. If she was able to adjust her assumptions of me, the implicit racial bias informing her instruction and the ultimate invisibility of her students was fixed.

*

I started to become very sensitive to these different nuances of mainstream responses to my students and their world, and struggled to accept that I had to sever ties with people who thought and felt differently than I.

I didn't know how to think about severing any tie with the people I considered home.

As with many white holiday tables, these issues sometimes reared their heads at my mom's house. At Christmas that year, the two "family members" who had posed comments challenging Gilbert's legitimacy to live in the US and whether his family was really hard-working did not hold any kind of power over him or control over our life choices. In fact, we felt kind of sorry for them and the ways in which they seemed to limit the quality of their lives through strong feelings based on ignorance.

My family was shocked by our cavalier attitude about the comments, and we spent the rest of Christmas Night, once everyone else had gone home, processing issues of race and culture in the US. My brother and sister had both moved to North Carolina for college and remained there as their careers headed in certain directions in the region. Despite my mom's liberal takes on global issues and the comparatively-backward approach of the US to certain things like class and gender, my sister had struggled to ward off some of the conservative values of the people she'd developed close bonds with—and this was the first time we'd had the chance to discuss things with her. Her future employment by the infamous Greensboro, North Carolina, police department would eventually position both of us as defensive even with shared perspectives underneath the surface, so in the years to come I would be very glad to have had the chance to process some of these issues with her. Even further down the road my mom and I would express a communal thank-you prayer to Jon Stewart for having drawn her back to the framing of the socio-political world she had espoused while growing up.

My sister was curious to know personally how it felt to receive critical questions such as those from the table's Rush Limbaugh fan, our childhood friend's grandmother. Gilbert laughed and pointed out that anyone paying attention in their own insular world would have stories to tell about the kinds of crazy thoughts that occur to us humans. This is the point, he assured her: to realize how human we are beneath whatever version of ourselves comes out of our mouths.

She wondered why he didn't feel the need to defend himself, and he countered that he actually thought that he had. He thought that perhaps by trying to read in her the circumstances that brought her to these kinds of racialized feelings, he had already countered some of her notions about him and others of his ethnic group.

My sister was getting more upset on his behalf—she had long been a fierce champion of the people, places, and ideas in her immediate world and was struggling to see why Gilbert didn't share that anger, especially since it was so personally directed at him.

"It all boils down to this," he'd said. "Racism as a noun is about social structures. Racist as an adjective belongs to actions and expressions. Neither word belongs to people. If you acknowledge that people—all people—are capable of complex and even contradictory points of view at the same time, then it makes it a bit easier to take when you hear some you don't like."

"But don't you need to act to change them?" she persisted.

"I think that's what I did. It's not always the gut response that gets you to the point you want to be at. I think of it like chess; I have to consider three or four of twenty moves ahead in order to get to the place I want to be in."

The evening was winding down and my mom had fallen asleep after her heroic completion of all activities, but my sister knew she still felt unsure as she acknowledged that it might be time to call it a night.

"Well, if that's true for Ellie's grandmother, what did you say back to Andy when he assumed because of your race he'd found a kindred spirit in crime?"

"I said 'See you later' as I went to grab my money off the bedside table."

7

JANUARY

J for Jeremy

It was hard every January not to wax nostalgic for warmer climes and the light of longer days. The sun barely broke over the horizon by the time we got to school and was gone again before I left to make the short trek home. The hospitable temperatures of summer would routinely bring us hibernators back outdoors and provide an automatic surfacing of the community for me, while in the stark winter it was easy to feel isolated and apart with the only communing possible involving formal participation—something that still eluded me.

If I'd had the inclination (or any goodness, some might have thought), I'd have found my way to church, as it was the location where my small community of students and families shared time together without reservation or pressures of assimilation. I watched appreciatively as families flocked in attendance both Saturday night and Sunday morning in numbers that would have been record-breaking in my family's congregation. As it was, the day of largest attendance experienced in my small parish was the back to back Christmas Eve lesson and carols service that my father transposed from his youth and from the English tradition, and for which he was organist and choir director. There was an intensity to his performance in these events that he articulated as his gift of worship, but that I always perceived as homesickness and cultural expression. These services he transposed faithfully reflected the ceremonial ones performed by elite English choirs in King's College in England and it felt even that this parallel between the secular significance of this cultural practice connected my family and our homeland as well.

*

Religion as a construct itself was selfish for me because it was an easy metaphor. I knew my longing for easy access to community and cultural practices existed in my mind as access doors to the deeper values of the community. My own immigrant parents had focused our cultural education on connection to our own church attendance, and so the metaphor was inherited along with my dual citizenship. Even in my own church community I had felt more an ethnographer than a disciple, and it was that lens that served as a conduit to my future academic studies and the framing that was guiding and dictating my approaches in the community that I longed to gain membership to.

In parallel with the institutions of schools, I knew also that both were human attempts to concretize value systems and authorship of history and centrality. Academically, I understood that legally churches could manifest their values and schools should not,—but that one could read our urban school districts for theoretical stances and politicized socialization. Churches comforted most congregants in a transparency not afforded schools, which clarified for me that my rages could be explained by the covert dimension of schooling—that so much of the true purpose and values were intentionally hidden. My faithless literacy of religion calmed the rage I felt at the educational institutions I believed in and which undermined the rest of my value system.

I was fortunate in all this that language barriers facilitated my own hidden agnosticism and its tandem academic distance.

★

Religion played out in the world around school in such significant ways that I was struck pondering how we might transpose them to our school community. My family's church was located far from my residential community, and so I'd never experienced much overlap between fellow parishioners and school peers, but I knew my students had those connections, and I wondered how we might serve as a conduit to deeper cultural practices without betraying the secular freedom in public schools. While I felt my hopes were somewhat curricular, I also acknowledged that there was a selfishness in my thinking—I wanted to be inside the hub of all that social activity. Churches were the spaces where families coordinated childcare, organized clothing drives, and created weekly calendars of activities parents could enforce on their children as protection from what they feared would happen to them on "the streets."

For a couple of years our school community had worked to organize similar efforts through parent networks and teacher-led drives at the school. Sadly, there were few families who saw us in that kind of light and who needed us beyond what they found in their parishes. As the years would progress, more and more families would find their community focus within our walls, but in our first years we struggled not to compete with parishes and the spiritual and material ways they provided for family needs.

I knew I'd had to grapple with my own intentions for integrating into this community.

In my own personal articulation of self it was true that I didn't much separate my academic life from my social one, so I was careful to check if my purposes for deeper absorption into my new community were anthropological or emotional.

Certain that I would never be able to claim certain authentic purposes, I refrained from attending. Without the official purpose of teaching as excuse for establishing deeper connections with the community, I believed incorporating myself into their church world would be interruptive in the best case scenario, and culturally voyeuristic in the worst. I feared a betrayal of their deepest values would surface every time I stood to recite their creeds, and that of all places I should be wary of falsehoods in front of their objects of worship.

I didn't grow up fearing a deity, but I could appreciate now that I should at least respect theirs.

I also knew I needed to respect the integrity of the academic fields I embraced, and maybe worshiped to a certain extent. In my ethnographic coursework, I'd heard repeated warnings against the temptation of "going native" and tried to hold that professional tension as well as my own intentions in constant scrutiny. I also had to hold up to the light the commentaries from family expressing discomfort and worry that my eagerness to invest in new communities and cultures reflected a void in the development of my own. There was also no articulated end-date to my immersion, and so their concerns about their own raising of me had tinges of sadness as well—that they might lose me in ways they couldn't yet predict.

I didn't have predictions for my near future either, and couldn't always make sense of my motives or what they might be evidencing about my feelings about my own roots. I recalled watching with my mom in the waning days of my college career the award-winning film "The Mission" which we followed with an intense conversation about the role of religion as the colonial—and genocidal, in the movie and beyond—force behind the inequities I was working to eradicate for the people I served in my teaching. The archetypes of different motives for colonization stood out to me as relevant to the work I embraced daily. Even without the parallels from the film, I thought a great deal about notions of enlightenment, civilization, and salvation. These notions and the wreckage they wrought in the film led only to wreckage in the film, and in each of the dimensions portrayed in the narrative I saw one consistent culprit—whiteness. Whether manifested in the institution of the Catholic Church or in the institution of public education, I had a pervasive worry about the violence brought to people not seeking it in the name of benevolent whiteness. I taught my middle schoolers to read incidents among us for impact rather than intention, and opportunities to understand this tension surfaced almost daily. Middle schoolers were also perfect examples of apologists for certain behaviors through mechanisms of "good intentions," and we worked gradually over time to understand the history of events among us purely in terms of the way they had been felt by each other.

In my critical reflections on my practice, I weighed my own intentions against impact and analyzed the values system I was institutionalizing among us, and tried to read it constantly for enforcements of whiteness. In our school's ethnic studies curriculum, we teachers worked daily to try to deconstruct the connotations of "enlightenment" in history, and construct a community with learning at the center that resisted hierarchies and judgments. I had enough access to the students' personal conversations that I was also aware of their developing critical literacy for whiteness and their own sensibilities of being empowered to navigate it safely and in ways that justified the sacrifices their families had undertaken in order to arrive in these cultural crossroads of Chicago, at a time when government forces were politicizing their own existences.

Pervasively, metaphorically, and symbolically, at my own cultural crossroads I used the Jeremy Irons character from the film as I had watched my church community consider its deities. With friends I made impolitic references to a necessary substituting of the name "Jeremy" for the third letter on the WWJD (What Would Jesus Do) lanyards I'd observed people wearing in other settings. The contradictions between his savior complex and the impact his immersion in the indigenous tribes of South America had upon his sense of morality, justice, and beauty became an allegory for me and a paradigm for critique of my community interactions.

I talked through this with a mentor—my former professor whose life had been dedicated to urban education and broader global justice. A former novitiate, she herself had pondered the structures a life committed to service might take. She knew generationally that perseverations on these themes did not always contribute to the quality of our service, and that in most religions the difficult parables are complemented by the joys of community. She wanted to make sure I salvaged time and space for myself so that I didn't burn out too early. She also reminded me gingerly, but without equivocation, that the story of this substituted "J" also arced toward a violent and tragic end.

★

I'd known how strongly I felt about the film and yet feared that here I was recreating its core conflict through naïveté and arrogance. Who did I think I was to walk into this community that I had no authentic connection to and try to immerse myself in its ways? Who did I think I was to imagine that I'd be wanted? Why did I think that it would be a good thing for anyone besides me?

Gentrification was taking hold on Chicago's south side in the mid- to late-1990s and there would be times ahead when I would feel angry amid stinging comments from local organizers and activists about my participation in the community, insinuating that I was just another white person looking to exploit a low-income community for my own gain and to ease an acute case of white guilt. I would fight those assertions from a place of hurt and fear, but that was more because I was being accused than that I hadn't considered this already. I saw the effects of what was occurring around me and was angry and resistant, but also afraid of speaking for a community that did not have one monolithic response to the political and economic turmoil surrounding it.

There were neighbors I knew who welcomed the opportunity to have coffee houses within walking distance of their childhood homes, as well as residents who railed against the middle-class Mexicans looking for fancy new condos along the university corridor. There were community members who embraced the increased commercial activity in the heart of the business district, as well as those who rejected the marginalizing of the disaffected youths that dispersed them to less-traveled neighborhood pockets.

Despite the linear definitions of gentrification across the city, I immersed myself in the spectrum of responses I heard frequently about local changes occurring visibly and rapidly. As I was considering purchasing a home in the neighborhood, I had a powerful exchange with a young activist mother who told me that she appreciated the battle against Chicago's tax-reward program for corporate developers, but wondered how accurate the claims of gentrification could be if the public-transit train system still didn't provide ample or consistent services to the community. In fact, she'd confessed, she felt more allegiance to me not for my participation in the community but because of the one indicator and practice that she felt was central to her life—that I'd taken the train for so long.

I thought maybe we didn't need to worry too much until our streets started getting plowed, the neighborhood indicator of centrality versus marginalization.

These different conversations were an indication to me that shifts were happening internally as externally. The fluidity of culture in all its marvelous dimensions would also include these political histories taking place around us. This was true for me as well, and gaining some clarity of my cultural role became increasingly clear as I watched artistic young white transplants take up residence in increasing numbers, their self-presumed benevolence confirmed for them as their residences in old warehouses turned rents ever upward. The history necessary to comprehend the impact of this phenomenon wasn't more than a decade old, and yet without any awareness of their signaling of gentrification, they patronized stores, developed conversational fluency, and talked about their virtue and tolerance in all kinds of local restaurants.

I knew that the Bronfenbrenner domains of identity put me squarely among them in a number of uncomfortable ways. If I began to feel any comfort or pride at the thought that I was both not artistic, nor carefree, I was quickly reminded that among the dimensions of identity that surfaced in political ways in Chicago, those were not prominent. That these new neighbors mostly interacted with each other and not I was also no act of resistance in the economic moment Chicago's south side was facing. The epiphany they provided me was the opportunity to register that in the same way I was assessing them by external membership in demographic categories, I represented to strangers the exact same invasive threat.

To my students, who'd wanted to absolve me of my own cultural background and provide honorary membership to their community, their generosity of spirit mitigated these tensions inside our classroom, and provided a relief for us all outside Urie's conceptualization of the macro-sphere by focusing us on our micro-sphere inside the school. I knew profoundly that my representation in the larger political shifts was culpable and complicit, but buffered by an acceptance that provided me access to resisting it with our families as much as I could, as often as I could.

The most moving element of their open invitation to membership was the confidence I saw the students express about their culture—as though honoring me as intra-group was as generous a gift as any that existed. I believed that to be true. The inclusivity and warmth I experienced daily in my new community was a healthy backdrop for me as I navigated the internal conflicts of encroaching whiteness in our midst.

I saw in this exchange the opportunity to extend a similar invitation. The exploration of the cultures that surfaced daily in our school made me develop an even stronger affinity for my own. Tensions I had carried with me for more than a decade felt resolvable among my new neighbors. I felt a deep kinship with the agricultural working class roots of so many of our school families which replaced the unease of feeling disconnected from the version of white America into which my mom and dad resisted forces of assimilation, sensibilities that I as the oldest seemed to have inherited most intensely.

Despite our rich connections to the people in our worlds of suburban Philadelphia, I felt keenly aware of the force toward erasure that the particular embodiments of whiteness in the US proscribed. What version of cultural traditions had my parents worked to maintain and pass on to us, and what political implications of this did they feel? I wondered whether as first generation immigrants, as opposed to my 1.5 generation, they felt at all a hyphenated identity: were they British-American? Did their acclimation threaten parts of their core identity to each other, to themselves, or to the extended family still at home in England?

I couldn't say for myself that I felt anything as concrete as any of that. What I had inherited most from my parents was a sense of being an outsider—of not being internal to any of the identities I declared. This was a helpful characteristic in the ethnographic discipline I had gravitated toward, but not much of a healthy conceptualization of myself outside of academic discussions.

I wondered as I watched from the window of the local taqueria what kinds of internal battles might be raging in all the variety of passers-by I watched with curiosity. Was the young thrift-store-dressed hipster self-conscious about her appearance? Was the hunched-over older man making his way off the bus angry at the free time the new residents seemed to have? Was the mother of four keeping a vigilant eye on all her young children frustrated at the reduced number of apartments available to her family and aware of the reasons why? I had to recognize that these questions were as much information I would ever have about any of them, knowing similarly that any parallel curiosities or assumptions would stop in the silence between us like the large pane of glass that filled my afternoon.

I hoped beyond the self-absorbed nuances of culture crossing and spheres of self-definition, that perhaps the fluidity of culture I knew my students embodied was the river I too could resign myself to. As the political culture evolved quickly around us, my participation in the community maybe didn't have to rest on any concretized internal definition. That I could work to understand the implications of my presence was the most important thing to keep at the forefront of my thinking, but beyond that any hopes for difference or absolution from complicity afforded no product either positive or negative. My most political event in my immersion was to let go of the outside positioning and worry about the movements I made on the inside.

The only path toward positive impact was to maintain a clarity of focus not on me, or the diversity of the people around me, but on the spaces in between where agency could be hatched and enacted in magical ways. We could inhabit a space of our own making, rich with knowledges and value articulations. We could name this space but were better off not doing so—the mystical power of the liminal that Anzaldua politicized and that extended through pre-colonial societies on varied continents could be ours in that remaining silence and stillness.

★

Not everyone knew exactly what I was up to. Like the hipsters on their bikes and the older men de-bussing, I too could be reduced to my superficial attributes.

I could quite frequently be called out on them. One of the earlier adjustments I'd had to make upon getting my job in the community was to the greater acceptability of commenting at women on the street. Beyond class and ethnic diversity, I'd realized in Mexico that past summer just how integrated this issue was to the norms of Mexican identity, and how quick in judgment and response I was. I worked to understand it not from a context of sexism but from a place of more equality and respect for women.

It was one of my biggest challenges to take the "güera" comments with a grain of salt. I was certain that I never once came across as "breezy" or nonchalant about it, but I felt successful in my attempts having refrained from engaging in bitter ethical debates with people who perhaps wanted me to—though I needed to recognize I had no right to decide their intent.

One summer day, the way I'd framed the issue was blown to pieces.

I was on my way south from the train stop, following the same route I'd taken every other day of the year—weather be damned. At the first intersection, I passed the taquería I consistently frequented for people-watching. There was a man just outside the back windows I'd perhaps walked past every other day. He was resting against the doorframe and sipping on coffee from a Styrofoam cup. As my knowledge about the community would evolve over the years, I'd come to learn that it might have been a sweeter breakfast drink called champurrado—a corn-based chocolaty drink—but in my ignorance I saw only what I myself needed, the steaming cup looking inviting to my bleary-eyed end-of-first-year teaching self.

Though I'd tried all year to avoid the stereotypical white-teacher outfits of holiday sweaters and appliquéd apple vests, that day I was in my denim dress over a white t-shirt—memorable not for the outfit but for the comment it provoked:

"Welcome back, Alice in Wonderland."

This was not the one-dimensional "güera" racialized descriptive comment I'd come to hear and take as a friendly reminder about my place, and lack of it, but an interesting dominant-culture reference that had caught me by surprise.

This man from a different generation and history had effectively nailed my presence in the community with a rich literary metaphor. I was charmed, befuddled, and stunned all at the same time.

I came to refer to various moments in my new community as my "Alice" ones—times when I would see things much bigger than they were, or frame myself in exaggeratedly off-kilter scenarios. This happened frequently in teaching—and perhaps most obviously when I was asked to see myself through the lenses of those from my own demographic—trying to make sense of me while I did also.

★

Whether or not I was Alice—or the most glaring example of gentrification in the neighborhood—or archetypal priests enacting a mission not articulated by their victims, I tried to engage the different metaphors for my own participation with anyone who'd listen. Those I kept closest to help me process some of the sudden and jarring daily dilemmas humored me at great length, but also reminded me that there were lots more important issues that I could spend my time worrying about. In my perseverating, I knew I was ascribing too much importance to my lone actions. I rationalized it constantly—to others, but mostly to myself: I was there because I wanted to give. Though no one had asked, I stayed engaged because I knew I had so much to receive.

★

In the end I didn't think that the learning I could partake in by attending different churches would help me draw greater conclusions about my role as a teacher. Not filling my empty Sundays with the community norms kept me honest about trying not to treat the symptoms of loneliness or fear of being left out with the medicine of religion. The illness was deeper—feeling that a true route to mitigating the whiteness and outsider-ness of my teaching lay outside the school walls and in my sharing of the students' community.

It kept me using the public transit system.

It made the Laundromat my saving grace.

The Laundromat gave me an excuse to be out in the community while engaged in universal cultural practice. Everyone washed clothes, after all, and I felt safe and contained in our tiny old-world Laundromat across from the school. With the broad bank of windows lining the main thoroughfare of cars, I found a spot to sit and observe my neighbors, visiting parishioners filing across the street, and the occasional caravan of sirens from the county jail to the local hospital. While trends in Laundromats were tending toward the 24-hour model—completely neon-decorated and filled with competing sounds from multiple TVs, my Laundromat was an old store front filled with roughly 20 of each machine, an old-fashioned radio by the manager's desk, and twelve hook-shaped steam pipes we'd sometimes use to practice sketching with our students in art-walk activities.

By the holidays of that year, word got out what night I tended to be found doing my clothes. The first to bump into me was Alberto—a sweet and friendly boy I'd known for several years. In fact, it was a memory of him from his third grade year that made me first consider moving to the neighborhood. I'd taken a different path to the train station that Spring afternoon and headed north on the boulevard. As I gazed at the centuries-old trees and the architecturally interesting two- and three-flats lining both sides of the street, I caught sight of Alberto in front of his house with a remote-controlled car. He hadn't yet seen me, so I stopped to check how he kept himself busy.

Within a minute or so he'd lifted his head and caught a glimpse of me from across the wide distance, and I watched as I saw him running through the space that had been between us. I wouldn't have been able to articulate if I'd expected him to be happy or afraid to see me, but he was running faster than I'd ever seen him—almost into traffic. As he sprinted, his way-too-large sweatpants threatened to fall to his ankles so I watched him hold on to them tightly even as his motion caused the coins in his pockets to spring into the air and across the parkways and sidewalks, mirroring my joy in the fountain formation they made.

I'd been able to get him to stop at the street and instead crossed over to his side. He'd shown me his car and asked me for several different English words to describe it, and I'd ended up playing with the growing group of students for several hours beyond the time I hoped to be still in the neighborhood. The experience had only been tainted by my slight fears of the train station after dark, but I needn't have worried as Alberto's uncle walked with me and the students the last half-mile.

I'd felt nervous about putting the students in danger, but no one seemed as worried as I was. And it dawned on me that I only knew the community in certain light and times.

I soon terminated my northside lease and parked myself across the boulevard from Alberto.

I let the lens of the Laundromat amplify my sense of this new home.

I didn't even pretend to do other things when I was there—and with Alberto's discovery of my routine, I waited routinely for whichever students would join me that week. Alberto and his sister and cousin were frequent visitors, and we spent the winter hours playing cards and talking about nothing much in particular. We shared random stories from pop culture and sports, as well as our collection of dimes the machines still took. We talked about books and stories but without any formal or informal prompting; we talked about weather and food. Mostly we laughed a lot—at ourselves, at the world, at our laundry.

On one wintry night Alberto's cousin Miranda asked me why I liked doing laundry so much and why when we had so much to do had I seemed so happy. I replied honestly and told her that she was a big part of that, and smiled for the memory of Pedro's ancestors as I told her also that it felt good to "do" —to accomplish the things in life that needed accomplishing without much complication. Miranda agreed that it could be fun to perform chores, but also that not all chores were done for you by machine while you hung out with friends doing fun activities.

She was right. I didn't like doing dishes like I had come to love laundry, or even sweeping—and yes, on occasion, some grading. None of those activities, however, could compare to my love for the weekly rituals here at our Laundromat.

There was no authority over anyone as we sporadically carted clothing around the floor, without interrupting the stories being shared. Routinely, other patrons saved us our corner and eventually the stack of games and books that lined it began to grow. By summer I'd see people in our corner at all times—chatting, playing, or just staring back out at me.

It felt like the best teaching I'd ever done.

★

The Laundromat was my veritable safe space—a liminal realm outside the formal expectations of either of the defined worlds my students and I inhabited—and I clung to it religiously. I looked for similar moments in my teaching life, but was hard-pressed to name any. For all of the ways in which we might have power really to educate, so much of our energies went into the institutional version we called "schooling." Despite the ways in which I felt like I was teaching in neutral without much evidence of disrupting the broader system, occasionally I had the opportunity to see us as others might.

That January we were being visited yet again by a team of students and professors eager to see our little world in action. These site visits always brought with them a cold aura of "objectivity." Were we to trot out a canned lesson that showed our good work—for the sake of the outsiders? Or were we legitimate in revealing the truths of our educational model as it existed in the exact moments of their visit? Would our self-narrative hold up under the microscope of outsider analysis? Would that framing matter at all to our work? Our lead teacher and supportive community assured us that we were to show only exactly what we would be doing were no one there, but at times this was painfully exposing. I knew full well that my teaching was only the sum of all the mundane minutes of our many days that resulted occasionally in true excitement—but only excitement for us who were in it. I couldn't imagine any outsider would see clearly the joy of our process from a vantage point of objective study through a random visit to my classroom.

For all those concerns, these visits offered nothing for us, even as we unpacked them. In the oddities of this particular visit, we were handed evidence of our efforts that might have otherwise eluded me.

★

We were knee-deep in our geography unit when there was a firm knock at the door. I had a designated "receiver" —sometimes called "ambassador" —who welcomed our visitors in. With the archaeological scavenger hunt instructions up on the overhead projector's screen, the students and I were assembled at our communal tables with a globe, topographic atlas, and textbook each.

Our half-lit room must have confused their protocols, because one of them took up the authority of turning on the lights before she stopped herself at the switch. Among the remaining group of three, we heard one whisper, "Where's the teacher?"

A sample of the students stared at the door, but the rest of the groups plodded through the activity. Not one student, no matter their reaction, gave me up.

"You're all just working on your own? What is the lesson?" Our ambassador took the lead and engaged the research team leader's questions and asked them if they'd like to see what her group was doing.

These events played out in the proverbial slow motion as I watched from where I sat with my students and our work. I felt dishonest in my silence, but delighted at the realization that the inversion of traditional teacher identity was so comprehensively shared in our classroom. We were in a lab exploration of what can happen when notions of teaching and learning blur, and collecting some data for ourselves on what responses that blurring might trigger. We knew in the informal space of the Laundromat that this was acceptable, but now had some evidence of the transfer of that to this formal space.

I finished the sentence I was writing and passed the globe to Noelle. I put my glasses on in some kind of universal gesture of teacherly authority. To the extent it mattered, I stood up.

"Game over," one of the boys announced.

★

I'd been so proud of that piece of our story that I recounted it like my own retelling of an important oral history. Though it allowed me deep joy in thinking about the students and their brilliance and humor, it also triggered a number of nagging questions: To what extent was my concession of authority still a centering of myself? What did I think the confusion of my colleagues had conveyed about the quality of the students' learning? Why was I so happy being noticed for not being noticed?

I realized in the dark early-morning hours before the students' arrival the next day what my contentment conveyed: with no direct purpose or result, I was happy for our moments of resistance. I was happy the interruptions we tried to effect had been public despite their hidden location. I was proud to have inverted the values that were so pervasively axiomatic among teams of researchers, working in different arenas of scholarship.

I was, in reality, happy to be Alice. I knew in moments of quick decisions, in fact, WWJD.

★

As the destruction at the end of The Mission and Alice's arc resulted in things I had no interest in experiencing, I also knew that our narratives here were not those stories. They were real time and unfolding, and hinged on salvations of our own defining—such as those of the Laundromat. The sanctuary of the machine hum and the communion-taking of books afforded me as much inner peace as any of the religions I'd spent time studying. Our sermons were discussions and the creeds collectively written over time. Our kneeling in pews was the perch in the steamed-up windows that lined the sidewalk and main avenue.

This small congregation would organize itself around clean clothes. I'd worry later about confessionals and people to process my sins with—the existential question of complicity in a world centered on whiteness. I'd leave those conversations for quiet corners and darkened conversations, knowing no answer would impact the course of events as they played out.

I needed one small communion to face the demons I fought for them, but also for me.

8

FEBRUARY

Everyday Pororoca

We were looking at the physics required to build a massive structure in the desert, when all heads turned in concert toward the alarmingly sudden crash in the hallway. I emptied the unseemly mix of dirt and sand from my cupped hands and walked gingerly to the door. An eighth grader appeared to have left class upset and thrown a couple of books at his closed locker, against which he was now leaning face forward. As I eased into the hallway I watched him arc his body over the splayed books, and repeatedly rest his head against the metal. The height he'd acquired rapidly this winter made the scene look oddly like the St. Louis Arch, and I wondered what frontier he was marking, and what welcome he had for anyone headed beyond him to unknown distances. The metaphor would be more fitting in the minutes and days that followed as we watched this young man and his peers process a future they couldn't yet imagine and whose dreams for continued opportunities had been thwarted. I nodded to the students and watched them estimate measures of friction in varied contexts.

I wasn't out there first, but Daniel was happy for the reinforcements.

After treating the anger and rage for what they were, we were eventually able to get to the source of our student's anguish—a rejection letter from the high school he'd hoped to attend.

The letter wasn't really so much a rejection as more of a refusal to waiver his low test scores and let him take the entrance exam required for consideration by district magnet high schools.

Without that waiver, our student and his peers in similar circumstances had only two distinct hopes for options beyond the neighborhood school: the new establishment of charter schools, besides shifting city demographics and teacher solidarity networks, held annual lotteries based on random selection and luck that hadn't intersected with his life so far, or navigate boundaries not far to the south of us, uprooting his family but placing him in closer proximity to arts and extracurricular opportunities that came with neighborhood enrollment in city magnets.

He faced all the responsibilities for his own destiny, but was afforded no control over the circumstances dictating it. We knew in those mournful moments at the lockers that his hopes not to go to our neighborhood school had proved fruitless, and that the frustration now at an unreliable and invalid standardized test would be woven into his high school career—apart from his creative aspirations and understandings of himself as brilliant and savvy, he was headed to an institution where his options for academically-challenging classes would only be offered in conjunction with this one false score.

Despite the previous years of understanding his scores to be among the lowest in his class, he had taken to heart that that measure was detached from the worth he felt in his own contributions and the value he felt mirrored back to him by his community of peers.

There weren't more than a few people in that class who thrived when it came to test-taking. Despite teacher interventions and attempts to demystify testing authorship and architecture, students varied in their capacity for preparation as they varied in their ability to imbue the high stakes with meaning. The meaning loomed all too large over us teachers as we strived to buoy the students amply with example tests and skills-inclusive units, and as we despaired at the number of students who underperformed— or for whom the tests underperformed in criminal ways—repeatedly year after year in ways we were only allowed to hypothesize, estimate, or guess.

In the Chicago Public School system, teachers were not allowed to review students' test performances and received scores only at the end of the school year. Even then, teachers were given numbers only as comparative percentages in the norm-referenced sorting of students, different from providing measures of their learning through actual results. Teachers as advocates were repeatedly left to try and help despairing students such as ours and the peers with whom he would now travel to entertain vague efforts to improve numbers that didn't exist. Our under-assessed student had struggled against the futility of studying and through an aspirational emotionality that the tests rendered prohibitive, and with no concrete data to process, we considered dimensions of navigating his second language in decontextualized and formal reading passages as the source of an intellectual paralysis that prevented him from attending to all the passages and questions required in the time allotted. As for the math sections, we feared that his belaboring of each procedural move in the completion of different problems kept him from advancing and having a good shot at all of them. He was a creator of beautiful things and an inherent perfectionist at heart, and we feared that his expansive mind also over-imagined his own inadequacies as a second-language learner and betrayed any authentic confidence in himself as a thoughtful decision maker who never tired of challenges and opportunities to improve.

While this emotional display was the first time I was personally connected to the heartbreak around the high school application process, it was only the beginning of my relationship with the issue that would eventually break my spirit for teaching and push me out of the classroom forever.

★

Two years later it would be Daniel and I shepherding our current sixth graders, pulling bricks over sand, in and out of high school open houses—a metaphor befitting our eventual expansive fears and the shrinking opportunities that would be afforded our students. We would fuel our cars and hearts with naïve optimism in and out of a dozen different open houses and two comprehensive high school fairs. We would enlist the good intentions of admissions counselors at two different magnet schools in the hopes of finding possible back-door avenues promisingly detached from the students' seventh-grade test scores. We'd invite desperate principals of new city charter schools to test their marketing skills in our classrooms and on our students. We'd watch as the lines blurred between neo-liberal capitalistic streaks and religious framings in a nearby Catholic parish as we heard the presentation from the newly-selected principal of a culturally-sustaining new Jesuit high school, whose model of tuition-reduction offerings blended ancient architecture of apprentice-based learning with new capitalistic state funding streams that moved money away from public institutions like ours into private institutions and corporate funders.

In the end our 25 sixth graders would end up at 10 different high schools and we would spend their ninth-grade year following them through their transitions into completely unique micro-societies around the city. Struggling with my own sense of empty nesting at that time, I would organize the students in monthly convenings back in my classroom to process their new experiences through a number of different guiding questions. Among the issues that would be elevated to prominence was the complexity of their racialized experiences within their schools but also across the schools in communities that represented the variety of intersectional communities in the large city of Chicago. We would discuss the ways in which race fostered changes in their social interactions with peers and with teachers. We'd ponder the ways in which these interactions informed shifts in their self-definitions—and the meta-awareness they were developing as they compared their new worlds with those of their long-time companions and measured the capacity for equitable education in each of the models of schooling available to them—from racially diverse schools, to local segregated schools, and across the city in various alternatively-funded options.

One of the things that struck me early in my teaching was how aware my students were of the norms of our school system—and the ways in which these norms might prove to be possible hurdles. Figuring that our students would be more likely to return to us as a collective if we planned formal meetings to process, we'd worked to build a practice that would elicit their critical reading of their experiences. We'd embraced new lesson plans for our prodigal students and centered for them famous theorists who would not only validate their experiences but help them to find the power and potential in even the most draining and difficult moments. To this end we centered several conversations around Gloria Anzaldua's *Borderlands*—a theoretical inquiry into border crossings that were mirrored daily in my students' schools and all their variations for Mexican American students. We studied their new experiences as texts in the traditional text-self, text-text, and text-world framing—just to make sense enough to survive.

Most of our conversations stretched over sessions and revolved around the ways in which students were categorized in their high schools—both socially and academically. At the public schools farthest from our community, students were coming into daily contact with racial, linguistic, and ethnic diversity they hadn't yet experienced. Their questions varied from the very specific to the vastly broad—wonderings about certain groups and cultural practices of inflection and playful banter, of fashion differences and complexities of cultural appropriation, of attention and priorities in worlds that attached high stakes to all of these domains. The liminal spaces between their new worlds and our previous shared home supported their spiritual questioning, but the opportunity to return to their own centrality in our former classroom provided safe spaces for strategizing around their own cultural practices and the ways in which they could prevent stereotypes and discrimination by understanding completely the architecture of the world to which they were acclimating. I myself had to adjust to a new architecture of my teaching life, and I reflected on the difference in light outside the expansive windows of our classroom. My memories of these students' younger selves were backdropped in my memory by the sunlight of daytime hours. Our shared learnings in these meetings were backdropped by the thick charcoal of wintry Chicago nights. My presence in their lives now backdropped itself and my opportunities to witness and support their shared understandings was rendered extracurricular and marginal to the day. I'd built a centrality for ourselves in this same classroom space that nurtured us for years, but I came to realize in the maturing network of young people in front of me, that I had fought not to face the border crossings evolving for me here in my own classroom—and that the distances of my liminal travel into the students' lives and back were extending like the hours of darkness imprinted on my sight.

In the Marxist fashion of Anzaldua's text, too, we hashed out which groups had been the most surprising to the students in their observations. There were the anticipated comments about hallway volume thresholds and academic expectations, but we were shocked by some of the overt ways in which the students' essences threatened to work against them—in ways both complete and definitive—while we were trying to help them maintain a critical eye and question everything.

We had to accept once again the blunt force of the colonial project's white normativity. Ricardo, our stellar achiever, reported that he had been informed by his English teacher that he'd better not hope for higher than a C because she couldn't assess him any higher, because he wasn't a native speaker.

★

One of these issues played out fairly publicly at one point in the year as the students still shared with me the central circle in my classroom. We had welcomed a new teacher to the school, a young Mexican woman who had recently graduated from college and whose cultural proximity to the students was both generational and racial. As a younger student in the city, her Mexican community was close in character to theirs though geographically distant. Her education took place in similar public schools to those we knew around us and her affinity for her communities rooted her locally for college, as well. She was inspiring in her accomplishments but humble and gracious in her interactions with other teachers, with parents, and with students themselves. After vacancies in the students' science classroom, her arrival was long-anticipated and profoundly appreciated. Students gravitated toward her and her classroom, and she was the subject of many of my students' essays that year, her sphere of influence extending even to those students who were yet peripheral to her teaching.

At one point during the year, on a quietly bright and snowy day, two of my students who often stayed to assist me after school were organizing my papers to be graded on the carpet of the reading area. I was sitting at my desk trying to make headway into the stacks they kept handing me—but felt easily distracted and fairly disinterested in the solitary nature of that seemingly endless work. As I tried to process the artifacts of my recent days' teaching, I listened to the boys' chatter and banter with half an ear. They were talking about homework and what I presumed to be new video game releases while they sorted my papers into stacks around the floor. I smiled without really lifting my head to them, and began to enter points into the grade book. I knew my slow pace as my tasks were not being visibly reduced though the topics of discussion in the back of the room had covered a range of subjects that could expand across days if they had them. I heard commentaries about the meals they were anticipating at home, as I was thinking about how young they still were despite how much they'd grown from our early ESL days in the boiler room.

"Ms. T! We have a question."

I glanced up to see them both facing me.

"How come you don't dress like Ms. Ramírez?"

I felt my face register the fast travel back across the years as I rested my glasses and pen atop my papers. I looked at the students but didn't have words for them, waiting to see how much they'd elaborate, and trying to determine the nature of my reaction as either shock, dismay, or jealousy.

I remembered a day several years earlier when I'd first got my classroom library grant and had taken the two of them with me to the north side to make a list of books they liked and felt I should spend the grant money on. I remembered the ways in which they'd fought over books as belonging to genders, and dividing their suggestions for my purchases into those best for boys and those best for girls. I had listened to them and thought that it was the first time gender as a divider had surfaced in our conversations. I realized at the time that their categories didn't resonate with me, nor did their impulse to categorize, but that I was happy to see them entertaining dimensions of identity and the power of books to elicit identification with others. I had hoped this gendered discussion might reveal to them the ways in which we limit our self-understandings knowingly and not, and the role of books in opening windows to new dimensions of ourselves when we can no longer appreciate ourselves as unique.

Inside that aimlessly adolescent conversation, problematic as it was in a number of ways, I hoped I was seeing an appreciation for audience and a thoughtful reflection on the students we had shared our reading choices with for so many years. I thought suddenly about those younger versions and ways in which gender had surfaced occasionally in conversation. The first year of my teaching was filled with curiosities about my lack of children and what experiences I'd had to inform that choice. The questioning resonated more at the time for me in terms of variations in cultural expectations and not in terms of gender, though I had been surprised after first announcing my pending nuptials that my students had adapted my title and replaced my surname with my husband's—and that I'd interpreted the act more as a cultural welcome than an articulation of gendered hierarchies. I realized now there were intersectional geographies that we could have parsed.

The intellectual wonderings across the many years of conversations were enshrouded however by emotions of hurt and surprise. I studied the faces of these two students who had known me longer and better than most of the others, and realized I had failed to capitalize on those previous opportunities to complexify gender, not simply to deepen cultural understandings about politicization of gender but also to reveal my own thinkings about gender equity and the ways in which women experienced victimization across cultures and interpersonal involvement.

Teaching had taught me to read myself for anger and be careful not to enlist it against students. I worked to recognize anger in my own life as a secondary emotion, and therefore an obstacle to processing true emotions in the contexts in which they surfaced. I had worked to shield my students from adult anger, knowing that it is the emotion adolescents perceive in adults most powerfully and clearly. I didn't want our room to be complicated by anger as deflection or as a weapon, and unpracticed as I was in sharing anger with my students, I was profoundly unprepared to feel it toward these two.

"You can go now. Leave the papers there on the floor and I'll get them."

It was probably the first time I'd ever spoken to them that directly or coolly, and they recognized the emotional shift in the room, as I recognized, and *felt,* that our shared understanding was perhaps less bi-directional than I had thought.

"It's ok, Ms. T. We're just playing."

"You can go play somewhere else. Just leave everything. See you tomorrow."

They stood slowly in silence except for a long glance of shared confusion, and moved sheepishly toward the door.

"C'mon, Ms. T. You know we didn't mean it. You don't have to be like that."

I looked down at my jeans and wool turtleneck sweater that I'd brought back with me from my grandmother's Cotswolds hamlet and shrugged—a gesture in direct contrast to the immensity of the loneliness I suddenly felt. I felt the years of trying to absorb persistently cruel forces of race, class, and age discrimination had been protecting them. In this moment, I'd failed to teach them their own capacity to hurt, and to recognize in the parity of relationships that we wield the wounds of socialization against those we know best. The comparative model of norm referencing student achievement on standardized tests was not less damaging than considering human worth against that of others', and I'd been unprepared to have to protect myself.

"If you can think of one time that I judged you for anything other than what you were deep down, then we can start the conversation there. On some other day. I will let you know when I've decided I'm ready to listen. Close the door behind you."

★

The story made it around the small school by the middle of the next day: that I'd kicked out of my room the two students closest to me in my daily experiences. In the wake of the event I had to carve out new ways to navigate those daily activities, while still facilitating them for others. In the reminder that the teaching responsibilities I bore were indeed work, I needed to check my emotional attachment and the ways it was impeding the responsibilities I had for my students.

I knew the work in front of me as labor and growth, and needed to reconcile the two.

The boys themselves looked pained and nervous the next day, but I paid no particular attention to them and went on with the things we had planned. We were beginning the process of creating symbolic pieces of abstract art that they could keep on their desks for the standardized tests in a few weeks. The students had large pieces of chart paper that they were to divide into sections that represented the different domains of their lives and different geographies they inhabited. We were going to try to distill the essences of all these successful identity elements into a symbolic piece of art, so that during the testing process they would have it as a constant reminder of themselves in full wonder and complexity.

The incredible high stakes of the testing process for middle schoolers in the Chicago Public Schools was unrelenting. Sixth graders were either passed or retained based on a percentile mark achieved in relation to all other sixth graders taking that specific test. The percentile marks of seventh graders were used to leverage access to selected-enrollment high schools around the city—the schools that received the most resources and provided the most attention in the transition into college. Eighth graders were graduated depending on these same norm-referenced scores, or forced to repeat their final elementary year—all these destinies determined by the week looming ahead of us.

Because I had students at the beginning of this three-year stress, I thought perhaps we could create an antidote to the pressure and the high-stakes by infusing students' creative art-making skills into writing activities. Students created large graphic organizers on their easel sheets and brainstormed all the different things they did well (according to their own perceptions) in the different spaces they occupied in the world—daughter/son, friend, sister/brother, student, athlete, artist/musician, mentor, family/community/"tribe" member.

This last category brought up much discussion before we headed off with our large sheets around the room. Students wanted to know why I'd used the word "tribe" so I put the word on the board and we processed its possible meaning within this context. We also questioned it for integrity of use, and the broader threats of cultural appropriation in a hyper-racialized society. The students had studied ancient civilizations that pre-dated colonization, and understood the governmental overlap with ethnic groups and cultural lineages. We placed the term and a question mark for impact in post-conflict worlds on our front board.

Students were quick to reference the people and places they called "home" back in Mexico, and despite the different immigration statuses in my classroom, almost all the students felt that there were people they associated with definitively across the border, and in ways that would possibly represent a "tribe" more than "community." In the analysis, students also acknowledged that they spent a lot of time with extended family here in their current neighborhoods, and that these specific networks were deeply important to them—and perhaps a better representation of the term. We briefly walked through the connection of ancient civilizations to smaller articulations of the students' perceived inner circles, and highlighted for ourselves an inquiry project to entertain later.

As we completed the contextual framing for ourselves, two of the students who had deeper contacts with gang networks asked if they could include those and we put the question back out to the class.

"But there's no blood relation there," one of the girls, Carla, suggested.

"That's not true," one of the boys countered. "I know gangs that are basically made up of brothers, dads, uncles, etc. That's as much family as all these others!"

"Can't it work then just to stick with the family group?"

I jumped in to try and keep an increasingly-emotional subject cerebral. "What tools can we use to categorize relationships felt as strong as family but without the blood relation? What could we say in that case?"

"Ms. T., that's right. That's the way lots of these gangs operate. To protect the people they care about."

Carla was getting upset. She lived on what was seen as a violent street—though to whom it was violent, adults never discussed—and was kept inside when not in school. "Then why do they make it so hard for everyone else to do the same thing? I don't get it. It doesn't seem like family to me."

"Let's step back then and think about other places where we might feel like we have family, or share a kinship—family-like feelings—with people we're not related to."

"I feel that way about church," Cecilia chimed in. "I love those people!"

"Good! Lots of people feel that way—and when we talk about world religions we'll process the ways in which they are interwoven into societies."

"I guess I feel that way about my soccer team," David confessed. "I see them more than almost anyone." David was our resident "fútbol" rock star. He had a scholar's depth of understanding for the nuances and global history of the game. He was recognizably and exceptionally talented. We'd organized as a class that fall to go to several inter-city matches and seen for ourselves what a leader he'd become.

"That's a good example, but you'll have to work that out on your organizer, because we have a section for sports. So think about how you might connect those, and what all our overlaps might indicate."

I wanted to get the students onto the floor and into the activity so I started to wrap it up when I was interrupted by Desmond, who hadn't looked up during the whole conversation but seemed to be still processing our exchange from the day before.

"I think you're my tribe, Ms. T. Even if you don't want to be, we're connected."

★

At some point in my own navel-gazing about whether or not I belonged in this job, in this community, in the eyes of the students, I'd forgotten just how sensitive students can be to adult input. In the high-stakes world we were currently stalled in, I had forgotten how our ecological developmental models are constantly negotiated and carefully maintained in the adolescent years. February in its own right had appeared the Achilles heel in kind interpretations of the work and people involved in teaching. Inside my own fears of a high-stakes job in which students' futures seemed all too volatile and dependent on the quality of my efforts, I'd forgotten to step back and realize how instinctively students could read me and my moods. While critically reflecting on my role in their empowerment and development seemed to serve me in my own growth as their teacher, my worrying about where I stood in the greater picture of things communicated an anxiety to them that I hadn't intended.

I knew that Desmond had tried to play with that anxiety and I'd shunned him. I had not crossed the distance of hurt and remembered to place myself in the context of our mutual explorations of identity.

I took my own sheet over to the area he'd found on the floor and started to make the circles of my own ecological identity. Desmond knelt on the floor, pen above his paper, and waited to see what I might do first. I put the words "work," "friends," and "family" above three of the circles overlapping on the left. I put his name in the intersection, set down the pen, and got up to peruse the students and their work.

★

Identity is a fragile fabric at the onset of one's adolescence. Even as I was wrestling with the different categories in which I was able to share identity markers with my students, I'd overlooked the ways in which they were doing the same thing.

I knew that they didn't need to determine whether or not I had a legitimate role in their lives as their teacher, but that they were instead in the process of individuating from their own inner circles as they manifested across domains. They were reading the kinds of spaces symbolized on their graphic organizers for ways in which they were reflected within them. It was an ecological examination of who they were becoming in the rich and complicated history of culture crossing inside a system designed only to compare them against whiteness.

Sometimes they were braver than I in asking the hard questions.

In my quick-trigger response sourced by gendered history, however, I'd read their inquiry more as a similar comparative evaluation of me. In parallel with the test reports, it felt like an accusation and not like their attempt to make sense of difference as it played out in their daily lives.

I still held firm beliefs about the objectification of women, and was working on trying to think about gender roles from within a place of cultural sensitivity. I was learning the complex ways in which women were both the center of power in Mexican families and second-class citizens in the traditional socio-political realm. I appreciated the gendering of elementary teaching to be predominantly female because it provided me with some breathing room in which to tweak the nuances of how I fit in to this community, and in general a freedom away from worlds dominated by the male gaze. Inside elementary schools, no one balked at a woman in the powerful role of teacher, though I was learning that there were other expectations of the female gender that I fell short of.

The issue of dress was one I never quite reconciled, or even knew how to frame without erring egregiously, so I found myself often dismissing its relevance and leaving the cultural nuancing for a distant time that never arrived.

The boys had brought it to me. Here were those questions in their fullness, presented as a personal challenge, by students I'd known closely across many years.

In form, I'd shied away from the challenge. In the shock and stress of the moment, I'd resorted to a latent tendency to "other" and failed to see the richness of the possible conversation I had avoided. I knew that I had deflected attention from our powerful teachable moment and drawn a line in the sand between us, a protective barrier against interrogations of that level of my being.

The only answers I would have had were that I'd been jealous and hurt. I didn't want my attempted connections with my students and community to be so easily brushed aside because of a difference of appearance, but also didn't want to acquiesce and give up my comfort level. Most of all, I was afraid of the inter-sectional bruising that might taint the in-process deconstruction of my role.

It was unfair to hope that the boys knew me well enough to see this already when it had been unclear even to me.

My thoughts of being transparent and predictable needed to be revisited. Desmond had recognized that too, and approached me from the shared spaces that resonated with him—we were both fairly reflective, somewhat shy, and primarily emotional in our processing of life events. I decided to ask him to stay after school so we could sit on the stairs outside the room and talk about things in a neutral zone, ignoring my growing understanding of the impossibility of this concept. I was aware, also, that the flip side to creating a safe space meant that I had to be confident enough to process the very questions I most struggled to hear—especially when I experienced through heightened emotions because of the personal connections I felt.

I tried to convey as much to Desmond.

"So I thought about things and I think you were right to ask me that question yesterday. I shouldn't have reacted the way I did, and I feel pretty bad about asking you to leave. But I don't know if you're interested at all in the reasons why I reacted the way I did—we could talk about it if you wanted. Fear and anger are common and unproductive responses to identity questions, as you know." I prepared myself for the big conversation.

"I think I have a lot to learn about girls."

Ecological models, intersectional bruising, and cross-cultural feminism would have to entertain me some other day, because sometimes students were just students.

★

Despite the beauty and intensity behind their symbolic desk adornments, and despite our attempts to break down the mystery of how tests are authored, and offer arsenals of "testing tricks" to help students maintain their focus on the larger goals, there would be devastation and despair in the testing sessions. As the students had encountered the core reading passage, they were paused by a term—pororoca—which was indecipherable by etymological analyses, and intentionally foreign to all sixth graders. Intended to assess their capacity for comprehension via context clues, instead they'd been assessed on their comprehension of the context of whiteness in US public schooling.

I'd also been assessed—our antidotes to the standardized tests hadn't been enough for the tidal wave—tidal bore as our own "pororoca" —that would wash over the banks of all the hopes and intentions that year.

We'd not lined the river banks for this, and ultimately eight students would still be forced to attend summer school and/or repeat a grade they'd completed solidly in all other ways. Once the results were given to us in the final days of the year, the distilled symbols of their strengths hung in the classroom like a mockery of us in our efforts to console the students who'd be staying with me over the summer.

It was hard not to take it as a large judgment—even indictment—of our insufficient work during the year. Like being cut from a team or not making it into a play production, the students felt dehumanized as much socially as they did academically. In the criminal mis-assessment of their capacity, they wondered what they'd done wrong to be singled out.

We would never be able tell them; there would never be anything to say.

As an assessment tool, we as teachers had no way of making sense of these test performances, since we never got to see the students' individual tests or annotated notes with the score reports. The sorting system of the bureaucracy based itself on a measurement tool intended to be academic in nature, but was instead linguistically and socially biased, and which we couldn't reference in our attempts to help them develop the necessary capital to move past it. It felt criminal in its impropriety. Under the umbrella of trying to help students get access to an education that was equal and fair, my students had been sorted purely by language skills and emotional fortitude—aspects of their young lives that were morosely beyond their control—and forced to endure the violence of institutional bureaucracy masked as "teacher accountability" discourse.

What the test results did convey was that our recent efforts had been like an unsteady levee against the country's raging tidal bore. The content of the heartbreaking passage had come to mean more in its symbolism than it had as a reading comprehension assessment. We saw the momentum-gaining accountability mania that was supposed to be the end result of our efforts rise up in the political storms and roar back toward us carrying the silt and debris of those it had washed away. We were powerless to control it and stunned by its fortitude. We were caught, in the end, trying to be anything but glued to our river banks.

★

There was occasional solace for us in the fact that we'd tried, and that some had made it to safe ground. Whether or not access to dry ground had anything to do with the fact that we'd made collages and fused colors to represent their identities, nuances, and complex strength, we'd never know. Whether or not students were buoyed by their assessment of their own vast knowledges was up to them to decide, and for us across the years to hold in balance with the constant feedback from testing agencies. Those corporate money-absorbing inaccessible positions of power could not ever see us—and, as was apparent, were never intended to care.

There would be no score report from us about their deficiencies, either, though we knew them profoundly. We knew they should care about the fact that Maribel had figured out the public transit system all by herself and taken her mother to a doctor's appointment. They should care that Cecilia cooked every night for nine people and translated her father's bills. They should care that Fernando got placed in an elite drawing program at a nearby university and took his cousin along so he could see what it was like. They should care that Desmond would learn to translate his favorite Neruda poems for the girl he'd later meet at the boys and girls club in an after-school program.

I was muted but knew. In a silence that echoed inside me, I believed all the sixth grade teachers across the nation knew more than they were allowed to say, and dealt with the testing assault as best they could.

It was this last nuance that I struggled the most to try to reconcile—that my hopes for my own cherished sixth graders had to manifest themselves in indirect hopes that the tail end of the bell curve be filled with someone else's students, elsewhere. Somehow, somewhere, 50% of sixth graders were not going to make this arbitrary cut, with disproportionate consequences attached. 50% was incomprehensible to me in its terribleness. My emotional investment in the 25 students in front of me was only repeated across the nation in variations on a theme, teacher to teacher and school to school. While the matrix of complex factors that might impede rising above that cut-off most certainly played out differently across sixth-grade classrooms, my silent pleas for less bias would need to be counterbalanced by increased bias for other students.

I had to remember that our anger and resentment were toward a system that didn't have capacity to allow them all to thrive simultaneously and thus save the competition for more appropriate arenas. I had to balance my personal anger at this unrelenting construct and dissect its methods so that I could pull them apart one by one.

★

The night after the tests, I went to the central Chicago library to look at all the encyclopedias I could get my hands on—hoping for the slightest remedy to my own intensifying rage. I wanted images, and contexts, and the etymology of the word pororoca to somehow assuage my anger and assure me that no sixth grader anywhere would do well on that passage. I talked with the librarians on hand for assistance and any texts they could find—I would take them in the next day and try to use our painful experiences as a springboard for further investigation. I wanted some lurking official who might set foot in our building to see that my students knew the concept of tidal bore better than any other sixth grade classroom, and that if they wanted to use standardized tests to make sure all students got a great education, then that's what we would do. Shy of getting a grant to take the students to the Amazon myself, we'd be the masters of tidal events for all of the Midwest—prepared should any of us make it out of this violent system and find ourselves shacked up alongside a large equatorial river. If they believed in competition, I'd give them my best competitive effort.

Metaphorically and quite literally, I wanted to dedicate myself to building the walls of sandbags in all directions so that we'd never get caught in this specific way again, and so that the students wouldn't have to pay so dearly for a system designed to monitor and control those who serve them, in this case me.

9

MARCH

Ides and Ideals

After a year of challenges, reflections, ruminations, and re-thinkings about race, language, classroom community, and even my gastro-intestinal fortitude, the Ides of March brought with them a chance for penitence and to step back inside my parable, this time with someone else as we engaged in school-like formal combat.

Our local branch of the public library system was a tiny storefront in a less-residential nether region of the community, tucked away on a northeast corner across from the "Carnicería" and the Dollar Store. In my first years of inhabiting the community, I'd never noticed it, despite the fact that it was mere feet from my walking path to the train, and on the busy polish-named street that connected every Spanish-speaking community from the loop to the far south west suburbs. More important than my recognition of public institutions was the students' recognition of informally public institutions—gangs in the area wrought tense perforated lines near the branch, indicative to me of the truth of lived experiences in the complete absence of pedestrians on a heavily trafficked street.

Learning of the presence of this public institution, however, renewed my faiths nearly universally and helped me complete learnings I had been reluctant to accept—the unmistakable misdirection of public services most intended in decades past to stabilize and center the poor but now criminally misdirected to the bands of elite communities whose needs for them were performative.

A hint of an invitation later was all we needed to make the quick trek to books lying low in the east part of the neighborhood.

My students had never been, though many of them had ventured downtown to the main branch. I wondered to myself as we marched there on a cold and windy day how many of them had not yet been this far east of the boulevard—and, indeed, many of them were nervous and unsure as we approached the building. Their lack of familiarity seemed tempered by the excitement of escaping the school building with some consistency and exploring this learning outpost in the outside region of the community which was easier to enter than to incorporate within the school-housed curricula. Our designation as a community-based school felt at times both true and untrue, as wavering levels of success and failure followed our efforts to extend ourselves outward. Bringing the community in as the more sanctioned alternative remained the easiest route to our moniker.

We found our way to the books every third Tuesday. The first week felt a bit unnerving—for me, as I had had 25 students walking busy city streets all by myself, and for the students, as they radiated varying levels of anxiety about the process of getting library cards. I hadn't for a moment considered that the students would both be afraid of exposing themselves or their immigration status, and also reserved about their reluctance to reveal the source of these contagious worries. When I'd paid attention in my teaching I'd got constant reminders of the differences between us and of my failure to convey to the students fully enough, or often enough, that they could trust me with such delicate matters and that I wouldn't turn them in. I had forgotten to be explicit that the process of getting a library card specifically was not a system to locate undocumented immigrants for removal and deportation, images we had seen personally and on the news, and more profoundly as the recognizable specter of the tentacles of the third Reich and its common first assault on othered communities.

If anything, I was afraid of their behavior that first day, and went over the norms and expectations we'd need to adopt as a group in order to maintain this privilege—and the students nodded dutifully and signed their contracts. The steps for consequences were listed in a checklist at the bottom, and we stapled them to the back of the front cover of their reading journals. These special "library" journals were transformed 50-cent spiral notebooks, and we brought them with us as part of the ritual. On the inside of the back cover we attached our version of Reading Logs—lined sheets for us to record our book selections and track their return dates, and then finally a column to list any recommendations or comments connected to the text and the context of our community. Both the contracts and the logs had been co-signed by parents, and we'd submitted formal permission slips for the repeat excursion required by the school to be left behind upon departure in the office.

Feeling pride in my preparation and attempt to facilitate as much enjoyment from the routine as possible, I'd not considered the need to include instructions for how to enlist help in the search for desired texts and then for the process of checking them out to take home. I had expected a bit of rowdiness to accompany a sudden sense of freedom from the confines of school, but almost all of them were fairly subdued. My braver student, intuitive about all things school, approached me eventually to "translate" a few of the broad apprehensions about being exposed, detained, and ultimately deported. Rendered invisible in this society and left to protect themselves in ways reflective of oral history traditions, my students had learned fear about registering for any kind of formal identification.

"Ahhh." I'd often felt amazed at how clear the situation might appear once I'd been offered the chance to see it through the students' lenses. I'd never not understood the history of the Malinche and Sacagawea in terms of the limited knowledges of the conquerors, but instead the tragic flaw of empathy these brilliant women held for their conquerors. The mystery was centered for me on the trust and faith in unworthy men that convinced those women to sacrifice themselves and their nations.

"I'll talk to them. Thanks, Ricardo."

★

My most recent arrivals—they'd been in the US only a couple of months by the time we first traveled to the library—were my first stop. Uniquely smart, sweet girls who were both effervescent and energetic despite the upheaval in their lives, I tried to offer them the chance to experience their learning as individuals, but tended still to think of them as a unit. Though their histories were quite different and their places of origin as diverse as theirs from mine, they still quickly found each other and built each other up to be the confident and outgoing students I gradually knew them to be. I wondered often how important their differences were to them and whether or not they'd have even been friends had their paths crossed in Mexico. Belén hailed from the Capital—DF to everyone—and was funny and strong in her friendliness. Noelle claimed French roots and was shy in her brilliance, and sweet in a way that made everyone comfortable. Their abilities to hold onto these traits despite the American definition of them as homogeneously Mexican-American became the lesson of my teaching career—how newness and oldness envelop each other and create new spaces outside those definitions.

Even among this group with ostensible ethnic homogeneity, the diversity of immigrant history had the potential to be very divisive. Varying derogatory names existed for students in all places on the spectrum of residency, and we spent frequent class-meeting time addressing this situation. It was part of the efforts behind the Huapango Dance they'd created in the first months—to build an awareness of difference and similarity into our community dynamic, and I was grateful for that shared history as I came to realize that this was an opportunity to look it straight in the eye again.

I called the two girls over to a desk with Jane the librarian and told them directly that I wanted them to know there would never be a moment when they were unsafe in my care. Their attention on us was intense and layered as they processed our assertions of complete safety and detachment from immigration policy. I re-introduced them to Jane, who had come to our classroom the month before to read to them and to get them excited about returning the visit, and we both reinforced to them that the Public Library system had no connection with any kind of local, regional, or national citizenship or law enforcement process.

I put my hands on theirs and told them it was an inalienable right to get to read, a nod to their studies of the constitution and the way I'd tried to characterize reading as the "pursuit of happiness." Despite what they might hear elsewhere, I said: no exceptions.

I asked them if they had any questions, and Noelle—the bolder, the future military program captain and valedictorian of our de-resourced neighborhood high school—hugged me. "All right, M.s T.," she said—her conversational English growing by the day. "You want us to tell the others."

"Exactly. And you tell them that the day they're too afraid to talk to me about these kinds of matters is the same day that I will leave teaching for good. I should be embarrassed that I haven't expressed this all to everyone before."

Noelle smiled—she'd perhaps thought this exact thing, but was too polite to ever express it. I winked back at her and sent them on their way.

Jane and I stayed put at the table, the two nice white ladies who spoke Spanish—who'd ignorantly and overconfidently thought that this would help us bridge the divide. It made me think back to my student teaching days and how overwhelmed I'd been by the amount of things I had to learn while on the job. Management and unit planning had seemed so concrete and unmoving as a student myself, and yet were entirely fluid once I stepped into a room with people in my care. I realized how bold it was to consider that I'd know ahead of time what kinds of things my students would need both in their academic development as well as in their socialization process—without knowing *them*.

Some of this plays out in all classrooms, and as I confessed to Jane, there is always the not knowing entirely what events surrounding the students will surface in classrooms. She nodded, as she checked her list of cards with my class roster. The reality I didn't know was that Jane had seen this kind of episode happen before at other Chicago Public Library branches—in fact, it was part of the CPL policy simply to use the students' school address as "documentation" for the card. She shared with me that in each of her placements she'd had to have this same conversation.

Despite her intentions, this information only heightened my frustration, at the scope of our hostility in the national sphere, and also at my blindness to it. I was bewildered at my continued lack of growth in these areas—and at the ways in which the divides between my students and me kept rearing their ugly heads. I watched my students as they'd started to mill about—as the students in conversation with Noelle and Belén began to wander the stacks in small groups—and do the things I'd hoped they would learn to do here.

Jane pointed it out, and I tried to smile—albeit with a straight face at the realization that learning to teach had once again been simply the process of deepening my sense of humility.

The students were allowed to take out up to three books, so at the end of each forty-five-minute visit, they got 15 minutes to check them out with Jane, fill out their logs, and write about their experiences in their journal. Jane called them up by tables while the others continued to work. As I mingled among the tables—to help students put their books in their "library bags"—special canvas bags donated by one of the university professors interested in our school's progress—students both shielded their writing from me and asked me to help them with it. They were allowed to write in whichever language they chose—but I recommended that they select the same language as that of the books they were taking out. Those who took out books in different languages got to make their own choice.

Despite my statements about writing for different purposes, and with different liberties—I didn't correct or grade their spelling, syntax, or grammar in journals—I still had to remind them not to "worry" about spelling, etc. At each table, my most conscientious students, and all of them to a certain degree, had wanted to know all the rules and were insistent about getting that information from me. I'd been trained to think that it was interfering with their creativity—that stopping the flow of what they were trying to say in order to worry about how they were saying it would thwart their development as writers, meaning implicitly at times also as humans.

In later years as I would continue to wrestle with this issue, I'd need to entertain the reality from my students' complex perspectives—that I was keeping them from their authentic search for the codes of the culture and language of power, despite my better intentions. My inclination to try and reduce the pressure on them so that they'd produce more was inappropriate and unfounded as that very pressure existed in the fabric of their existence within a society about which they'd already absorbed and understood so much.

Often in vain, I tried to strike a balance. Our classroom was filled with labels and posters that were also labeled with other words of interest. There were random categories of words as high as the 16-foot ceilings and I urged students to look to them in those moments of curiosity and/or frustration. I also wanted them to take risks—to trust their instincts and make guesses, because the process of trying to build within our languages would help them tremendously as they began to internalize all the rules.

At one of the tables, a communal version of this process was happening already. Students knew the "silence" rule of the library, so they sat as closely as they could to Geraldo. Confident in his own language acquisition, Geraldo was our classroom's master of spelling in English as well. He had a particularly intriguing system that he conveyed to the others at every opportunity: he sounded out English words for other students as they would be pronounced in the Spanish phonemic system. He was phenomenally more popular than I was for all my moralizing about risk-taking. I'd gleaned over the course of the last months in our trips here just what kind of power he had due to the popularity of his proximity here at the Library.

I decided to leave that group alone. No one ever taught me about these kinds of democratic principles in my linguistics classes, and I realized just how amazing our meta-cognitive language skills could be, and the exceptional knowledges my students owned and exhibited that I'd not fathomed.

As I approached Ricardo's table, he raised his hand to get my attention. In my struggles to disrupt a coloniality that felt alive in our journeys of just a few blocks to get here, I knew as clearly as I knew anything that I was a living, breathing, walking archetype, and no investment in tandem public institutions would mitigate that truth. I headed over and saw that Ricardo's journal entry was a letter to me. Jane called his table and I was left alone with the journals—the other students having closed theirs up for privacy, Ricardo clearly wanted me to read his:

Dear Ms. T:

Did I tell you we like the library? Noelle called it her "refugio." What's that word in English? I know you think some of us don't trust you. But we all do. I like to bring my family on the weekends—and I don't know if you know a lot of other students do the same thing. We don't tell you because we're afraid you'll stop bringing us. Anyway, we want to know if you and Jane are related. Does she eat meat?

Love,

Ricardo

I smiled to myself and remembered my first year teaching. Ricardo's older cousin had been in that group, and so he was here making an inside joke because he'd heard the story before. My students at the time had wanted to bring me different foods as offerings of gratitude and also to show off how great their family culinary practices were. Some also wanted to help me learn more about Mexican culture. Touched as I was, I had to confess to them that I was vegetarian at that time. This was as foreign to many of them as if I had said I sleep hanging upside down. It became quite the issue in the class—in journals, in any kind of kitchen-based ESL activity, and at lunchtime. I fielded constant questions about it, and tried to convince them that it wasn't a strike against my overall character. Ricardo's question might be evidence that I never really managed that last part.

Similarly to our own extensions into new people and places, it was in late winter of that year that a friend of mine came to spend the day. He was considering becoming a teacher and had heard me talk a bit excessively about my experiences. He came to help out with projects and centers, and arrived around 10 a.m. By 10:02, the students could no longer refrain from asking questions about him. Nancy Drew, Hardy Boys alike—there was no better sleuth than an early adolescent. The first question in the interrogation had been whether or not he ate meat. I laughed long and hard—and then had to backtrack to make sure they knew it wasn't meant to be laughter *at* them, but more my amazement at what a big issue that continued to be. My own idiosyncrasies were less fascinating I was certain, but what compelled me persistently was their anthropological study of me and of a broader "us," and their brilliance at recognizing patterns and looking for the limit to characteristics shared by "like" groups. For years after, students extended the sociological, psychological, and ethnographic work and employed the story and its tandem incidents to cause me to laugh, and then at times they'd use that enjoyment as leverage to get out of something they'd wanted to avoid. There were also innumerable lunch-table conversations that stretched from keen focusing on the lives of our former visitors to the broader hypotheses about how weird white people were in general.

Ricardo had now recalled the cross-cultural analyses and broader cross-social-science study, and brought it up at a time that seemed relevant. He hoped these earlier paradigms might help me perceive my missteps in cross-cultural borderland travels as fraught, but that it would be all right also to laugh at overlooked common fears about the INS, just as it had been appropriate in terms of the white-people assumptions and the fear that vegetarianism was a foundational cultural practice of late-adolescent white people, or was frighteningly and powerfully contagious.

★

Part of the routine we'd established with the library excursions was to stop at the bakery on the way back to school. While the library trips started out as a way to allow students more choice in their selections for Reading Workshop, they'd grown in importance for me personally and helped me in other dimensions of my teaching. Part of what I struggled with in this incredibly dense and crowded community was the lack of opportunities to participate in pro-social ways. For me, belonging to the library and using it were acts of civic engagement—of participating in the things that make a society strong and foreground the public good above individual possession. Undeniably, our disinvestment in our collective was manifest to terrible effect in both the increasing inequities within both the library and school public systems. Within Chicago proper, wealthy neighborhoods benefited from expensive and elaborate library facilities, blocks from well-resourced schools, while poor community libraries stacked hand-me-down books on the shelves in buildings in disrepair. At some point I hoped to arrange to take the students to other library sites connected to other field trips so that they could start to assess this inequality for themselves.

The other element of the routine was my hope to make their memories and affective associations with reading as positive as possible—and as interwoven into their lives as I could. Stopping off for a treat at the end of each visit seemed like a step in that direction and an effort to weave the opposite of structural systemic paucity of resources. It was just bread, but perhaps an indication of the social kindnesses our city was supposed to want for them. I wanted structural benevolence for ourselves as teachers also. Those beautiful new schools next to newly-filled libraries would never suffer a year with an administrator whose purpose was to undermine creativity and research-based teaching, and we knew our low status every time we were addressed as problems to be solved on site and by a district working to fix our wrongs.

Each rotation to the library required newly-assigned "caretakers" for our walk down the busy boulevard and these students were charged to help shepherd their peers back to our school safely and soundly. The caretakers also got to pay the cashier and help the bakery staff serve us as quickly as they could. Despite the importance I felt for this activity, there was a nagging doubt in my mind that this was not how I should be spending valuable "instruction" time. The Chicago Public Schools had vast and complicated matrices about the different amounts of instruction time required in different subjects at different grades, and I feared in general that my approach already had me way off the grid, and that bakery time would surely put us in a no-good category. Though no one else had yet raised this issue with me among my peers, we had a new principal and I felt cautious about drawing too much attention to myself.

Sometimes on the walk back I gave the students a topic to discuss with their "partner" —the students walked in two single-file lines, each student next to the person they chose to chat with. The topic this time was Chicago weather. It was always ironic to me that our students and their families had to come to this cold, dirty city from beautiful small towns and farms—and I was curious to know to what extent they liked it in Chicago, for the complex matrix of things those feelings would encompass.

Students talked about the temperature in a lot of the conversations I was able to overhear—it was March after all and we were still dealing with freezing temperatures and different forms of precipitation, as is the norm in Chicago. March was not the happiest of months across the board here in the northern midwest, but for my students there was a heaviness to their conversations. I participated in coat drives at the school and in community parishes and thrift stores, but hadn't realized the pervasiveness of ill-heated homes and inattentive slumlords. Cold was more than an inconvenience or unpleasantry, and snow-day policies reflected the district's understanding of this. Most school "closures" were simply an acknowledgement that teachers would struggle to make it to the school buildings. But facilities managers and other staff people charged with school administration were made to open the doors to the buildings and offer spaces for students to spend their days of non-learning in the warmth and comfort of their classroom and school sites.

As the conversation drifted from challenges to nostalgia, I recognized the patterns of heritage I'd come to appreciate. The diversity in the students' hometowns/points of origin was consistently fascinating to me, and I listened curiously as the students from Guanajuato talked about the road between their two towns. They'd long-ago made this connection but loved to wonder if their paths might have crossed had they both remained there. It was fun for me to imagine, since I had just spent a few days recovering from that same illness that plagued all my trips to Mexico in the city of the same name, a veritable college town with *posadas* and cultural activities that kept its residents, students, and visitors engaged and active in the city center nearly once a week. I was moved by the fact that the students were talking about these public investments now and here as they trudged through the slush-strewn sidewalks. I understood the strategy of warmth such reminiscing could bring, as my heart thawed at the memories and as the students' reflections echoed my clearest recollections of their home state: everyone together and outside, cobblestone streets laid long ago and attended to lovingly serving as foreground for the nightly promenades for happy pedestrians and a warm glow of gratitude for a city that values the public good over individual hoarding of capital and resources.

I was remembering my stay there and wondering how well I'd do in a visit to the rural parts of the state when we began re-entering the building. As we entered the foyer at the base of the stairs, I walked between the lines and reminded the students that they'd have to continue their conversations in letters at the Writing Center when they finished their work. I made it to the head of the line and Sarah, the school wonder-woman, came out of the office.

"Big Shot." She made fun of my enrollment in grad school.

"Hi, Sarah. Were we too loud?" I asked.

"La Directora wants to see you."

Our previous principal and lead teacher had both gone by first names, so it was a form of resistance draped in irony that we all referred to our new Principal by her title. Mexican, white, faculty, staff—we'd inserted a shared idol into this year of parading crosses.

"Ok." The students were silent. They'd quickly readjusted back to an autocratic form of schooling after all our efforts to try and give them responsibilities necessary for our democracy. "I'll just take these guys upstairs and get started on our next lesson. Who's coming up to relieve me?"

"I don't know yet. I actually wanted to give you a heads-up."

"Thanks, Sarah." I nodded to the students and pointed to the top of the first stairwell. "Don't worry," I told them, thinking that maybe it was our last stop at the bakery after all.

The students were nervous anyway—there was an odd history unfolding this year. Two of my colleagues had already been suspended—for things no one had even heard of let alone understood to be worthy of suspension. Union delegates and higher-ups had been to the school now on three occasions to try to investigate the sudden rash of issues, incidents, inquiries, and any relevant outcomes. At one of these hearings, our union representative successfully fought the threatened and pending suspension and now La Directora walked among us with her own public scar, though that mattered to her less than the strike against her on record.

At a different hearing, the union representative was unsuccessful in their support of the teacher's claims of innocence, and so that teacher had been suspended for a day without pay, and forcibly banned from the school. There was a banality to the hostility that unsettled us most. We'd fought the racialized inequities of our system of schools, but not personally experienced its bureaucracy as violent. Yet teachers suspended, forced from their classrooms and students, had shifted our perceptions and afforded us a deeper glimpse at our students' lives. The aggression that was antithetical to the community we'd been working to build, however, soon began to enervate us, and we started meeting regularly off-site and off-the-record to try to rid ourselves of the unelected interim to make room for our own permanent principal hire by year's end.

It had taken us a while to remember that outside this world of our own making the routine power distributions and the systems they protected emanated cold and were sharp to the touch, a metastasized winter that felt like our eternal March.

In the month leading up to Sarah's kind warning, these private meetings had taken on a furious urgency—the formal Local School Council process to elect a principal would be about to be begin full swing and we were not even yet granted permission to consider opting out of the interim situation. La Directora was starting to pick up on the activity and accelerate her own strategy of threatening to suppress any and all activity that she could.

I guessed I was next.

Sarah gave me a heads-up because she'd already been through the worst we'd yet seen. As the central person for the whole school, we'd become accustomed to using her for all of our needs and she always graciously and generously obliged us. She mothered students needing moments outside their classrooms and received anyone sent to the office. She fulfilled our constant requests for copies both ahead of time and when a sudden need arose unexpectedly. She served as nurse, mother, truancy officer, and cultural liaison to all parents, guardians, and neighbors. Her official role and job description sat underneath all of that and that she still managed to serve all these complex duties defined her more for us as hero than "School Clerk" or "Assistant to the Principal."

For all this, she was the easiest target for La Directora and the first to be put into play. The school managed to rally around her and get her suspension reduced from five to two days, but it was a learning process for all of us to realize the frightening impact of Sarah's place in the formal hierarchy of the school—it took all of us to stand behind her in order to clear her of the inappropriate charges. There were few avenues for Sarah herself, despite the fact that not one of us would survive a day without her—our anguished and unearned privilege aside.

That year we'd quickly learned a few lessons about leverage. In fact, the days she was gone, the students and teachers and families refused to do anything other than the bare minimum and everyone wore black. Students were challenged and threatened for expressing their support, but we were able to curb any rampant abuse of power on their behalf by threatening to call the press.

Things had seemed to subside a bit after that. We'd thought it had settled. Word spread quickly that we'd been wrong, and that our next moment was upon us.

The students were starting to get antsy and worked up in anticipation of having to defend me, but I quickly tried to deflect to other things, and ice any burgeoning plans.

"It wouldn't be too smart to give her reason to come after us. Let's play it cool." The students got into their groups for the social studies research project, and I brought the cart out with the resources we'd borrowed from Jane in a previous trip.

When I was eventually called down, it was more than I'd been ready to expect. La Directora had my permission slips from the last several Library trips in front of her and was poring over them looking for one in particular. She pointed out that there was a clause missing on January's trip slip, and challenged me for putting the students in danger without having cleared it through her.

On each of the other slips, I'd included the clause that states that we had school permission, but forgot in light of the Sarah incident.

She told me she'd already notified the Board of my "crime" and that they'd recommended that I be suspended for a day without pay. I argued that it seemed steep when every other excursion had been okayed and that I was always transparent about the trips—giving her the dates and times and contact people in advance.

"That may be true. But you are asking me to give you the benefit of the doubt, and I'm not sure that I have a clear enough sense of your character to do that."

Me either, I considered saying. Instead, I started to object, but to no avail.

"However, Maestra, perhaps you would like to demonstrate to me that you are of an ethical caliber high enough that I could forgive you this instance and defend you to the Board."

I waited.

"You can tell me the extent and content of your meetings outside of school with the other teachers and rabble-rousers."

I'd been new to the exercise of leverage in our own pursuits of justice from disciplinary action, but not known to anticipate any in return. I was even worse, I knew, at acting and had most likely revealed these simplicities about me through a cursory read of my face. I took a moment to remind myself of the coolness I'd suggested my students demonstrate previously. I needed to heed my own advice.

"You see—I know that it's mostly the white teachers who are meeting, and that you'd rather have a white principal in here who can turn a blind eye to your loosey-goosey methods that fail to help these students get a leg up. I know that you all like to think you're doing the best for the students but that's really just because you've never had to work very hard to get where you are.

"But I know how close you are with some students and their families, and so maybe you're ready to do the right thing. Maybe you can start to see things from our perspective."

I was horrified and flushed with anger and shame all at the same time because I was being challenged on my concern for the students and insulted simultaneously. I was also flummoxed because it felt like she'd read my deepest fears, not unsubstantiated, and was now employing them against me—and I hadn't given her that credit at all in our year together.

This was all something I had never even considered, as is often predictable in politics. I'd had to reestablish my schemas, as I perceived for the first time that La Directora had been true in her articulation of a pro-community, if not traditionally progressive, agenda behind her actions.

While I considered the realization that I'd dismissed her entirely because of a difference of pedagogical philosophies, I managed to stand and assert that my character was of high-enough caliber that I would not stoop to being blackmailed, and that if she proceeded with the charges then I would use the full avenues to fight it allowed to me.

I quickly headed back up to my classroom.

Standing at the door, I saw my students suddenly as I'd never seen them before. What I previously had seen in my own classroom as "productive and meaningful chaos" I now saw as possible negligence. Students had large sheets of paper and different resources in front of them that I'd asked them to assemble, and they were shuffling through the packet of graphic organizers I'd given them to find the one best suited for their research projects. For the most part they seemed to be happily working and, ostensibly, learning, but I suddenly saw them instantaneously as La Directora might see them—rambunctious, disorderly students who needed a lot of different options because they couldn't meet the demands of normalized assessments. Perhaps she'd interpreted their mini collectives around the room as evidence that they couldn't work individually and get important things done—a skill of high value in our educational system—and that they couldn't memorize extensive details of historical material in order to take a simple test. Maybe she'd made the assessment of them already that they couldn't be counted on to use a standard outline—a skill universally implemented in high school classrooms across the city—and that they seemed to do very little without talking to their peers about it first.

Was this a progressive and empowering way to see them, from within the same socio-cultural circle of power? Or was it an autocratic grab at power at the expense of me and my students? Had my cultural lens really softened me to think that I was expecting great things of my students and empowering them to higher levels of status via their education, or was I making myself feel better by pretending to help those less fortunate than myself? These questions were beyond the scope of one teaching career but I knew the metaphors necessary for me to check myself. I needed to have considered more deeply how others would check me, and how would I then name that?

I stepped back into the hallway and turned my back against a locker. The gift of such moments of quiet reflection had been few and far between in my elementary teaching career, so I decided to try to clear the fog from my own head and leave the chaos to someone else.

Oftentimes I needed my students for clearer understanding, but in this particular situation I needed space to see through what had just been presented.

I took two deep breaths and tried to find the conviction that had helped push me past previous obstacles, though I recognized the differences here as the need for self-defense. I'd not needed convincing to engage in a fight on behalf of our students against obvious inequities and injustices, but this fight had been framed as in support of our students but against me. I was the problem and the impediment to their happiness and success in this fight being leveraged at me. I knew the first strategy was to believe deeply in what I was doing. But had I ever believed deeply in what I was doing? I knew why I was doing things, but not that there was some factor of value that connected directly to me.

I knew some things, though not the question in front of me at the moment. I knew most clearly that my students were learning things that mattered to their successful navigation of a historically cruel world, as well as to their own personal understandings. I had lots of evidence of them analyzing the world in increasingly complex ways. I could produce documents that would speak to their definitions of themselves as brilliant and as learners. I could also produce these artifacts in a variety of formal languages and informal discourses, and were also able to communicate worldviews and emotional connections to knowledges through the media of arts. We didn't do these things so as to build a case directed at testifying for me. All of the events, activities, and explorations belonged to them and existed only for them. In this vein I also acknowledged that a lot of evidence would not be available to an outsider until life had established it more permanently in anticipated experiences. I had no issue with this truth of human learning and resented the personnel action that made me consider it here and now.

I took a third deep breath and struggled to remind myself that this was the gift of committing oneself to teaching—guessing, reading, and planning for students without need for personal and immediate gratification that any of it has hit its mark. Whether or not I returned or introduced more traditional methods in my classroom, this would still be true. No matter which approach I took someone somewhere would have a criticism to offer about it.

I realized that this wasn't so much the part that had bothered me.

It was the suggestion that my whiteness was a large problem and that I'd been blind to it in my own naïveté and egocentrism. I thought I'd done as much as I could to "member-check" my own teaching—asking my colleagues, engaging with the families almost constantly, and questioning my own positionality in my choices.

Deep down, I had known it was not close to enough. Now, from someone whose opinion I had not respected or trusted, here was the full challenge—out loud and in front of me.

I did the only thing that it made sense to do—I went to back to the space that I could use to measure this interaction, my classroom.

As I stood there awash in the sounds of my students working and laughing I realized that this was the teaching life I had always wanted—warm, productive spaces with ample opportunities to explore learning through the different intelligences. I acknowledged how much of this stemmed from my own personal memories of warm and open elementary classrooms that pushed me to learn and didn't focus so much on measuring my deficits or strengths. While I knew that those memories locked me into acting on my historical privilege and from an outsider perspective, I felt that I'd done some thinking about transposing those beliefs into my current context.

I knew I hadn't been persuaded away from it yet.

There were plenty of examples of other issues which I'd come to see differently by opening up to the perspective of my new community—the blue police lights the city had adopted to help patrol crime-heavy areas being one. I felt deep anger the first day I saw the blue aura atop a dangerous corner at the system that would penalize and police me and my neighbors for the poverty of our collective community. I was outraged to understand the hidden message of blaming the victim and was discussing it one day with the parents of a couple of my students.

They'd respectfully disagreed with my feelings. They wanted me to know that their fears of the violence that their children could be subjected to took priority over any kind of civil rights issue they might have felt existed in this case. The parents told me that they had had no time to wonder about what were the deeper causes of the violence around them, as they had the pre-eminent and immediate responsibility of protecting their children.

Besides, they'd told me, if the whole community is not like that—like the "gang-bangers" or other perpetrators of violence—then how could the system have caused this to be? What allowed for the difference?

This, I realized as I sat on the perch outside my classroom, was the heart of my learning and at the core of the lesson I was getting that day.

I wanted to be someone who could see the larger issues but also the nuances of individuality in my students and in my world. I wanted to be someone who could fight the police lights but struggle alongside my students' families for their safety and security. I wanted to be inside the spaces of subtle individualities while also appreciative of the forces beyond our control that were worth learning to fight better.

I had to bring whiteness to the act, but use the act to mitigate whiteness.

★

The day of my suspension I spent the morning at the Bahá'í Temple just north of Chicago—a spiritual and architectural destination along the shore of Lake Michigan. In my one and only flying lesson a couple of years earlier, I'd asked to be allowed to see it from above. For several years I took my students there for an end of the year fieldtrip—to look at the ways in which the religions of the ancient civilizations we studied had been integrated into one belief system that premised tolerance of diversity as the fundamental religious endeavor.

As I walked around the building and through the Visitor Center that day, I realized how much less of a place the Temple was to me by myself. It had meant a lot to me in years past mostly because of the conversations triggered by our questioning and reflecting on the role of difference across time. I was moved during each visit by the opportunity to stand inside living history and architectural beauty, offered with text and pedagogy authored to include rather than exclude.

I realized what many people had told me long ago—I appreciated the opportunity to hammer out difference in multiple contexts and therefore felt compelled to immerse myself in it.

I knew therefore about the academic and interpersonal openness necessary to engage with people on their own terms and in their own locations.

I knew knowledge was shaped by experience and experience by knowledge, and that the extrication of one of these from the other could lead to failure. This was the answer I'd been looking for since the harsh day of the personnel action. Just as I had learned to appreciate the nuances of difference among my students and new community, I had to learn to see the nuances in the different ways they read me. I had fallen into formula, and La Directora had been right to challenge me on this, but she'd been wrong to decide the results for herself before any inquiry. In the research necessary for her own learning, she'd been wrong to manipulate students and the advocacy they sought purely for her own gain and greater access to an increase in her power over others.

Despite any motives I perceived, I was grateful for the pause. She'd been right in her challenging of me, something I was only able to see as connected to the questions at my own source once I had moved beyond self-defense—once I had let go of the fixed notions I had settled into and could appreciate an invitation to improve as ultimately promising for just my students and me.

I knew she'd wanted answers from me that vindicated her time with us, just not the ones I'd had to give her. In the methods she was implementing, I knew she'd wanted not so much to hear my take on my own practice but to have access to information in her own work to understand it and assess it. That increased power might come of that seemed more the byproduct of her disciplining of me than the objective. In her asking me about the oppression of our students that I might be participating in, her actions appeared based in a search for their rights and opportunities that I didn't disagree with. If on the surface, she'd wanted to find data that would support her hypothesis about the detrimental impact of whiteness on our student body, I hoped I would have agreed with her and offered myself as data. We only knew we shouldn't trust her completely as an ally was because she was focused so intensely on the professional positions she saw at the end of these inquiries, and not the students' presentations of themselves.

On one level, I appreciated her search for information about her own choices and philosophies, but questioned at what expense she'd pursued them as well as to what extent she was looking for those answers to come externally in a school whose skeletal structure foregrounded individualized learning and internalized empowerment. We hoped our years with students would culminate in more questions than answers, and saw the potential damage in the images of us she'd pre-constructed. Students, families, and teachers in our school committed their learning to the deconstruction of pre-conceived understandings of the world not based in experience.

What I knew in my heart now was that I could process the interpretation of me that didn't see through the layers of uncertainty and privilege that was in my teaching, and in my life on the outside moving inwards in my new community, I'd come to see it was all about the opposite.

I'd learned to accept that we should instead live inside the questions, no matter the source. In fact, the surprise at being exposed inside them meant having more people with you as you teased them out.

10

APRIL

Unplanned, Imperiled

To me the scary part of opening up my classroom to a student teacher was more the exposure of my less than traditional style of developing curriculum, structuring class learning, and integrating subjects through projects. While I'd seen many ill effects of lack of planning and foresight, I also held increasingly fast to the belief that some of my best teaching was shaped through direct engagement with shared thinking, and best when tailored to the needs of my students as they were revealed over the course of days, weeks, months, and a year in general.

I was nervous about incorporating a teacher candidate into this system and afraid that I'd be remiss in not providing her with pillars of a strong foundation from which she herself could grow her own intellectually engaging and perhaps non-traditional classroom—and then worry when she herself didn't perhaps have rock-solid plans or concretized pillars to provide also to teacher learners.

I hadn't been the first choice of the university, either, so I don't think my read on the situation was less than accurate. Wary of my issues in the previous year as well as my unorthodox approaches, they'd tried to place Geneva with another teacher in our cluster, one who'd had great rapport with students and an air-tight curriculum for the many years she'd worked with older students. But there'd been some broader issues in her first placement, although the information coming to me was vague, and I didn't quite know what to make of the unwritten feelings by the university professors regarding the dramatic shift, in the ways that I was antithetical in my teaching to this colleague whom they'd earlier seen as an ideal mentor.

I was also painfully aware of the increasingly hyper-evaluative lens on teaching and having experienced even localized punishment was developing a new level of self-protection from the judgment of others—not healthy judgment that guided necessary criticality in one's reflexive practice, but weaponized judgment by levels of corporate and governmental discourse that instrumentalize teachers' roles in a narrative about broken schools and broken families in the act of breaking them further.

Teaching doesn't always afford time for ruminating, and whatever the reasons—positive and/or negative—for choosing me, once Geneva and I were left to ourselves, I realized how glad I was to have her.

In my five years in the community, with the difficulties and successes, I'd felt consumed by reflections of my teaching implicated by my cultural background and its role in my pedagogical choices. I'd wondered frequently about the ways in which I was perhaps not connecting my methods to the traditional ways of schooling that the students were used to in their Mexican communities. I'd wondered if my discomfort with the absoluteness of authority afforded me by the parents and children had taken away from my students' natural inclination to take education and school intensely seriously. And I'd wondered if my position of privilege had infused my curricular choices and served to deculturalize the students by subconsciously dismissing more traditional methods of direct instruction and skill-focused learning.

But because teaching necessitates constant action and reflection I'd taught through these issues and tried to improve my sensitivities to any evidence that I'd dismissed and mis-taught the students, and tried to allow students the opportunities to choose their own approaches to learning and presenting to me what they'd learned while also having a more open approach in the classroom.

My initial fears that I would be exposed to the university and myself for being culturally inappropriate as well as insufficiently traditional in my expectations of my students' learning were quickly dissipated in my first conversation with Geneva. I'd asked her what she was looking for in a classroom and how she hoped to proceed with her teaching in this new context, and her answers overwhelmed me with hope.

She confessed that she'd been somewhat aware of how different things were in my classroom from her previous placement, and that she was wanting to make real connections with students so that she could learn how to "read" a classroom and prepare materials that would be challenging and engaging for her future students. She said that she was also eager to try to add to her toolbox of strategies some of the ones that weren't typically taught in university classes, which she'd loved and whose professors had expressed the magic of experiential learning.

We talked about her own schooling experiences as a young immigrant and she was deeply reflective about the different ways in which schooling failed to meet her needs. She had been bilingual and biliterate early on, but encouraged not to grow in Spanish. This was what led her to request our school as her placement site—she was deeply committed to promoting learning in both languages.

She was also careful to admit to me how much she hoped to see non-traditional learning. When I probed her for details about this, she embellished her statement by saying that she'd seen in her previous placements how bilingual students were often given intense worksheet work in English in order to try to

"catch them up" in the language skills they were "lacking" in what we understood as the code of power. She thought much of that approach led to inauthentic exploration both of the language and the content of different subject
matters through a constant dumbing-down of the curriculum and its persistent
reductivist approach to rote memorizing.

As we talked about some of the philosophical perspectives we shared, I invited
her to consider jumping in to her teaching as early as she felt comfortable. While
the university had her signed on in the fall for observation hours, she was eager to
begin assuming teaching responsibilities before the official start date in January,
and so we began to set her up for sharing instruction in our Social Studies class.

By April she'd become such a concrete part of our classroom that it was hard
to conceive of her not having been there at all. We'd accomplished units like "A
Cruise Through Ancient Civilizations" in which she'd designed the room to
represent each of the worlds we were going to visit through study and a passport for
each child documenting their successful exploration of each culture. We'd published
newspapers from contemporary versions of those ancient societies that discussed the
connections that existed between the historical and contemporary versions of those
societies, and we'd also integrated three-dimensional renderings of the biomes and
environmental characteristics of each of those locations around the world.

It dawned on me over the course of the year how polarized some of my
thinking had been before Geneva—how I'd essentialized the extremes of traditional teaching to be "Mexican" and progressive teaching to be "white" —and
about how stereotypical that thinking had been, and how damaging to my role in
the collegiality of the school and how limiting in my understanding of the complexities of my students and their expectations of adults. While I had differed in
approaches with Geneva's first mentor teacher, my dear colleague, I had ascribed
some of our differences to being cultural and was attentive to trying not to make
them a divisive issue between us.

What Geneva provided as a bridge between worlds was an awareness that
perhaps my attempts not to be offensive had been just the opposite—by not discussing pedagogical differences I was making assumptions about the reasons
behind them and prejudicing my analysis about our shared and unshared degrees
of enlightenment about teaching.

★

I'd been feeling swaggerish since the suspension, too assured by everyone's kind
words in response to the harsh personnel action that I'd been unjustly treated, and
also emboldened by the thought that perhaps the worst that the year had to offer
had now happened—like some weird universe-based balance sheet—and that I
was possibly untouchable from here on out.

There were also a lot of different things to worry about—the students' results
from the ITBS, the segue to seventh grade, different units I'd hoped to cover but
were now either being inelegantly combined or selected out. April felt like

triaging of instructional best-laid plans with some hopes that my power over curriculum wasn't being abused, and that the choices I was making wouldn't lead to critical gaps in their future lives. I'd taken out a series of activities on the demise of civilizations—and the ways in which once-strong societies fall inwardly, often catalyzed by surprisingly small events. As I rewrote the last several weeks' plans, I wondered about the ways in which the students whose fates I held in my hands would meet varied fates—who among them would rise into leadership and who among them would create professions not typically seen in the current bifurcating economy; who among them would know unparalleled successes and which of us, myself included, would see our efforts crumble under their own weight.

It was a suitable pondering as I was headed for the greatest evidence of this in my own life, a couple of weeks into the last marking period.

Because we were collaborating with Gilbert and working on visual arts units, some of our biggest projects were shelved until this last quarter. We welcomed Gilbert into class on Tuesdays and Thursdays, but were struggling against time to complete the work—and more importantly struggling to secure that we had concretized the students' learning. Geneva and I took an extra hour on a Wednesday for students to have extra painting time, unchaperoned as we were. Despite our best efforts, we'd added on the task of creating scenery for a play the intermediate cluster was putting on, hoping that it wouldn't take us too long to create some of the natural world—trees, a lake, a large animal or two, the sky, and some flowers—and that perhaps we could fold it into some work on biomes we'd begun earlier on. I was working against our efficiency with a stubborn commitment to not allowing any activity not connected to deepening students' understanding of some big concept. Behind in our products, I was agitated and rushed, thinking that I was using class time for less-than-meaningful child labor, and my guilt was quickly overtaking the atmosphere in the room.

It was clear that I'd sufficiently underestimated the amount of work and I was trying not to realize how little learning had been happening those chaotic days. The frenetic energy caused by all these factors was impeding our progress, but my hopes that we were closer to finishing than we were kept us barreling through, and not airing some of the frustration building among us all. The only hope of reducing the anxiety among us all seemed to be to split up the projects and relegate some of them to the rooms where the young thespians were hard at rehearsing.

I stayed in the classroom with two large groups of students as we worked to hustle through some of the smaller "completable" tasks—a turtle, a mushroom, a stump. We had a random assortment of butcher paper from the "bodega" and were organizing that collection of students into yet smaller groups when one of the girls I'd known since second grade, a quiet and extremely gentle girl named Olivia, was put in charge of sorting out the paints for her station.

I often relied on Olivia for the orderly aspects of teaching—she was extremely gifted in organizational patterns and her skills complemented mine but also highlighted for me the complexity of identity. I related to Olivia in her sensitivity and fondness for work, but I differed from her in terms of approaches to tasks and people. Olivia fascinated me, and the affinity we shared for academics was a bond that didn't need expression, for us shy girls. Olivia often "volunteered" —sometimes without vocalizing it—to tidy up my desk, or organize the papers that had accumulated in the stacked trays. She was quick to get to the chalkboard by midday, and had a notepad she filled with remnants of instruction that I'd left up there following different lessons. My chaos both upset her sense of order and offered her a central role in the classroom that didn't require any activities she didn't enjoy. I worried where the line might be between opportunity and exploitation, but she among all the others was much more at peace with her leadership in this realm. While previous teachers at our former school often mistook her seriousness for frustration or indifference, I knew her quiet to hide only immense generosity and careful attention to thought.

Olivia was still reserved enough at the beginning of the year that I hadn't understood her complexity until a few weeks later when we started doing Writing Workshop. Teaching is a front seat at times to the best dramas in the world, and so it was watching hidden parts of Olivia's character revealed in her writing. I'd recalled advocating at times for Olivia in her primary classes—hoping that teachers wouldn't mistake her silence for lack of knowledge or ability. I was concerned in the early parts of the year that in my own instruction I might err similarly. I was aware of, yet somehow not adept enough to prevent, public moments when Olivia wasn't ready to respond to my question in large-group discussion. Olivia was a bellwether in our class, directing and reminding me to stay diversified in my methods—trying to hold her needs in tension with those of students for whom more speaking than writing opportunities facilitated better language acquisition.

Olivia also kept me clear about what I was assessing—both formally and informally—in all my instruction. If I was looking for content knowledge, then perhaps I needed to craft a way for her to present it that didn't require speaking in front of others; if I was looking for speaking skills, then perhaps I needed to craft safer ways for her to produce. Her unique brilliance and sensitive nature kept me focused on best practices of language instruction—clear articulation of purpose and detachment from elements of instruction that might impede it, and that a tendency to conflate mode of learning with content being assessed could crush a student's language development process without a teacher ever recognizing it. For Olivia the routine became easier for me over the year: if I was hoping to assess her learning as clearly and cleanly as possible then I needed to incorporate constant opportunities to write, write, write.

Our work to diversify our teaching strategies spread across our classrooms, too. Daniel had long been concerned about Olivia and what appeared to be lack of interest and effort in his math class. Olivia was respectful and attentive as she sat and listened in math, and seemed occasionally to enjoy working in pairs and small groups but didn't carry with her the spark he had seen in her in language arts. His intuition and concern were made concrete when he held assessments ranging from projects and presentations to individualized test performance. All his strategies that worked so magically with students who'd never known they enjoy math as a subject were unsuccessful with Olivia, and he despaired at her lost learning.

One day a few months into the school year, one of the prompts for Writing Workshop had been to tell the story of a prized keepsake, to describe it in detail and tell the story about how it came into possession. Olivia wrote diligently and at the end of the week when I perused the samples they'd selected for me and revised and edited, she had also attached the artifact. It was an award she'd received in Sylvia's fifth grade class for greatest improvement in math. Her perfectly descriptive and figurative writing told of the ways in which she'd been in charge of helping her mom with all the arithmetic that appeared in their daily lives and had brought that drive into the classroom. Several changes in life events including the completion of fifth grade as well as her mom's independence in computation shifted her sense of self and an affinity for the math identity she had embraced, and she confessed that she had no longer felt like trying.

She knew she was good, she said—but she just couldn't make that matter.

There were gender issues surfacing, too, I surmised, given some things we'd known about Olivia's extended family throughout the years. Olivia lived with her younger brothers and mom consistently, and with her dad and older brother when they weren't busy in local gang activity. Her father had also recently opened their home to her cousins—the oldest of whom would later be incarcerated for life. There was a lot of aggression in the house, and while Olivia and her mom—both remarkably gentle and introverted—had acclimated to their new living arrangements, I feared that this acceptance might lead to resignation.

At the first conference of the year, I tried to present Olivia's strengths to her mom in an effort to encourage her to provide time and attention to Olivia's need for help in homework, but felt both immediately ridiculous and gallingly ineffective all at once.

I recognized a certain detachment in Olivia from the situations she was facing and began to see a bit differently her resilience and coping mechanisms in my class. In our micro-society Olivia was still engaged in routines and invested in learning in the ways she could. She was never unkind to her peers and was intentional in her care to remain respectful in her interactions with others. While she had made perhaps subconscious decisions to detach when it came to certain subject areas or activities, she was still an active participant in our community, and I felt incredibly proud of her if not a little bit awed.

The missed communication in our shared experiences were all mine, I knew, and my efforts to communicate my appreciation for Olivia were often ineffective as well.

Most of my interactions with Olivia that year took place in writing. It felt easy and natural to have ongoing conversations in her journal and in other pieces of work she did both for Writing Workshop and other activities. With all the other students and issues in our classroom, I often didn't push beyond this arena, and decided almost by default, along with Olivia and her mom, to let her choose her moments for participation and withdrawal.

By the time of our second report-card pick-up night in early April, I felt a synergy with Olivia and her mom and felt that she was aware of her own talents and needs, and that I could spend our conference praising her for her incredible writing talents and expressing that I felt certain she would expand her comfort zone when ready.

It didn't occur to me that I enacted a complicity in her silencing and oppression until our chaotic art day in mid-April when we were spread too thin trying to live up to promises and deadlines, without much intellectual excitement for ourselves.

Up to my neck in paint and paper—and students in several spaces around the building—I used the PA to call down to the office to alert them to one of our students needing to get a new color from the bodega when there was a squeal of laughter behind me and then a large crash.

I turned around to see that in her efforts to run away from Marisol/Amelia's playful threats of chasing her with a wet paintbrush, Olivia had run right into the tray of paper cups filled with paint and caused it in its entirety to take flight from the table and make its way upside down to the floor.

The emptiness of the hectic activity led to an emptiness in my intentionality, and in that blankness of fear and frustration, I sent Olivia out of the room. I knew I did not understand the events that had happened, and wanted to get some straight answers despite there not being enough time to process them carefully. As the embodiment of a judgment I did not feel, my response was to keep the highly-verbal student inside with me and send Olivia out. Ease of interaction with Olivia had also caused my own carefulness to lessen, and my separation of them both, and of Olivia from me, was quick and without remorse.

I knew that some of my students were still bubbling with energy so I called them over while Amelia and I tried to pick up the mess. Delia was standing by glaring at me, taking constant stock of my lesser moments. In no mood to deal with this situation on yet another level, I barked at her to at least contribute somewhat to the solution rather than standing there like my critic and making things worse.

She quickly turned to walk away and snapped back that I might want to make sure I see what's up with Olivia before getting everyone else pissed at me.

Joanna knelt down to fill in for me, laughing while telling me I wouldn't find Olivia in the hallway. I tried desperately and in vain to think just when it was that Joanna left the classroom without my knowing—and decided to let it go for the moment while I went to reconnect with Olivia.

Joanna had been correct and Olivia wasn't, indeed, there.

I couldn't see her anywhere.

Like a mother in a department store unable to locate a toddler, a sharp and sudden fear grabbed me by the throat and squeezed short squeals from my throat and tears from my eyes. With our room tucked away in our far-west corner of the second floor, I'd always felt protected and safe in our seclusion, but I was overcome by the flash of Olivia across the years, and all too slowly realized all the different ways in which a twelve-year-old girl removed from a version of herself she loved could seek her escape.

She was not in either washroom. She was not in any of the classrooms on the second floor. She was not outside the back door.

I had no idea if she'd walked through the portal that separated us from our neighboring school, but knew I needed help and would find it in the office.

"My students are upstairs without anybody, Sarah."

Gesturing to one of the teacher aides, she responded both to my comment and my fear. "What happened?"

"Call next door and ask them if they've seen a sixth grader. It's Olivia."

Pushing the security guard in the direction of our next door neighbor, she calmly asked, "When did this happen?"

I'd only ever had criticism for the seemingly extra staff peopling our previous school's office rather than engaged at work in a classroom, but at the moment I wanted an army of them.

"And then call the cops."

"Let's call her house, then the police. Sit down."

I didn't want to be in the office. I heard La Directora's voice about my arrogance and inefficiency and lack of representation and didn't think I could absorb it all. I headed back upstairs. Like Olivia I felt a brief sense of glee at my ability to defy protocol and head out on my own. More like Olivia's last moments in my classroom, I was steeped in a public version of myself I didn't feel I could inhabit. I wanted nothing more than to find Olivia as quickly as possible—not to bring her back into this mess but so that I could join her in an escape from all our mistakes and failures, mine accurate and hers misassigned.

Daniel was standing outside his door, an eerie silence inside. My room on the other hand sounded as though there were four separate fights brewing, with Miguel firmly planted in the doorway.

I moved in the world differently than Olivia, but I loved routine and the peace I felt when I knew exactly what to anticipate across a day. Olivia's needs were an intense version of mine, and I suddenly realized that was why I so trusted her with my things and with my space—and more importantly with what many might see as my shortcomings. I had lost Olivia the minute our day lost purpose and strayed miles from our values and patterns, but she had been resilient in her work with others and unfortunately for her more quiet in her agitation than I.

It had so quickly unraveled, and I tried to piece together the events as they stood: I had lost a student. A student I loved got up and walked out of my room and out the door in the middle of a school day. This had occurred in a "stolen" art session, and was immediately caused by an accidental spill of paint. That would be the newspaper 5Ws/1H version, but my emotional interpretation of the episode now conveyed to me that the rest of the news story had some hard truths to tell. While I'd hoped to create a permanent refuge for Olivia that reflected a peaceful life she didn't yet have power to author in her home, I had also annulled her authorship of it in our classroom. I saw clearly for the first time that my read of Olivia was tinged with a righteousness about her world and a self-aggrandizing view of mine. What I'd hoped was shared governance in my classroom could now be distilled to a selfish need to be a hero in her story. I knew now that Olivia was taking care of herself and fulfilling needs of other students in the class, and that when I had sacrificed time and learning and then amplified my botched read of the day with aggression and isolation, I had imperiled her in such a way as to make the public statement of walking away from it all.

I felt hot with shame. It could be grief or lividity in any of the following seconds, but the heat filling my lungs and throat was the unwelcome physiology of shame.

I'd been stalled by my thinking, a public paralysis when others were looking to me for direction and activity. I looked to my right, only to see La Directora heading to me and embodying the certainty I was missing, so in the hurricane of emotions I took a seat right there on the top stair.

I'd seen misdirected coping mechanisms from middle school students for enough years to know the stream of consciousness now bouncing around my head as my own self-soothing.

It was probably moments just like this one that reminded her of her own positionality, and also maybe justified all that principal-preparation hurdle-jumping she'd had to complete before getting this position, because this seemed to be the kind of moment La Directora had been waiting for—she appeared clear and focused on trying to get me back into my classroom and put a tourniquet on this situation, one with a lot of potential to spiral way out of control.

She sat down with me—pumps, professional business suit and all. "I realize I've only known you a short while, but I'm guessing you've never had anything like *that* happen before." She extended a hand toward my shoulder and laughed.

I'd been so entirely caught up in my worst-case-scenario imagination, by my misplaced aggression, that a laugh seemed like a language I'd not heard before.

I managed a thick, "no" in response and rested my head on my knees.

She admitted that it was the first time she'd seen a student leave a building mid-day, and thanked me for giving her something to round out her training. She said she hoped for both of us that there was a quick and safe resolution, but that for now I had to try to go back to my other students.

I was certain my face looked as though I'd been seizing and asked her for a few more minutes.

"Maestra." I hadn't realized it previously but apparently she knew our use of the formal title for her. "Let's take a look at things from the students' perspective. Think of all you've been through. You sat there with them in that church and said farewell to their family. You've included them in the process of making sense of that grief as well as processing all the other issues that have come up."

I looked up because she was trying to talk about the suspensions. I couldn't be sure but perhaps she was communicating a few reflections on that process, too.

"You should be there with them in this. You don't get to walk away. It's your turn to sit in the chair."

I didn't know that she knew about the chair—the one we'd had at our disposal for students who needed some bolstering up. In class meetings, both planned and spontaneous, we'd organized the class into a circle around an individual student while the rest of the class told that child and each other what they liked most about that person. I'd been nervous about introducing the activity—it had felt a bit primary to me and I was sure my pre-adolescents would rebel against it. But it was clear that I'd failed to give them credit for their maturity and ability to recognize how important it was sometimes to be transparent about building each other—and our community—up as we went through our days.

I also hadn't really given La Directora, Susanna, any credit for noticing such details about my teaching or about the work we performed inside my classroom walls, and felt remorse for again needing to see things in a way that made me more the hero than I ever would be.

As for the chair, I knew I wouldn't be able to sustain what she was suggesting but felt buoyed enough to go back to work. I touched the hand she'd placed on my shoulder while Daniel shrugged confusedly and returned to his students.

The first to greet me was Joanna.

Joanna was the loose cannon in my world until my own usurping of that title today. My efforts to contain her by predicting what issues might arise and by laying out for her my transparent expectations had helped us draw a friendly truce, but I was troubled by the lack of connection between reining in her behavior and seeing evidence of her growing academically. While Joanna had forced me into refining my own management system—more than any other student she was my reminder of how quickly I could lose all control just as I had in the previous year—I was not reciprocating that teaching and clearly struggling to help her achieve the same learning I was seeing in other students.

Similarly, while staying on top of Joanna's every move had proved exhausting for both of us, in the end it had also prohibited independence in her growth—as an adolescent, and as a member of our mini-society.

After so much activity here was my chance, I was soon to find out.

The need to control proactively had lessened my ability to see Joanna's core humanity. As I entered the room, she was quick to my side with a generous arm flung across my shoulders and a sweet chortle about playing hooky.

In the years to come Joanna would remain in my classroom along with Olivia's cousin as sixth graders. No test would come close to assessing her real strengths, and even my intended-to-be-holistic efforts would often miss them. The humor and clarity I heard from her at this moment, however, despite all the chaos she threatened on a daily basis, proved again a wisdom beyond all the rest of us. She could avoid presentation of academic data, but proof positive of complex knowledges was always quick to surface.

"Some people just gotta give in."

Was she talking about me—giving in to the emotions? Giving in to facing the students? Giving in to my anger and frustration about starting this whole crazy mess? I thought for a moment she was hinting at my need to throw in the towel and find another life path.

I couldn't tell to what extent she was also talking about Olivia—giving in to a world that never read her correctly or seemed to meet her needs.

Many of the students wanted to know what had happened, as they'd been engaged in their own busy work at the moment of conflict. I called them all to the rug and we started from the beginning—not with the details but with a question for them to recall a moment when they'd become somebody they didn't want to be, responding to outside pressures that made them temporarily lose sight of a more important truth.

The students had a lot to share, and we huddled for the longest amount of time we had all year. Geneva and I inverted the feedback session and reflected how even after a short while a destabilizing event can subside into a funny story. In her wisdom she intoned that it was one without a conclusion, so far.

Sarah quickly learned that Olivia had in fact gone to her home. Our security guard had been dispatched then to make sure that she was safe both physically and emotionally, and ultimately the police had not been summoned. Years later I would think of the possible peril that my panic could have caused. In my desperation to secure safety for Olivia, I could have escalated the event and invited a different level of harm. Police in our neighborhood saw in my students obstinate hurdles to others' safety. The lens on Olivia's self-saving act would have been truancy and citations and a wholly exaggerated version of my error during the day. Triggered similarly by chaos, suffering, and disinvestment, my community bore the burden of violence structurally induced by poverty and racialized marginalization, that is then aggressed by institutions of law enforcement that have less of a clear sense of the people in their charge than I had had after the paint spill. The innocent are shunned and exiled, human events that at worst might be tiny infractions are escalated to fatal events, all to ease the agitation of the powerful in charge who know there is no justification for their authority other than privilege, access, and titles. I'd been out of control and far from my core work as a teacher, and Olivia had been violated by it enough to walk into physical danger—none of it her fault and all of it her burden.

Our security guard told me he'd tried to bring Olivia back with him, but her father was indignant and unbudging. After listening to his side of the story for half an hour, he returned to the school to provide me a report. I read it as code for warning me of the father's anger, and wanted to rail against a system that encircled me with care and protection and imperiled the innocent emotionally, educationally, and physically.

It was apparent to Olivia's father as well as to me that I had a lot of explaining to do, but also somewhat clear that our current situation was bigger than that afternoon's mistake. Olivia's dad was threatening not to return her to school, and had had his hunches verified about schools as enemies of his family. The guard winked and said I shouldn't worry, but yet again I saw the perversion of a rule system that attributes blame and innocence through intersectional positionality, and continued not to understand at all what had happened—responding to us through learned biases as well-meaning white lady, and troubled city kid from a gang family.

I recognized in myself that I felt hopeless enough to want to escape, angry at the misconceptions and frustrated by the willful ignorance of what is obvious and always witnessed. Years later a student exactly Olivia's age would be playing in a park with a toy—and be fatally shot by an officer who required no evidence to enforce what he'd misunderstood and heard vaguely misreported—and to weaponize pervasive anti-blackness in the fatal shooting of the child.

I had asked Sarah to call the police. Afraid for her, I had no capacity to step outside my own normalized read of society and its institutions and had nearly invoked hyperpolicing.

Olivia lived a door down from one of the more-feared corners in the neighborhood, where reports of gang activity made their way not only through the grapevine to teachers at school, but sometimes also to the local television news. Activity had heated up there in fact over the past couple of years, and uninformed discourse attributed blame to her family and the relatives who had joined them from the southwest.

The corner was also directly across the vast expanse of boulevard from our school and was fairly visible from passing cars and pedestrians. The teachers in our school who had grown up in the neighborhood narrated stories highlighting the legendary nature of the location for decades, most of them expanding their commentary to causality and the connections between low rents and dilapidated buildings that remained attractive to people who earned their income in "anti-community" ways.

Though many episodes had occurred within feet of Olivia's house, I didn't feel personal danger when passing near it, though communications at all levels of discourse worked to reinforce constantly the untruths that ensured peril for my students attributable purely to their intersectional race and class positions and refused to ascribe me blame even in front of many. Beyond acts of the day, I also recognized the factors that worked to protect me perpetually in such volatile and destabilized pockets of the community—and my role as a teacher in a nation where nearly 90% of teachers are white women, and white women are perceived to be innocent and in need of constant protection, had a lot to do with that.

I thought about redemption and reparations on my walk to Olivia, and wondered if today would herald a moment in history where a white female teacher got her due.

I scanned the house—a painted-over storefront with a circle of chairs visible from a small window in front of a kitchen area—and knocked on the open door. I couldn't make too much sense of where the house continued from there or how people in their family unit were arranged for daily activities as I was called in. Olivia's mom had not yet returned from work, but her dad was steady in his urge to protect his daughter—jaw firmly set and hands planted firmly on his knees. He didn't motion for me to sit, and I stood by the still-open door.

He expressed mostly shock at how a school in the US could allow a twelve-year-old girl to walk out of its door, and I agreed that it seemed to me to be one of the more horrifying things one might consider as a parent. He wanted to know what kind of aggressions I'd taken on his daughter so that she would feel the need to escape, and I explained as best I could in my trembling Spanish about being overwhelmed with all the activity of my class and then suddenly snapping and taking it out on Olivia. I told him how my long connection to Olivia had always been a bright spot during my day and how I'd blindly assumed—incorrectly and unfairly—that she would always understand my motive, even under great duress. I tried to share in his version of the moment with him and commented that I was sure he had too felt at certain moments that he knew his daughter only to find out that she was growing and changing into someone else all the time.

I tried to tell him that I knew that Olivia had given me a great learning opportunity—and that I should never assume that the hard work to reach a student was complete and then bankable, but that instead one had to constantly re-establish connections with students and see them as changing people who needed to be interpreted anew and given space to tell who they are along the way. Olivia sat and watched me from behind her father, waiting to see what more vulnerability I would reveal and how I would endure the intensity of her family.

Her father remained incensed that there could be someone he'd trusted with his daughter who could make such an error as to cause her to imperil herself on the streets of Chicago in the daytime. He argued that for all the issues he'd had to face in this world, never once would he have guessed he'd be dealing with this. Olivia looked down at the floor and we both shared a long pause in which we let her dad's comment sink in. This was true, apparently, and the unspoken accusation in the air that I'd been more aggressive than local gang leaders—perhaps precariously with one of their own —lay heavy between us. If I were going to try to get back in the family's good stead, then it was going to have to happen right now. I expressed that I agreed that it was a serious error, but that I felt that my previous connections to Olivia and shared experiences of her life had made my ignorant act all the worse. I tried to reassure him that I now understood her complex character all the more deeply and would appreciate her needs much better from here on out so as not lose my head again with her. I tried to plead my case that this was in fact the main reason for my visit —to make sure that Olivia had seen my efforts to come to her on her terms. To try to make things right enough for her to return to my class tomorrow.

He snuffed out a reply, but by this point I was watching Olivia for signs of recognition. She made no comment as I returned my focus to her father.

"I understand the anger I must be responsible in bringing out and for that I'm sorry. But there are many other teachers at the school who would probably agree to take Olivia into their rooms if I'm the issue. I don't want to come between Olivia and her learning."

"You are the issue, that's true."

"So I don't think Olivia should be further punished by being kept from school for something that is my mistake."

There was a brief smile in Olivia's eyes, and a severe nod from her dad.

"I'm going to go—I want Olivia to have plenty of time before she decides with you what she wants to do tomorrow when she comes back."

I was in full control in the face of fear mode, and the Joanna revelation came calling back to me.

"Also, please know that I hope this is the last time anything this terrible happens to anyone in your family at school or elsewhere. It's the only hope that helps abate the lasting shame I'll feel with all of you."

Nothing left to say, I slipped back out the door, and back into Olivia's good graces, I hoped.

Eventually the horror of the day faded into a funny memory as the weeks progressed. A couple of other teachers made Olivia well aware that they'd be happy to talk to her and mediate anything she wanted to say, if it came to that. I stood quietly in the background and offered her writing prompt after writing prompt until the day she dared to discuss things in her journal.

> Dear Ms. T,
> How are you? I'm fine. I'm happy the year is almost over. Are you? I always feel happy to be done with school for a couple of days but then miss it. This time I won't miss a lot of things but I think I will miss you. I know you are sad about what happened with the paint, but I am not. I was mad that day and didn't want to get yelled at for something that was an accident. I was happy to have a friend to laugh with and didn't mean to spill everything. But no matter what, every time I'm happy something bad happens. I was just starting to believe that maybe I was wrong about life. Now I'm not so sure. Are you happy? Are you afraid ever of losing that happiness? Sometimes I want to be a little student again and you could teach me English and I could learn a lot more and not be so afraid.
>
> I am sorry if you think it's your fault. I wanted to stay in your class because it is good for me. I wanted to tell you that I wonder if you think I could be a writer some day.
> Write back.
> Love,
> Olivia

How could it be that Olivia could see me as the cause of her loss of innocence and yet still care what I thought about her writing, or care whether or not I had ever felt like she did? I didn't even know how I would survive or who I'd be in a situation like hers, and tried to think only about the questions of how we reveal ourselves in writing—and what the implications might be for someone as opaque as Olivia worked so hard to be—but also about the ways in which we access an aquifer of commonalities through narrative. I hoped even in that moment that perhaps I'd spurred her to sear me publicly in nationally-read essays written across her career as an elite writer.

11

MAY

Structure and (In)/Verse

There were days when even in a language and literature class, speaking and listening seemed like Herculean activities. Days raged around us in the long transitional month, and I was compelled simply to distill ourselves into a core purpose, removing the extra words that weren't ours, and center ourselves on the page like stanzas.

After a winter of Monday-less weeks and Spring Break and testing, May landed like a year unto itself amid a heat wave's worth of discomfort and claustrophobia. It felt clear that the delegation of May as one of the longest months was not decided with schoolchildren in mind. In Chicago it has always been chronically the month of high-school nerves and placement anxieties.

In a month of students and teachers partnering inside these structural antagonisms, the purest of May efforts is to remove excess.

Despite everything one has planned for, the relentless decisions in May belong to someone else.

While I and a generation of my peers had made the difficult transition to high school accompanied by the safety net of not having to choose one for ourselves and then hope they choose us back, Chicago schoolchildren have historically had to make this critical "decision" exceptionally early—using their seventh-grade test scores and grades through the first quarter of eighth grade.

The pressure was enormous in those first years that our school had an eighth grade class. For the most part students from our neighboring schools had no choice as to where they were automatically placed. Our local high school— famous within the public school system for its remarkably low completion rate— was the "default" option for our children: students went there if they didn't have scores, means to relocate, or access tickets to enroll elsewhere. Students around the city historically lacked advocates as all counseling resources had been depleted to nil, and with no one to speak to the dimensions of a student's knowledges beyond the least reliable or valid assessment I'd ever seen, destiny was determined by forces unseen as well as inaccessible.

As we grew with our students into the upper grades, the precariousness of this situation grew for us as well. While our curriculum evolved in the opposite direction of the standards mania of our public school system, we had very few secondary options that seemed curricularly and culturally fit for our students. The unique qualities of our school that had long been a source of pride and energy now felt hurtful in our most vulnerable of places—the imagined futures of our graduating students. New to the high stakes of this process, it would be a couple of years before I was responsible for helping students cross this dangerous canyon and land in a place that best suited their academic/artistic, multicultural/multilingual, and personal/interpersonal needs.

This sixth-grade group and I would be guinea pigs together in a couple of Mays, and the competing emotions would threaten my trajectory beyond the professional. Eventually, it would be this issue that would cause me to look at other avenues of advocacy. The heartbreak was too severe, and the ramifications of my advocacy and incompetences too difficult to sustain.

Poetry had never been introduced in any of my teacher-preparation classes as a way to examine the roots of urban education phenomena, yet that May it was the only catharsis available to me. I was in search of a metaphor to help me transpose our reality and left with the act of trying out various versions of the truth.

Words had never felt so empty, so I shaved all but the essentials off—wishing for a poet's agency with the words defining the students, me, even what purpose we embodied. The internal words were hot and angry, but the grief they appeared as too large to hide. I named everything I could muster and then pared it all down. Private in nature and often writing just for myself, that year the desperation to be read authentically pushed them into the public sphere, with a prayer that somehow that would be all there was.

HARD WORK
"Ay, Maestra, yo corto a m'hijo en ocho pedazos."

She laughs, and I smile
knowing how easy it had been to forget
the warm breath of spring
gently heating the cement wall we leaned upon
for so many seasons.

In the gust of the back door closing
I feel the light of eight pieces
falling from my hands.

The sun bakes my bones free of the October chill
camped there
since the moment Mexico was the only answer

and a child's hopes
were the leaves falling around us –
Leaving only the bare trees
of our advice
protection for no one:

"Hard work will always pay off."
Around the trunk they'd gathered,
armed only with numbers
against the wintry gusts of disappointment
from the cold front of bureaucracy.

"It's not enough...."
"We're sorry...."
"We'd love to help but...."

The fears like seeds falling on icy ground
had rattled inside me
swirling into a tornado of failure

It's not enough?
I'm sorry.
I want to help.
I can't.

I can't.

———

But now April had slid in quietly
and its soft breeze wraps us in an embrace of relief
as we gently lose the heavy coats of guilt.

She sighs as she sees her son
open the back door to us in pair.
I would smile too if I could
but I'm not ready.
Spring's good news
brings summer
but also the hint of the next fall
and winter
on its other side.

Those seasons are promises for this private woman
who gives her words less to me
than to the wind:

"They want my son."

I watch them float past me
into a gentle urging
to this lone tree
to present itself
as another promise fulfilled
for another hope nurtured.

They want him –
Seven high schools.

Even from the maternal branches
some inner teacher to check the math:

"Señora, porque ocho pedazos?"

She laughs –
at me
with me
for our predictability, like seasons.

"Si maestra.
Siete más uno –
The heart stays with you."

—
He's ready to go.

"My heart is mine,"
his caveat in a good-bye embrace.

There's no math for this next season
Or formulas. Or proofs
to learn.

It's time to go.

We switch roles at the door.
I lean against its heavy hinges,
its tendency to stay closed,
and keep it open
one moment longer.
Night descends on a cool breeze
brought in from somewhere

we've not yet been.
with her final words to warm me,
protect me,
I let the door latch.

"So much
hard work:
ours has been good."

★

"The dangers of caring too much" was a constant theme among the veteran teachers at our old school. It wasn't until that May that I began to sympathize with
them and see within myself the potential to distance myself and my reality from
what my students had to endure and navigate. Prior to having to shepherd these
students into suitable high schools, I also had to relinquish them to other teachers.

While every year my own teaching had seemed clearer to me and I'd seemed to
reach my hopes of higher quality time with students, by the end of each May I
stumbled away from images of teaching without the context of the students currently sharing my space. It was a paradox of anticipation—the relief of a long-awai-
ted summer and the dread of starting all over again with students I didn't know. May
was a clash of emotions lit by the spark of fatigue, and as the opportunity to step
outside ourselves neared, the images of our current selves loomed large.

To keep us focused, we immersed ourselves in poetry, taking on the challenge
of reclaiming language.

ORDERING
Catalogs opened and sprawled
over empty desks
in the echoes of another final day.

The familiarity of the urgency
in the ritual
cannot be skimmed
or fought.

A teacher buys pencils
dreams of writers
anticipated books
unlived years.

Faces fill the images
my young
are missing

from visions
as my mind edits them
their presence
my activities
as my life.

Loneliness keeps
pages blank
eyes empty
contact numbers for questions
unable to be answered.

Who could dream of books now?
In contrast to the
will be
I want to buy
what was.

With no help from the index
a hope
too unaffordable
not to buy.

That they be long-cherished
again
in hands held dear
through dreams
around plans
of new to come.

★

Having granted ourselves the freedom to re-envision the schooling program, we also were solely responsible for addressing the needs of each and every student. And looping proved to be the issue that brought most of this discomfort to the forefront. While certainly there were students with whom I had developed a productive rapport and close advocacy, there were also students who were stifled by my instruction and resistant to my teaching. Looping myself with the class as a whole would perhaps create as many problems as it solved—and if we believed in the human diversity of teaching as its core power, we should investigate all options to make the best use of our autonomy and freedom.

Freedom was a complicated concept for us—while the previous year had been overwhelming, with no skeleton to keep us in place as we navigated too many opportunities to become anew, this year we'd received an authoritarian principal who saw her role as instructional leader as the antagonist to teachers in protection of students who were not experiencing the concretization of her pedagogy and whose teachers must be forced to work better. Post-conflict, like the worlds of our humanities curriculum, her departure was now imminent—present enough to whisper new plans, but distant enough to dream them. We had to see ourselves first, however, and investigate for ourselves the fault lines in our work that required something new.

The intentionality of school relationships forged partnerships where none might have materialized in other worlds, and across the school we watched our adult world fuse with that of students, not just by their inclusion and the equality we espoused—but also in the form of compatibility issues and struggles to define productive responses to them. Because we had actively constructed cluster models that depended upon teachers collaborating and working closely in all aspects of their teaching, when incompatibilities surfaced, all school citizens suffered.

I was immensely fortunate in my pairing with my team teacher, Daniel. At the start of the previous year, when my anxieties were at an all-time high and my sense of being unprepared unparalleled in my life, I had formulated a quick opinion of him in response to the terrible fate that prevented him from attending our first day of school—which of course was our first day working together, and his first day meeting the students. Friends in later professions would speak to the barbs of othering that surfaces in panic and high-stress conditions. I could see in myself an instability that fostered judgment and reflected it back to me in intersectionally racialized ways—I feared the labor of both groups' first days but even more a year of not being enough. Humor and grace would reveal themselves to salvage more than just that first week, though the interpersonal stakes would never be that high again. More persistent stressors, such as my rabid and rampant blind spots and a complementary casualness from him, forged a true partnership that was visible to students and families, and tended to by all.

Sometimes our collaborations were simple reinforcements—the two-parent model where students could take a message a bit differently because two separate adults were giving it. This worked well for the majority of students—the simple transparency of our shared philosophical and pedagogical perspectives contributing to an overall calm and safe environment in which to experiment.

But our collaboration was also ours to exploit—in pranks and in dangerous theorizing around our categories.

Our first April Fools' Day in the new school and as team teachers, one of the students who carried more stigmas and ascribed negative traits than others, Jaime, decided to join me in a prank on Daniel, an original prankster whose art was interpersonal relationships and who could play them in ways I naively couldn't see. Jaime came in early before school started—ostensibly to complete some work he'd not done the day before—and we acted out our routine that we'd practiced gleefully almost as an outlet for frustrations at his struggles with meeting his own goals, and I meeting mine. We mocked up the crescendo of an argument—hinting at escalation not just in the moment but over the course of the year. At the height of the prank we had acted ourselves down the hallway to the space just outside Daniel's room. Jaime loudly moved ahead and pulled Daniel out to declare he was done with the school. The urgency new to Daniel, he paused his all-too-knowing students and moved into the hallway to place himself emotionally, physically, and metaphorically in the middle of us. As he flipped his head back and forth in search of way through to us, appealing to our better senses, we both raised our arms and at the last minute turned them into a high five. We laughed, hugged, and moved swiftly back to class to leave a shaken Daniel to face a class all too eager to keep this secret from him, who now got to help him transition back into his true teacher identity.

Daniel was furious for a day, but I defended my case with the reminder of the similar kind of unfortunate prank he'd pulled on me in the zócalo of Mexico City. Walking back one night from a performance, a group of us was just ahead of him on the sidewalk when Daniel decided to pretend to accost me and grab my purse. Without recognizing it had been him and a joke, I reacted physically and hit him with it, about to yell for help. He had pleaded his case on site to help me transition out of panic and see clearly again, recognizing that those instincts had shocked us both. He had been remorseful, and the event produced many insightful conversations about context and fear, and what we are capable of without knowing. In the moment, however, I'd smiled knowingly but questioned his humanity. He now did the same.

The thing that struck me as I thought back on our exploitations of our differences was how easily we were able to put our social positions on the table and both work with them and joke about them, highlighting nuances of the process in our teaching and social lives.

★

Our close collaborations in the school would also yield unfortunate casualties. In all the efforts to design and build a school from scratch into something both rebellious and common-sensical, different characteristics in individual personalities became imperative. An intense ability to be visionary and push toward lofty goals with drive and unrelenting force was a great asset in our collaborations, but not the only one. A small but tight-knit community might suffer more of those, however, than usual, and the petri dish yielded conflicts worsened for perceived affinities elsewhere.

Recognizable in its purity for early adolescents, at this juncture it was our middle school cluster that suffered.

Ian was newer to teaching than the rest of us on the team, and also one of the most creative and efficient teachers I'd ever seen—his ability to organize and innovate his curriculum surprisingly compatible. His keen focus on maximizing minutes with multiple opportunities for engaged learning was a talent I dreamed of harvesting. His intense dedication to his students was undeniable.

In his first year in the old school, his stalwart nature and strength of commitment helped him bring gifted teaching to 34 of his first graders, while the 35th experienced the 4-month long process of being diagnosed with a condition that put himself and his classmates at risk. Like most people who believe intensely and without reservation in their work and philosophy, he created ways to be the protector of everyone, and brought a family in crisis into a stability of mental and physical health when that had seemed unattainable. He was an inspiration to us for his singular focus, but suffered in the transition into a democratically-led administrative model and a teaching life founded on collaborations with others.

Because the reduction in class size was a primary commitment in our new entity, we had to forge teaching clusters of four teachers for three grade levels. These were spaces for cooperative teaching and shared instructional opportunities, but also spaces where individuality of choices worked against students who needed the adults outside their classroom walls to complement the work inside—and for each teacher to be open and willing to play both leader and follower roles.

When we processed the reality of our middle-school cluster, we could see that we agreed philosophically and pedagogically on many things—truths that might in other circumstances maintain the collaborative. What we both philosophically and pedagogically believed, however, was that the human component of teaching that surfaced in personality and capacity for shared experiences was an essential part of the work. This essential part of our profession, however, was destroying a small collaborative of committed and creative teachers. Because we were critically examining social structures in our school model and in our curricula, we also understood that this essential part of our profession did not always have space for intersectional positionality when the relationship informed by those identity traits could not survive the differences. The teachers in our cluster were each different in intersectional identities of race and gender, but the racial location struggling the most with the other locations was the identity found at the crossroads of whiteness and masculinity.

In terms of the collective fight against both patriarchy and white supremacy, we were eager to take stances and leverage fight behind them, but this sureness was compromised when we faced the sense that the fight against these might be also internal—to our cluster, with our students, and within ourselves.

Almost in direct response to the dispassionate and jaded feelings about teaching at our former school, we enacted our beliefs quickly and easily in the architecture of our new school, each person's intensity intended to separate us from the apathy we perceived in a district setting up its citizens for failure. Yet the study of political movements hadn't helped us prevent the inevitable, however, and it didn't take long for the intensity to backfire on us. We were starting to turn the same anger and frustrations that fueled our resistance efforts on each other—and to essentialize each other in our conversations and disagreements.

Our cluster, the four of us, stood out as a peculiar example of the difficulties involved in trying to teach for social justice across different demographics. We were a Latina native to the community, a white woman crossing and adopting into the community, a Latino native to neighboring communities, and a white man who'd been raised in community crossings. Two of us had grown up in divorced homes, with very different SES statuses. Our Latina had been born in the neighborhood and raised as an only child by both parents, while our Latino had immigrated in his pre-adolescent years with five siblings and happily-married parents.

Every collision of viewpoints stood like a study of race, class, and gender in teaching—the petri dish of intersectionality in grassroots activity. Not surprisingly the strongest and most persistent collision surfaced in discussions of acceptability of behavior in different concentric circles of community.

It was clear not just to us that we couldn't agree on a discipline code for our classrooms, and so we had to parse out to what extent race and gender and class informed our opinions and whether or not we could stand outside the things we felt we normalized and expand our perspectives to include the others'.

Eventually the long process of deliberation and positionality navigating developed into a long downward spiral, farther from reconciling our situation. Our team of teachers was on the verge of irreparable damage as we pursued mediation and some resolution to the debates that raged within us.

We thought carefully about the parameters we should establish for our efforts so as not to compromise the larger project of the school and community. We sought out mediators and mentors who understood the philosophy and pedagogy from which we framed our work, so that our core vision would not be challenged in the process of rebuilding our professional community, and so that any repair would be authentic and powerfully connected to our process of growing together. None of those efforts panned out, and our school had to consider implications we didn't feel ready to consider. Stubbornly, we tried to sustain the effort, and ultimately we were informed that we needed to find ways of planning escape hatches so as not to build a foundation of learning upon raced and gendered hurt.

Our larger community feared that we'd end up ruining that which we worked so hard to create.

We had to face our own immaturities as people and as an institution, and learn that there are times when the act filled with the most courage and the most strength is letting go.

I knew that May that I was enmeshed in this struggle but from an antithetical emotional space. My identity in the work was intertwined with their roles in it, and didn't know how to salvage the structure we had built and let go of the reasons I had contributed to that effort. As I watched the layers of intention and purpose erode my small professional collective, I learned to see the threats it might pose to the work I wanted to survive longitudinally. Though I had spent years priding myself on my connections to my students and my authentic interest in their education, I was starting to get in my own way.

*

In response to the destructive indifference of our host school, many of us took our jobs as students' advocates extremely seriously, but in the end our intensity threatened to keep our students from advocating for themselves. We ran the risk of projecting our measures of success onto their constructions of themselves and their futures, and had veered too closely to the space within us all that longs for interdependence and companionship. With our students facing the discomfort and power of the rite of passage that would come with graduation, we were acting in ways those accompanying loved ones through difficult transitions understand—our instinct to prevent pain was in danger of being its cause.

Noelle had blossomed into a strong community leader and an incredible academic talent by the time she began preparing for high school. We knew as teachers and parents that her talents had been under-represented as she had been such a recent arrival and therefore not assessed in the standard manners necessary to apply to magnet and/or special schools. She had no scores to use in her applications to the competitive high schools, and so was rejected across the board. Even arts programs were unable to process her applications, and for no other cause than having immigrated in adolescence; her options were starting to look slim.

Noelle was unremorseful as she committed to enrolling at the local high school. We teachers lined up to talk to her in an effort to establish some alternative that we hadn't yet imagined. Devastated as a group of professionals who felt we knew the situation into which she was walking much better than she, we nearly severed for good our connection with one of our kindest and most brilliant students.

Because we cared so much we couldn't hear her steadfast perspective that she was angry that we didn't think she was capable of becoming her best in any situation. "It's not the school, Ms. T.; it's the student."

I knew this deeply to be both true and completely false. I believed that schools could be wonderful places where intellectual exploration facilitated the development of complex identities while adolescents developed meta-awareness and collectivity on their developmental trajectories toward adulthood. I believe equally as strongly that the myth of personal responsibility was often used to underfund schools and communities and then blame those students and families whose life circumstances prevented their exit from these structural inequities.

In the short time she'd been with us at the school, Noelle was the one student who'd been eager to share analytical reflections about cultural values that surface in schools and also remain hidden. I knew despite my fears that she was telling us something much deeper than my framing—that her sense of self was stronger than the school and that her commitment to the person her family had helped nurture into being would prevail even in the direst of circumstances.

Our relentlessness had yielded us an incredible school, and so our behaviorist selves fell into Pavlovian traps. We presented case studies of students who'd made the same transition from our middle school cluster to that high school, and who had both been thwarted within the school and had grown dispassionate enough about learning to make the self-preserving choices to escape its negative forces.

Still, she insisted. What we wanted for her she would make from whatever circumstances she found.

We trusted her, believed in her, but didn't yet know that Noelle indeed would have a tremendously successful high school career, and would go on to higher levels of schooling than any one of our alumni. We grappled with the dearth of options available to her as symbolic representation of the ways in which our efforts to teach toward a certain aspiration of equity and justice were curtailed by the system within which we worked. We could not break free of the constraints of the bureaucracy, despite our unique successes in carving out a space that buffered our students from them. No matter what we were able to construct within our classrooms—and then in collective efforts across classrooms—we still had limited options for shepherding the students into the next and critical stage of their academic careers.

For many of us, the political elements of our work—facilitating students' self empowerment —were the aspects we liked most about our jobs. As I watched year after year as students left us for programs where they were criminally mis-assessed and often derailed from their dreams, I felt the longitudinal equivalent of May erode my hopes and energy to push for changes even in my own work.

I hadn't anticipated this outcome, and I certainly hadn't thought it would precede hopelessness about my role in the system.

If I was simply going to be another teacher to shepherd students through to the local high school, then I didn't know how well I could reconcile my participation and role.

Colleagues and friends warned me of the dangers of getting too personally attached—of mirroring the defeat I felt back toward the children. I was dismayed many times over by this possibility and tried to retreat back into the spaces in between the two forces I felt pulling at me.

In my writing program with the students, we took time on Fridays to work-shop different pieces by the students. Our protocol consisted of allowing the student to hand out and read his/her piece to the class and then ask for specific guidance and feedback. Students then had to absorb silently the comments from their peers and take notes for further revisions of their work.

At my lowest after the completion of the high-school selection process, I myself had written a poem about authority and community, as well as about moving into the moment in our grammar curriculum where we could begin to use creative license and break certain grammatical rules. On a day toward the end of the unit, toward the end of the month, this was the piece I chose to workshop with the students themselves, current participants in reflections inside the stanzas, students of the rules I was trying to dash, and future high school applicants bearing the hopes of their families, their school, and themselves.

lower-case i

In the classroom
All rules
Rule

Capitals and capital
Follow traditions
To keep all parties
Calm
And reasonable

learning is home where
there is no hierarchy
of capitals above the rest
and rules of creativity
disintegrate
and set free
to be
small as a wish

In the classroom
First must be
Large
Larger
Than the meaning of what follows
With all the answers
For questions
Not being asked

at home in my classroom
learning could be lower-case
with students for students
level in space and place
a normal
piece of a sentence
for the same questions
and breaking of rules
no difference between letters
same lines
with the same value
of both strength and whimsy
hold and release
of a dot in midair
above a strong bar
and space to either side

Not this stoic staff
Bound by lines

> Fixed ground and sky
> Parallel and never meeting
> Apart.

I asked the students for two things of all the things I needed—their analytical interpretations of the meaning next to the poem on the front of the page, and their personal responses to it including feelings about "voice" and "message" on the back—and was rewarded with an unsuspected outpouring of candid feedback on my teaching. Some of them saw themselves in it—how often I'd reminded them of conventions of writing in English. Several saw my habits—how I asked for "calm" in the classroom to let people have room for creativity; how I didn't like enforcing rules during Writing Workshop; how my writing on the blackboard always sloped and was never even; how I tried to pretend I cared about any of that stuff.

Interspersed were other students who read back to me that they didn't understand, because I seemed to like asking questions and liked being a teacher, and that they themselves loved finding out answers. They wrote back that they were confused by the parallel between lower case and equity—they said it helped people read to have upper-case letters, that they were tools that helped people reach deeper meanings without confusion. It helped make sense of ideas and expressions. Capitals held some power that was good.

I found yet other students who read that the poem connected to the way teaching made me do things that were contradictory to my beliefs. They wrote that they could tell I wanted not to have to play by the rules at times but that I had to, even if the rules weren't mine. They expressed concern that I was being dramatic. They didn't really agree that these aspects of teaching would lead me not to like the classroom. One insightful student thought that the parallel lines of the capital letter version of me were the two aspects of who I was—white but in a Mexican school—and that I didn't know how to be both.

★

Noelle found her way through to the top of her class at her high school via the military preparation program. In meetings with her over the years, she tried to communicate to me how clear a choice that was for her—how she could grasp the broader political issues around the military's role in a high school while still making that system serve her needs. She had found a group of students who were good friends to her and hard-working, and who appreciated her commitment to excelling. She reminded me frequently that she had a supportive network to back her up and help her assert her self-definition across the school. In her own efforts to stand between the two parallel parameters of her own world, she was living out a truce that I would look to for inspiration and role model repeatedly in the decade to come. She stood gracefully between what was and what might be and grew into her own tall "I".

12

JUNE

Spartans

Minutes seemed visible, like humidity particles in the air of our classroom as June arrived both more quickly and more slowly that year. While I knew intuitively and from pervasive teacher discourse, time travels differently for students, and with the archetypal adolescent developments taking place, the world outside us was paralleling these personal shifts, and it was time to merge inside and outside nature and get out of the classroom.

On the last day of allowed field trips, we said goodbye to the backdrop that had framed us and hit the road for some outside relief. It would never cease to amaze me that there were funds for air conditioners in every administrative office within this large urban bureaucracy, but none for the students who funded the whole system. Our room was hot and baking under the sun hitting us from all angles—reflecting off the pavement that permeated, defined, and surrounded us in our industrial neighborhood. It was summer, however, and we were looking for real-life learning experiences and also trying to ease our real-world woes.

I recognized that how students learn was the hot topic *du jour*, but I'd have gambled my bus pass that not one educational theorist would ever see these conditions as optimal.

One of our out-of-school curricular experiences took us to the Children's Museum downtown. We got the somewhat apathetic guided tour along with busloads of other students—pointing out the unmemorable alongside the experiential. For all the wonders of the museums around the city, my students routinely remembered mostly artifacts and creations they'd been able to get their hands on. In the elements of childhood that are universal, securing experiential hands-on learning opportunities can be more competitive than securing district resources. As we sojourned through one of Chicago's most-visited tourist attraction, we made a silent communal decision to concede time and space and hands-on activities in the museum and bank our leftover time to explore the Pier before heading back to school. Uncertain about the options available to us at the Pier, I'd been optimistic and brought the students' sketch pads and pencils. After a quick walk along the waterfront outside the commercial kiosks, we climbed the stairs to the conservatory on the top floor and stood inside the crisp and clean oxygen its green plants emanated and that could not be found in our community. The blue sky sparkled through the glass above us, and the for a moment I felt a burst of joy in our elevation above the fray, and a flash of sadness knowing that in the same cycles of nature and civilizations we'd been studying, the nurturing of the young people with me in that sparkly air was about to mean letting them go.

Not trusting myself to words, I pointed out the benches dispersed beneath the plants and trees, and tapped my imaginary watch to signal the start of their thirty minutes the sketches required for their observational portfolios. We'd studied different plants and their roles in the ecologies and social structures as we studied the early civilizations curriculum of sixth grade, and integrated arts in the practice of sketching to enhance our observation of details. The students were excited about having some independent time and about compiling their portfolios after this last activity in the year-long project. I shared their lack of familiarity with mainstream Chicago destinations, and took this opportunity to improve my own capacity for detailed observation and watched them in their practice. I saw students using shading techniques and experimenting with their own styles as they'd developed over the years with our visual artist—habits I'd learned to appreciate as reflective of their artist repertoires—and took stock of the intensity of both their focus and contentment, while noting also the way they continuously shifted trying to make space for their peers on the benches that couldn't quite accommodate us all in number.

We were looking at the last twenty minutes of our session when a group of forty or so students flooded the conservatory—perhaps with similar ideas to ours. Two teachers followed the predominantly white group of students and I considered approaching them to see if they would like us to tighten up our ranks and concede some of the seats on the benches for them. Heading in that direction, I was derailed by the squeal from a nearby pair of girls and the fight that was ensuing between several other students swinging their bright yellow schoolbags at each other. I couldn't make out the school district for the logo that reminded me of my own middle school Spartans—the first time I'd thought about the school logo since my last day on its campus, I guessed. But this was not the first time I'd considered how different my adolescent world was from my students'.

It was around the age of these different souls up here in the Glass Public Penthouse that I recalled starting to recognize ways in which society assessed people in terms of socially-constructed factors connected to money and social status. In the excavation of my own geologic educational layers, those sixth-through eighth-grade years would expose the seismic rupturing of coming to terms with social class. There was a cruel irony in the fact that it was in middle school that I started to see myself in our hierarchical society organized by income and wealth and the intersectional demographics that sustain it. While I embarked on expanding my internal sense of self, I could keenly recall considering how these external markers seemed to matter more—to ourselves, to each other, and to the adults we were being socialized to replace, but I was slow to understand their fundamental purpose in the school system that shepherded us into adulthood. I could see later on the sorting set up by the consolidating of our district middle and high schools, and how we were all thrown into the same pool and sorted by how well we could swim to the top, our school a cog in the wheel of US individualism.

While the segregated school system of my students had separated these two groups now meeting today from each other, I was also glad for my students that they were safe from that kind of nefarious sorting—at least in their daily experiences. Underneath it all, Chicago Public Schools was a system wide version of what I'd experienced, students experiencing the tracking of income and privilege from school to school more than from program to program. While this rampant segregation was a particularly evil monster to fight, connected all the way back to the Brown v. Board of Education decision, in that moment I recognized the freedom our separation had given us to craft a curriculum that spoke specifically to the culture and background of our community—and how special that was given the current direction of education policy.

★

Debates had raged around that time in the world of education about self-segregating by race and gender, and our school community was not spared the concerns within our faculty, either. One of our teachers—Latina but not Mexican—struggled openly and painfully with the lack of diversity in our population and in our curriculum. She wondered what kind of service we were providing to a generation of students who would indeed need to acculturate in order to find success in their next stage of schooling.

This was never an easy conversation for us to have—nor was it linear or contained in one frame. As we worked to push our students and their families in their acquisition of linguistic capital, we were painfully aware of the new efforts around the city to create elite dual-language programs where students benefited from having to learn the new common language among them in order to function academically and socially, but premised access to linguistic capital for wealthy monolingual students through the busing and possible exploitation of students from bilingual communities. Our school model pre-dated this version of politicized bilingual programming and didn't benefit from district resources as those schools did, but also employed language use outside of essentialized discussions of diversity and multiculturalism that seemed always focused on the benefits to white students, and didn't often include students in our immigrant communities. Internally, our separatist demographics kept us from employing the interpersonal motives most heralded at these dual language schools, said to increase language acquisition through social and academic experiences.

District policy in our community schools was premised on an assimilationist philosophy, antithetical to what was now being promoted for white communities. Because we were already innovating beyond district transitional approaches, we weighed the benefits and costs of some of these other programming alternatives—as was being done on a national scale. Ultimately, in the collegial discourse necessary to construct a school-wide policy, we embraced those scholars studying the subtractive nature of schools for Mexican students and the history of schooling as a tool to deculturalize non-white children and families and decided to face these specific challenges to our community and build a solid culturally-sustaining and -rich curriculum for our students alone, and forego this possible pathway back into the district's graces.

Besides, many of us argued from the Marxist framework, students in marginal places in society have an inherent awareness of how life works at the center, and don't necessarily need to be schooled in the culture of power in order to know its ways. We couldn't be sure, anyway, that the white students into whose worlds district Spanish-speaking students were bused would be able to appreciate the complexity of life in the margins or the brilliance of its children who learn to navigate knowledges, values, and hierarchies in a life curriculum that cannot be shared no matter the model—that the white students seeking linguistic capital for an increasingly globalized economy would not be able to see no matter the sacrifice of the Spanish-speaking families allowed only to visit.

★

My students' lack of surprise at the rowdiness of these suburban Spartans confirmed these conclusions for me. Perhaps they'd had so much intense immersion in white culture through my singular presence in their lives that they were no longer stunned by situations like this one. After all, who were these white suburban students but younger versions of myself? Had I been indirectly preparing them for this moment, a hidden curriculum even to myself? Less intriguing to me was the question of the Spartans' seeming lack of awareness of my students and their quiet and studied concentration, but I was struck by the sudden possibility that they were a reflection of my own blind spots. How many times had my students—past and current—felt invisible in my classroom and presence? More painfully, how often had that feeling been correct?

I scanned the beautiful space in front of me and considered how an education system that self-articulates itself as a vehicle for equality continued to render my students' knowledges as invisible. It felt profoundly unjust that my students would know this much about the world and not get recognition for it, let alone academic credit. We were studying the Humanities and I could see the gaping hole of crediting their humanity in ways both formal and informal. We had designed culturally-sustaining arts-infused curricula and together stretched ourselves as faculty and as a community inclusive of students and families, but I now saw some hubris in that self-assessment. In the models of instructional design being enforced in the district and held central in new efforts to focus on accountability, our revolutionary ethnic studies curricula seemed now to be missing the key stage of planning—a careful assessment of student knowledges as tools to enhance opportunities to demonstrate excellence, while also affording spaces to provide exposure to new learnings not yet presented in students' works. The resistance was not solely against standardized testing and inauthentic history curricula, but also about the witnessing and surfacing of knowledges of white institutions and their methods, values, and purposes beyond that which we as agents of the state understood ourselves.

I saw us here in this space amid the terminology and academic language of the universe's lesson plan for me, the vocabulary on the blackboard to guide my study, the word of the day yelled at me by a sudden imaginary PA system: "conservatory," "observation," "individual variety," "creative decision-making" and shut my eyes to the shift in my own worldview and the understanding of the educational inversion that had been at work beyond my grasp. I realized that no system had held me accountable in the ways it mattered most to me.

Beyond this remorse, I also felt waves of both pride and sorrow for my students as I watched the brief scene unfold before me. The Spartans hadn't been in the conservatory more than a few minutes before the teachers opened the doors and snapped at their students to leave. And yet, I'd traveled fifteen years backward and forward again to see my students and the whole enterprise of teaching with new eyes. I was proud of them not just for their composure and their maturity in a public and social space, but more so of the depth of the understanding that lay beneath that comportment. At the same time, I was saddened to realize how much of that version of childhood my students had not had the privilege to experience. I wanted for them the brilliances I had just come to recognize, but also the healthy and stress-free years without persistent worry or fear. I saw in my students' dignity an adolescent developmental trajectory beyond their years, past the self-absorption afforded to the Spartans, who had experienced our shared space without any apparent recognition of being "read" by society, without any need to consider ways in which others' implicit biases might bring them harm, and place them in peril. By parental instruction or accrued experiences, my students demonstrated a deep awareness of society's persistent pathologizing of them—and demonstrated their humanity and intellectual brilliance also as protection from the dominant narrative. They had the maturity to assess these new environments for their personal safety within them, and I was impressed and embarrassed to acknowledge how much farther along in their development they were than I had perceived, and that any of us Spartans had any hope of paralleling.

Heavier than any of this, however, hung an anger that dimmed the previous sparkle I had felt and laid out for me alternative versions of my children free to

experience the gentle playfulness they experienced in our shared space and unaware of any peril connected to journeys into the center of our city, or of the
hierarchy of socially structured racism conveyed in Marxist circle framings.

★

I tried to venture into a discussion about what we'd just seen as we headed back
to the buses, wondering if I should convey my sadness at their innocence lost, or
appreciation for their expertise on whiteness, or even wonder at the metaphors I
finally understood in that penthouse of glass. I watched their chattering and
considered the unrelenting whiteness still within me and understood that I should
listen and work to refrain from stealing any more joyful experiences by projecting
again white normativity and imposing negativity that might dim their sparkle
here back among ourselves.

To elicit some reflection, once we got back on the bus I threw out a general
comment about the other visitors to the conservatory and waited to see where
the conversation went. To my surprise the students were mostly curious about
dress and other superficial issues: How did they all get the same bags? Why did
they use Spartans as their mascot—were they Greek-Americans? When I posed
the questions about what societal expectations might be for both groups, the
students were thoughtful but not entirely interested. They mostly wanted to
know why the other students weren't yelled at or physically ushered out of the
conservatory. At an end-of-year picnic the previous year, our school had been
criticized and aggressed by a neighboring group of students referencing in general
our students' behavior—though it hadn't quite been clear what the offending
actions had been and why we had ruffled the feathers of the other school's cha-
perones. This time around, my students were curious to know who was in charge
and maybe what kind of purpose there was to the other school's visit.

The students had been troubled the year before by the complaints about their
behavior. We had tried to play it off as just part of what happens when resources
are sparse and up for grabs—there had been a lot of children in a field the Forest
Preserve usually only reserved for one school—and suppressed any discussion of
implicit bias or social policing of non-white bodies, though I was never certain if
that was to shield them or elude our own discomfort. As for the Conservatory, I
tried also to steer the conversation back to how proud I felt of them for not
reacting to the other school group and for demonstrating confidence and maturity in staying focused on the work we'd brought. I confided in them that many
of the people with whom I myself had grown up—of whom I'd been reminded
by the other students—would perhaps have anticipated the exact opposite of
what happened. The students smiled, shrugged, and returned to their private
discussions, possibly letting me know that this was not news. What I understood
in that universal adolescent expression of frustration at adult ignorance was that
they were perhaps also letting me know that I shouldn't really be proud of them.
If they'd acted up and had a raucous time of it, what would it have meant?

Would I have thought less of them as people, or understood them to be demon-strating age-appropriate behavior? The truth was I couldn't even guess. I knew them to be the people they'd been at the Conservatory, and would have been shocked to see them behave otherwise. I was drawn to them for this fact and others that came with the same assumption—that they knew so much more than they would ever be given credit. They smiled at me even though I myself had never given them full credit either. Even as we as a collectively resisted society's narrow definitions of "smart" and "worldly" in which students like ours never seemed to be considered, I had still framed my lens in reference to it. If we naively persisted in the hope these biases would be ultimately erased, or that one day students like mine would epitomize those words and be exemplars of an education based in the definitions of both their cultures, I still needed to complexify any yardstick I was wielding to measure it or name it. In the years that would follow, as I would sit in the back of their high school classes, I would watch the system we resisted work to maintain itself despite social efforts to chip away at it. The possibility that on some level we understood some of our shared future experiences illuminated for me that this learning, like all of them, needed constant attention, and I knew that I wanted it to frame my life and help me never to forget. Beyond any group articulation of selflessness, fundamentally it was why I kept coming back.

Indirectly I possibly also hoped that maybe in the meantime I could provide them spaces where they could blow a gasket on a field trip every once in a while without having to worry.

★

It was a hope that had pervaded all the efforts to get to that point, and yet also worked against us. As a school we knew that the dominant discourse about underprivileged students focused on the troubles they faced and the ways in which they found it hard to escape them—and then blamed them for it. Funda-mentally, we also knew that many efforts to help those same students—our stu-dents—find success within schools still failed to problematize the schooling system at large for its role in the oppression wielded against our students. Discussions about the low test scores of students like ours focused on efforts to try to raise those scores by filling in perceived gaps—not by problematizing the tests that failed to elicit from my students the vast expanses of information they already knew and the ways in which they understood why society only privileged other kinds of learning.

In weekly meetings we wrestled with these issues as well and tried to keep ourselves from the temptations of fatalism. When the hurdle of working against the system proved too difficult for us, we talked about the surprises—the moments when what we expected turned out to be antithetical to what was really happening. We sustained at least a presence in a world that didn't want us as we worked to keep each other from proscribing a fate this broader society had already written.

If not always, we let ourselves know that sometimes we succeeded.

★

As with any counter-normative movement, there were moments of horror for us as well—moments when our frustrations and anger fed righteousness and bitterness toward each other. In the face of limited access, like the students in the Forest Preserve, we got distracted by the smaller nuances of difference among us and for long spells spent our energies on issues of little importance to the students. As the stakes for our students' success climbed higher and higher, and we perceived the stakes of our own efforts to follow suit, our intensity of commitment proved as much a handicap as asset.

Several nationwide and local events played their own parts in this, not least of which was the changing climate around bilingualism and the immigration patterns that fostered the issue. While the country wrestled with the political and moral nuances they perceived and intentionally misarticulated, we as bilingual and bicultural teachers dealt with a shrinking understanding of education, and of the philosophical implications of narrowing pedagogical decisions as we were. As the nation increasingly articulated an affinity for whiteness as the one dominant culture, schools intensified ways to pathologize and render deficient those of non-white heritage. Rather than embracing the talents of language- and culture-crossing inherent in the make-up of every immigrant child, we faced an increasingly venomous discourse about the inherent value of the speakers and participants in that border crossing—beyond contemporary political events. The linearity we had hoped for in our social justice pursuit proved unfounded and naïve, and we watched as history played out in its cyclical ways toward weaponized culture clashes and deteriorations of empire. We hadn't learned everything we'd needed from the exploration of the Aztec world, or their neighboring societies—they had lessons for us still.

★

The hope that sparkly day that our students might one day be seen as equal in the full meaning of that word enough so as to interpret the experiences as odd and uncommon proved to be a historical artifact for us and eventually for teachers and students taking our places. These same underlying philosophical differences persisted beyond us as the foundation of the bilingual debate as well: rather than appreciating the multiple assets that young children from other heritages bring with them to this narrowly white and one-purpose culture, we establish more and more structures to problematize those knowledges and misidentify them as precluding all necessary access to our dominant culture's framings of its values and norms, and call it education.

It was this aggressively prescriptive notion of culture and its erasure of true academic understanding of culture, language, and intellect that I found my students to be engaged in daily —in both large and small ways. My students were intrinsically aware that they were perceived frequently as more than their individual selves—that their actions and presentations would be perceived in light of the broader political issues that surrounded their existence in their own country, that they carried burdens beyond themselves. If they were bold and carefree, that would be overstated to be part of the culture of poverty in which they were being raised—that children in low-income homes wouldn't be able to comport themselves in mainstream society even if they were somehow provided entry. They had a Marxist awareness of how the center of society thrived and perpetuated its dominance over those at the margins—and this deep understanding that worked against any child-like impulses. While I was always proud, and at times sentimentally moved by their maturity and decorum, I realized that I was enabling a system that not only imposed external pressures but also simultaneously worked at erasing years from their childhoods.

This enabling, my embodiment of the state, stood on a good day in tension with my work to invert whiteness in their educational lives. I knew that my measure of their value was always tainted inherently by my whiteness—seeing their strengths within this framework was important, but not the level of empowerment or agency I'd hoped to facilitate. We were not the change we wanted to see in the world.

In my classroom I had to be clear that my goals were not to see them acting like the students at the Conservatory—there was a security, certainly, in those confident and privileged engagements with the public sphere, but no signs of deeper awareness as they could not see clearly both the efforts and knowledges of my students, but also the myth of meritocracy that lay underneath us all. I thought about all the ways I had watched whiteness interact with immigrant children in kind but incomplete ways. I watched society being friendly and kind within a system that maintained our community in servant positions. I was witness to the persistent reveal of the lie of white benevolence upon which both our school system and social justice network was based. It would take years for me to fully understand this as intentional and even more years for me to appreciate the torment my students would feel as they watched their cultural graces—their kindness, warmth, patience, determination, and gratitude—be employed against them in the educational institutions that misunderstood the integrity of these values as vindication and as co-signing on to structural inequities.

★

I thought often of the original inhabitants of that mountain village and the day one, or many, of them had placed a metal idol imbued with meaning and pride and appreciation for their history inside a brutishly undecorated cross forced upon them. I wondered what conversations had led to that moment, any efforts to resist that had been thwarted, and how many efforts to convey their full humanity had been ignored. How much had transpired before the forced parading of the cross would never be visible in the artifact or even the transgression that helped them survive such dehumanization. Despite the painful recognition they must have felt of the erasure of themselves and all their acts of refusal, even in the singeing of the symbol of that erasure, the colonial project that had descended on them would still center itself—in fear, in avoidance, and in the authoring of history—and never know what future generations would seek and appreciate—their brilliance and resistance, and commitment to survival in the face of harrowing odds.

What name was worthy of that particular form of resistance then? In the year following that visit to the cloister in the mountains I had engaged in this question with people in my world who had come from different socio-economic positions. One of them whose insight I deeply valued, my old college friend—brilliant and critical in his analyses of current globalization patterns and trends—interpreted the event differently than I, in a way that exposed even more intersectional lenses than I had seen before, and I wanted to know why. In the privilege from which he framed the debate, he had surprised me with an anger that made me examine my parable all over again.

"It's because people have not challenged outright these colonizing trends that we're in this mess currently," he'd asserted.

"I don't think so," I'd countered. "It's a little unfair to assign blame to the victims, don't you think?"

"While it's not their fault that they were colonized, they have to be responsible for their actions in response to those forces."

"Ok. Let's assume somehow that's right—but isn't it from your position of privilege that you judge them? Your sense of the system is that if you fight things, they can be stopped. For many people their actions in response to aggression only work against them. There's no reason to expect that they will reap any rewards from fighting back—only further violence, aggression, and oppression. Maybe it's the colonizers' responsibility to rein in their own actions."

"But they never will—they have too much to benefit from it."

"True—and can we blame those victimized by it for seeking out their own best interests and going with a more peaceful resistance? Especially if their main purpose was only to maintain their family/community security and still be able to maintain a worldview that was built into their existence?"

"But for generations that in and of itself was forever changed—and opportunities for their descendants ever changed. Time is a colonial weapon, too. And they gave up the best moment to fight it."

"But it's a moot point if there are no descendants at all and the lineage is thwarted entirely. If the only other option is death—and the erasure of any legacy or descendants or continuation of the outward culture—aren't they wise to choose to continue their cultural and religious practices in secret?

"Aren't they wise to choose themselves over some moral value?"

I had an image of the woman who'd placed the idol, gendered in her enslavement and forced sanding and washing of the wood. I wanted her to be a hero, but was fooling myself if I thought my intensity of argument was academic at all. It wasn't even selfless.

I was hoping to be absolved myself.

★

I felt very close to the struggle of the ancient people of the mountains and also recognized the ways in which I perpetuated the colonization that had attempted to erase their culture. But if I had learned anything in a year and lifetime of mistakes it was to be clear about the directing of blame in this emotionally-complex scenario.

It did not belong to my students.

While the mountain society had indeed chosen a form of resistance that would speak centuries later to the version of parallel unfolding narratives in different global contexts, then perhaps those heroes had been committed beyond their own self-preservation or that of their immediate descendants. Perhaps their commitment to their beliefs had transcended the ways in which they needed to see those beliefs reflected back to them in their new reality. Perhaps they had had a grand sense of humor and appreciated wide and far the ways in which they'd stumped the chumps, like the mockery of the Spaniards in the famous pink masks, who'd exercised power in a myriad of ways over them.

★

In my own teaching life, I knew I could claim no side of the debate exclusively. I knew that I was no more responsible for protecting our small treasure of a culturally-relevant school inside the cross of the large oppressive public school system than I was for the racist and colonialist bureaucracy against which we fought. Both were entities beyond the scope of my one classroom in the collective of our one small school, but the considerations of both sides of the parable helped keep me focused on the work ahead. Steeped in the notions of metaphors as beacons, I knew that as I processed my actions and beliefs within that frame, I was also moving closer to the core of who I had hoped to be.

I'd hoped all along to find my core at one end of the spectrum and had instead stumbled upon it in the most surprising of places—the murky middle. I'd entered teaching with the assumption that I needed to be solid in my curricular and philosophical foundations so that I could provide an education of empowerment for them, but had forgotten to leave space for them in the equation. I knew I'd hoped to build my teaching around notions of equity and justice for them, but was alarmed to acknowledge that the more I tried to do that the more elusive notions of how to teach critically might continue to be.

Questions helped me understand that I would be hiding idols from myself unless I found a way to stop looking exclusively for answers and see the complexity and hope that interruptive teaching could be.

It wasn't the first time I realized the potential for deeper meaning once I let go of all the structures I'd thought I'd need to be an effective teacher, but it would be the essential one I would hold on to.

In embracing my uncertainty, it turned out, I was more a teacher against oppression than when I had felt entirely sure and righteous, despite the fact that much of that dissonance was the result of my own weaknesses. It was within that paradox—finding myself certain about the need for uncertainty—that I placed my teacher self and let the discomfort guide me into better work on behalf of my students. In the epistemological diversity of my classroom and community, I had learned that no sooner could I recognize concretely the learning as it was happening for my students than I had to step back and facilitate a different avenue of access to a different level of understanding.

I needed to make sure we stayed "in-between" and tore ourselves off the cliffs of security and reason. We needed to try to be the returning tide rather than its victims.

★

I felt the debate as it had played out internally in my life in a variety of contexts.

My most constant manifestation of this issue was with another teacher at school. Deeply traditional in her approaches to discipline and curriculum, she was also troubled by some home issues that affected her ability to arrive at school on time and prepare sufficiently—whatever that might mean—for her class. Students were often given extended periods of "free time" and were frequently found in the hallways and other locations around the school when they were supposed to be in her class. This was accompanied by the fact that when students were called on their behaviors, there were inflections and articulations that I struggled to comprehend.

I seemed to be the only one, and I paid attention to the fact that so few of our parents ever complained about the situation. In the one instance when a few families planned to talk with our principal about events in this classroom, they had trouble reaching out to other families to share the burden. Almost always, the majority of parents expressed an appreciation for all they had at our school—and for the talents this teacher did have—and did not want to appear ungrateful or overly demanding. Instead, they took other approaches that included volunteering in the room, sharing in the teacher's personal struggles, and offering suggestions for ways in which they could contribute to curricular projects.

This was hard for me to take on multiple levels—professionally, I wanted a different experience for my students and felt righteous about the work many of us had put into creating a unique learning environment. I felt empowered to want to change things particularly at the level of sixth grade both because it seemed too critical a time to "lose" and because I received the students from this classroom and felt that I faced challenges of lost time to establishing norms for my classroom that had already existed in the early years of their study with us.

Personally I was bewildered mostly by the lack of outward resistance to this teacher because it made me question to what extent I should trust my students and their parents in the feedback I received about my own teaching. Perhaps what I perceived as responsiveness was simply a version of schooling they were kindly "enduring" or through which they were biding their time. These tensions afforded me the unpleasant opportunity to question again my read of the partnership, and I wanted to find ways to invite honest exchanges about their students' learning in my room. The layers of difference between us, mirrored in my tension with other teaching styles, made this pursuit often very difficult—and added to my understanding of dimensions of culture even still: I was never certain whether parents' values of deference to authority complemented their kind attention to my feelings or whether parents were grateful for a shared enactment of care. More acutely, I pondered whether parents wanted their children to acculturate to white society and believed they would have that access through my presence in the classroom, or whether parents were dismayed that I couldn't assume pure responsibility for my work and needed to ask even more from them in the education of their children.

None of these was ever clear, and when the parents chose not to complain about the other teacher, I understood this not to be superficial laziness or passivity, but from a matrix of positions that I could not inhabit and could only barely perceive: wanting not to add to the teacher's troubles, sharing a cultural connection and a shared value system beyond the ways in which they were enacted in the classroom, and a gratitude for the native-language and arts-traditions this teacher provided.

For many years, I failed to see my own positionality in these two repetitive arguments as contradictory—but in reality they were. In the arguments with my college friend, I inhabited the point of view of the idol-worshipers and supported the quiet resistance of my church-going, family-centered, and unwilling to rebel community while he saw it as complacency in their lack of resistance.

Within the school I had performed the role of the priests, failing to complicate these moralistic and white-normative tendencies in regards to this other teacher and ultimately assessing the situation in ways that imposed my own cross on the community.

★

The gift of that sparkly June afternoon in the Conservatory grew in value in my life beyond even the opportunities for shared community. In future years I would come to realize the challenges of cultural normativity that even adulthood brings. If I had been able to see my students as ambassadors of new cultures being lived into being I might have seen the transformative power they might have had that afternoon and beyond as culture-crossers, agency in what they could effect as change and not just recipients of a model that belonged to us adults. At that moment the promise was that they were being raised within two disparate societies—the one that enveloped them in this "chosen" land and the one they bring with them manifested in their home lives and histories. Hidden from us in discussions of crossing cultures in schooling is the rewriting of it beyond hegemonic forces—in a way we might only hope for—that they will instantiate more complexly than our generational epistemologies allow.

That day in the Conservatory they were responding not as children, but as ambassadors of a complex society more brilliant and knowledgeable and for future truth-seekers to get to excavate and celebrate.

★

Those questions and answers came up again not long after our field trip—I was still riding the wave of good feeling that promised to carry us through to another summer, and had planned our final mural projects for time during our final weeks. It'd been a fun and gradual process earlier in the quarter to plan and coordinate the content of the murals, following our theme of "Journey" to the end of ours.

The students had lots of freedom to present their interpretations of the notion of moving through time and space to me and to the rest of the class, and then once their proposals were approved, their group could set out to plan the visual rendering of the topic. For two of my groups the overwhelming drive was for presenting the geographic, emotional, cultural, and educational immigrations from Mexico to Little Village. Both groups used the visual of the Río Bravo to tie in their smaller images into the broader theme. Both groups would get long-lived rounds of applause at the unveiling.

Another group decided to interpret the notion of journey as it had played out in the growth of their present country, and many students in this group were the ones with whom we'd worked to parse out notions of bigotry and racism among the diverse demographic known as Latinos. Led by David, this group centered their visual rendition around the Statue of Liberty and the barbed-wire along the Mexican border. The contrast in the two trajectories of our country—the philosophical humanity of Liberty's welcome over Ellis Island and the antithetical "keep-out" that was growing in the southwest and beyond—was realized in bold hues from opposite sides of the color wheel, and clear symbolic images—of eagles and open arms—but cloudy people. It seemed to me that there was some asking for forgiveness from those they'd perhaps offended—with their earlier jokes about INS and historic slurs—and it was incredible to see them use this activity to speak to their peers so directly.

The last two groups were just as conceptual—and risky in their proposals. All year I'd been peppered with questions I hadn't really stopped to take note of—on the way to lunch, during lunch, after school, on bus trips, and in quiet moments—from my newer students about the birth of the school and the process it took to get us up and running. Like parents of inquisitive toddlers, I'd fired off answers to the questions depending on the time and place—and the degree to which I'd been preoccupied with all the details of getting a class through the day—without really registering the interest or curiosity.

But apparently the stories had mattered, because I now got to see them realized in this final visual form—there was our logo at the heart of the panel with the different art forms radiating out from it. Beyond those inner circles lay different curricular presentations from over the years—the Corridos at the Museum, the folkloric troupe in full force at an assembly—with other more standard tools of teaching. There were students all around the perimeter with families of different orchestrations, and the muted and impressionistic tones conveyed both the cultures and languages represented in our school and stressed in the mission statement. Intended for the girls' washroom as part of the beautification efforts, this mural ended up outside the office on request of the Principal for all those arriving at the school to behold.

Our last group had taken a more personal approach to the theme of journeying. My resident philosophers, they'd taken to heart the fact that beauty is a troublingly normative word for girls—even though it was there in the grant proposal without my realizing it—and that we'd had to face two sad instances of this in the last ten months. Sixth grade seemed yet too early to me to have to face anorexia, and we didn't really deal with it as a group, but some of the boys friendly with one girl picked up on it. Other girls were sensitive to Cisco's fears of the sun and covered up in all weather to try to keep their skin as light as possible. Despite our attempts across the curriculum to try to address this issue, one student held fast to her feelings and rejected any discussion.

So my final quartet—Desmond, Ricardo, Cisco, and Pedro—took it upon themselves to portray girls in healthy pro-social and ethnic-identity development stages—and they asked that it be prominently displayed along the main wall of the girls' washroom, underneath the high windows that brought in the light from the parking lot. At the beginning of my own adult trajectory, I'd stood in that parking lot and gazed upon this building—not knowing the learning it would hold for me—but thinking about its massiveness in the densely-occupied world of my new students. I'd looked up at the windows to see if there was anyone watching on the numerous occasions that I slid across the ice ungracefully or dragged my weary bones at the end of a tough day back to the train. I'd had no consciousness of the layers of complexity in what it means to migrate, learn a language, and grow into a multicultural identity in those early days, and recognition had hit me squarely how unprepared I'd really been to face the years that had lain ahead of me.

I challenged the boys to think about how they could speak for and to girls from their male position, and gave them a couple of female peers to check in with in their planning. As a way to be inclusive, they told me ahead of time, they'd like to incorporate mirrors at different heights that would work as the faces for each of the girls in the mural. They wanted to leave open the soul of each girl to reflect back to their peers who they are and might be.

I would have declared it to be my proudest moment as a teacher, but there was so very little of me inside this event that it felt too self-indulgent to assert even that level of ownership.

I'd just never been more content as a teacher, I guessed. I felt a peace in the manifestations of the young people around me growing into adults—and allowing me to do the same. I thought to myself that this was the "education"—the "drawing out of" —that I'd long ago sought, but I wouldn't have known to look for it in its formal indirection. Nowhere in any lesson plan had I written this goal or objective and lain out the steps of my procedure that would bring us here.

The quartet provided evidence they'd arrived. Somehow while I had been busy constructing the bridge over the river it had flowed in its own path—with me just lucky enough to schedule an activity that would allow me take a look.

I had a momentary urge to measure it somehow and get to the core of it so that it might be replicated later on in subsequent years. Maybe I needed to con-cretize data so that I might be able to build something this strong and powerful in future groups of students, but let myself realize that I might be ruining and ignoring the art of it all by trying to place it in an ill-conceived frame—that of some recipe or formula for my own teaching.

And so I accepted it for what it was—a moment that happened—for those students in that time. I was lucky to have seen it—to have perhaps had the chance to throw a can of water on the seeds planted long ago by someone else and watch the start of a bloom that would then be nurtured in ways beyond what we were doing in that moment on that day, behind those windows I'd pondered as an outsider.

★

The murals went up on a hot and humid day almost unfathomable in the con-crete desert surrounding the school. It was also a day when almost every other school system in the country was no longer in session, but there we were—faces and bodies dripping and struggling to muster up the energy for the occasion. Somehow the powers that be that think they can make up for this country's structural racism and economic oppression by punishing low-income students with long school years have never stood inside a poorly vented school washroom in the third week of June.

I knew that someone somewhere must have had a formula about how this was all equitable and equal—how the "instruction time" in Chicago Public Schools remained shorter than in other more well-off districts elsewhere, but I had a humidity-triggered temper and didn't buy it. We were all tested in our mini-society against ourselves more than against anyone else, but the space we all needed between us was elusive for us as the weeks crept on. We were ready for the July 4th weekend by the time school let out, and then after that seven of the students and I would reconvene here again to try to give that stinking test another try.

Stickiness and crankiness aside, we had put our theme on the wall, and that day was a good day.

We were hosting important funders—big name families who give routinely to urban teachers for projects such as this one. They saw us grateful and proud, but tired. All their grants should have been completed and documented by mid-May, but I got yet another pass this time. My reputation for perpendicularity to bureaucratic processes had preceded me—the books that almost got taken away, the deadlines for documents I managed almost never to make, the receipts I never turned in to get the promised monies.

Any concern I might have had was baked out of me that day. I'd been inwardly steeled in ways unspeakable for me, and only communicable in images: students visualized for us the hypocrisy of our current society, celebrated an educational institution of the state that wanted fully to resist that, and four boys stepped outside themselves and imagined the challenges of growing up female in diverse economic and political situations and gave the small gift of imagining better things in a better world. And somehow trying to see outside of my own normalizations—beyond that which I inherently expected and believed in the world and opening it up to the read of others from other experiences—had become a theme for some students themselves.

They'd also lived inside their grief and projected the would-be futures for the sisters and cousins they'd lost, and memorialized them as they would be reflected by all our girls for as long as the school was there.

I realized, too, how timely the activity was—it being the time of year when I needed to give to the students my own imaginations of where their own trajectories would take them by giving them my interpretations of their current selves in all their complexity and conveying some notions of where I thought that self might grow. I clearly hoped to witness much of that within our small community and perhaps beyond it, but also needed to let go and not stand in their way.

They had their own parades to start and parables to make sense of, just as they'd made mine possible.

They'd shared our space, brought truth to the complexity of cultural interpretations of the term education, resisted us, believed in our resistance of forces outside us all, sparkled in clear and unclear ways, and established themselves at this point in time, Siddhartha in the river, on walls that would ideally outlive us all, next to windows whose mysteries remained now for others.

EPILOGUE

Like my former students interpreting the sparkly clean-air penthouse of our last excursion together, my current students as future teachers have a sixth sense about inequities in the architecture of public education, as stemming both academically from a centered focus on research in their preparation for the career, as well as from an Honors level critical analysis of their lives in Chicago. Most of them have had a front-row seat of their own in urban classrooms. They know academically, personally, and professionally how to read the school district policies of our urban center for assertions of value, importance, and support. They know that these data point to one consistent argument about the intentionality, hegemony, and longevity of the colonial project. They know what it's like to live inside it, and what it's like to mitigate its violences.

Now they want to commit their lives to that task.

In an era of underestimating teachers, and implementing that underestimation then to blame them for the very social injustices they long to erase, my undergraduate and graduate students engage the minds of young people in an eternal act of hope that my generation's will to dismantle these structures might afford them successes in our wake.

Scholarship suffers enormous gaps in appreciating and understanding fully the art of urban teachers' layered navigations of its oppressive pillars, yet my students perform this art each day. Even if scholarship were able to fully grasp the science of their applied understandings, the work would still be theirs to advocate for— by inserting critical pedagogies into traditional framings, and by implementing expansive theories into classroom practices that foster learning in the ever-complexifying minds of young people. It is my hope that articulating this one, lone academic journey of teaching written to honor the intellectual, emotional, and cultural practices inside the real work might fill the gaps left open by quantitative data sets and subsequent detached analyses.

In the criticisms of urban teachers and urban schools, these nobilities highlight the direct contrast in their mainstream portrayals. In an era of political turmoil, and resurfaced racialized divisions, it might be said that current American culture is at war with itself, making schools and my students' classrooms the battle lines of this contest in values. Teachers are currently responsible for creating worlds that support collectivism and developmental processes, focused always on the life-long process of individuals in gradual improvement, while broader society seems to be deteriorating. Teachers fulfill these charges as agents of a society that hinges on antagonizing ideals, with one side an ongoing construct of ourselves as individualistic and product-oriented, and the other a focus on learning and doing well, for their own sakes, as well as for a broader collective.

Within this heightened context, different discourses attempt to provide solace as much as information. Rebecca Solnit (2017), in reflecting on a pivotal moment in this political era, wrote:

> Some of us are surrounded by destructive people who tell us we're worthless when we're endlessly valuable, that we're stupid when we're smart, that we're failing even when we succeed. But the opposite of people who drag you down isn't people who build you up and butter you up. It's equals who are generous but keep you accountable, true mirrors who reflect back who you are and what you are doing.

It is in that spirit that I offer this text to them, and in a structure that I hope is helpful.

Each of the twelve chapters here is constructed upon the lived experiences of my teaching and the ways in which I found the learning and unlearning within them to parallel the most meaningful scholarship in critical race studies in education. In my aspirations to be both accessible to practitioners and honoring of their deep and disparate knowledges, each chapter attempts to present data and analyses of structural inequities still perpetuated in post-conflict colonial school sites by the very schools that espouse justice and name themselves central to its pursuit.

We know differently.

Practitioners understand profoundly that we in schools are *not* central to pursuits of equity in a vast number of ways. We are asked to enact hierarchies of social behaviors as agents of racist states. Urban teachers enact their crafts through inhumane working and learning conditions designed intentionally to result in their exhaustion. They serve as the lone public good available to disinvested urban communities, and yet are marginalized through anti-blackness, xenophobia, intersectionally-gendered expectations of themselves and their efforts to reconstruct a world they know only how to imagine.

Beyond the content and vehicle of this book, I am troubled by the increased reminders of the colonial project's brutality against minoritized and marginalized students. Since my years teaching and learning with my students, they have grown into adults whose lives are magical in their unfolding. In their places, of course, are new children whose lives have been riddled with violence and oppression in increasing volume. Chapter contents connect the legacy of schools to today's heightened racialized inequities and violent bureaucracies experienced by children across the nation. Tamir Rice was killed at the same age as my student who left my classroom to go home; the migration stories of my students' parents and family members would today become holocaust stories of devastating encampments on our southern border, and possible fatalities in the circumstances fostering those, and in the harrowing conditions experienced in the pilgrimages themselves. Legal institutions seek out teacher records to justify murders of innocent young people.

This narrative is not intended as a salve or enabler of this system. It describes no heroes and wants none. It is a narrative toward destroying both teacher-hero genre and any need for it. Intended as a tool toward the dismantling of systems, these words hope to be only historically interesting or significant to that end.

Looking beyond the narrow world of teacher education research, there is hope in scholarship advancing critical framings of other public institutions in colonized contexts. Historical and cultural framings of the human endeavor to deconstruct inhumane institutions extend far beyond the parameters of critical educational scholarship. In the paradigm shift of the last several years toward a historicized analysis of racial and economic justice, vocalizing the daily lives of professionals and their classrooms in this contested territory may also resonate far beyond the limits of our participants.

The words herein intend to support multiple paths through grassroots, pueblo explorations of research and scholarship. In a pedagogy and philosophy centered on marginalized experiences, these words intend to present both a bridge for access to scholarship detached from community agents, while also highlighting the fundamental tensions in concretizing these ideals. In recognition of teachers as ultimate scholarly contributors to critical knowledges, these words also intend to honor their daily deconstruction of the colonial project as they reflect, theorize, and build new visions for their students in its place.

For the ones I know and have known, and those who know beyond me: this text is for you.

References

Solnit, R. (2017, May 30). Rebecca Solnit: The loneliness of Donald Trump: On the corrosive privilege of the most mocked man in the world. Retrieved from https://lithub.com/rebecca-solnit-the-loneliness-of-donald-trump/

FURTHER READING

Anzaldúa, G. (1987). *Borderlands/La frontera: The new mestiza*. San Francisco, CA: Aunt Lute Books.

Anzaldúa, G. (1990). *Making face, making soul = Haciendo caras: Creative and critical perspectives by women of color*. San Francisco, CA: Aunt Lute Foundation Books.

Ashton-Warner, S. (1963). *Teacher*. New York, NY: Simon and Schuster.

Ayers, W. (2001). *To Teach: The Journey of a Teacher* (2nd ed.). New York, NY: Teachers College Press.

Ayers, W., Klonsky, M., & Lyon, G. (2000). *A simple justice: The challenge of small schools*. New York, NY: Teachers College Press.

Ballenger, C. (1999). *Teaching other people's children: Literacy and learning in a bilingual classroom*. New York, NY: Teachers College Press.

Bell, D. (1995). Who's afraid of critical race theory? *University of Illinois Law Review*, 4, 893–910.

Clandinin, J., & Connelly, F. M. (2000). *Narrative inquiry: Experience and story in qualitative research*. San Francisco, CA: Jossey-Bass.

Cochran-Smith, M. (1999). Learning to teach for social justice. In G. Griffin (Ed.), *The education of teacher: Ninety-eighth yearbook of the National Society for the Study of Education* (114–144). Chicago, IL: University of Chicago Press.

Cochran-Smith, M., & Lytle, S. (2009). Teacher research as stance. In S. E. Noffke, & B. Somekh (Eds), *The SAGE handbook of educational action research* (pp. 39–49). London, UK: SAGE Publications Ltd. doi:10.4135/9780857021021

Crenshaw, K. (1989). Demarginalizing the Intersection of Race and Sex: A Black Feminist Critique of Antidiscrimination Doctrine, Feminist Theory and Antiracist Politics. *University of Chicago Legal Forum*, 1989(1), 139–167. Reprinted in The politics of law: A progressive critique, 195–217 (2nd ed., edited by D. Kairys, Pantheon, 1990).

Csikszentmihalyi, M. (1990). *Flow: The psychology of optimal experience*. New York, NY: Harper and Row.

Cummins, J. (2001). Empowering minority students: A framework for intervention. *Harvard Educational Review*, 71(4), 656–675. Reprinted from *Harvard Educational Review*, 56 (1), 18–36.

Delpit, L. (1995). *Other people's children: Cultural conflict in the classroom*. New York, NY: The New Press.

Eisner, E. (2002). *The arts and the creation of mind*. New Haven, CT: Yale University Press.

Faltis, C., & Hudelson, S. (1997). *Bilingual education in elementary and secondary school communities: Toward understanding and caring*. New York, NY: Pearson.

Fleischman, P. (2004). *Seedfolks*. New York, NY: HarperCollins Publishers.

Freire, P. (1968). *Pedagogy of the oppressed*. New York, NY: Continuum Publishing.

Freire, P. (2004). *Pedagogy of indignation*. Boulder, CO: Paradigm Press.

Freire, P., & Macedo, D. (1987). *Literacy: Reading the word and the world*. South Hadley, MA: Bergin & Garvey Publishers, Inc.

Gee, J. P. (2001). Identity as an analytic lens for research in education. *Review of Research in Education*, 25, 99–125.

Gorski, P. (2008, December). Good intentions are not enough: A decolonizing intercultural education. *Intercultural Education*, 19(6), 515–525. doi:10.1080/14675980802568319

Grumet, M. (1988). *Bitter milk: Women and teaching*. Amherst, MA: University of Massachusetts Press.

Gutierrez, G. (1988/1971). *A theology of liberation: History, politics, salvation* (C. Inda & J. Eagleson, Trans.). Maryknoll, NY: Orbis Books. (Original work published in 1971)

hooks, b. (1994). *Teaching to transgress: Education as the practice of freedom*. New York, NY: Routledge.

Horton, M., Kohl, H., & Kohl, J. (1997). *The long haul: An autobiography*. New York, NY: Teachers College Press.

Hulme, K. (1986). *The bone people*. New York, NY: Penguin Books.

Kingsolver, B. (1998). *The poisonwood bible*. New York, NY: HarperCollins Publishers.

Kozol, J. (1985). *Illiterate America*. Garden City, NY: Anchor Press/Doubleday.

Krashen, S. (1998, June). Comprehensible output? *System*, 26(2), 175–182.

Kumashiro, K. (2004). *Against common sense: Teaching and learning toward social justice*. New York, NY: Routledge-Farmer.

Ladson-Billings, G. (2001). *Crossing over to Canaan: The journey of new teachers in diverse classrooms*. San Francisco, CA: Jossey-Bass.

Ladson-Billings, G. (2003). Racialized discourses and ethnic epistemologies. In N. K. Denzin & Y. S. Lincoln (Eds.), *The landscapes of qualitative research: Theories and issues*. Thousand Oaks, CA: SAGE Publications.

Ladson-Billings, G., & Tate, W. (1995). Toward a critical race theory of education. *Teachers College Record*, 97, 47–68.

Leonardo, Z. (2009). *Race, whiteness, and education*. New York: Routledge.

Lugones M. (2016) The coloniality of gender. In W. Harcourt (Ed.), *The Palgrave handbook of gender and development*. London, UK: Palgrave Macmillan.

Marx, K., & Engels, F. (2016). *On colonies, industrial monopoly, and the working class movement*. Montreal, Canada: Kersplebedeb. (Originally compiled and edited by The Communist Working Circle in 1972).

McIntyre, A. (1997). *Making meaning of whiteness: Exploring racial identity with white teachers*. Albany, NY: SUNY Press.

Michie, G. (1999). *Holler if you hear me: the education of a teacher and his students*. New York, NY: Teachers College Press.

Michie, G. (2005). *See you when we get there: Teaching for change in urban schools.* New York, NY: Teachers College Press.

Miller, J. L. (2005). *Sounds of silence breaking: Women, autobiography, and curriculum.* New York, NY: Peter Lang Publishers.

Murrell, Jr., P. C. (2001). *The community teacher: A new framework for effective urban teaching.* New York, NY: Teachers College Press.

Noddings, N. (2002). *Educating moral people: A caring alternative to character education* (4th ed.). New York, NY: Teachers College Press.

Paley, V. (2000). *White teacher.* Cambridge, MA: Harvard University Press.

Pinar, W. (1994). *Autobiography, politics, and sexuality: Essays in curriculum theory, 1972–1992.* New York, NY: Peter Lang Publishers.

Schubert, W. H. (2009). *Love, justice, and education: John Dewey and the utopians.* Charlotte, NC: Information Age Publishing.

Spring, J. (2013). *Deculturalization and the struggle for equality: A brief history of the education of dominated cultures in the United States* (7th ed.). New York, NY: McGraw-Hill.

Turner, V. (1995). *The ritual process: Structure and anti-structure* (2nd ed.). Piscataway, NJ: Aldine Transaction.

Valenzuela, A. (1999). *Subtractive schooling: U.S.-Mexican youth and the politics of caring.* Albany, NY: SUNY Press.

Weiner, E. (2009). *The geography of bliss: One grump's search for the happiest places in the world.* New York, NY: Twelve.

Weis, L., & Fine, M. (2018). Critical bifocality. In D. Beach, C. Bagley, & S. Marques da Silva (Eds.), *The Wiley Handbook of Ethnography of Education* (91–112). Hoboken, NJ: John Wiley & Sons, Inc.

Wellstone, P. (2003). *How the rural poor got power: Narrative of a grass-roots organizer.* Minneapolis, MN: University of Minnesota Press.

INDEX